What others say about this book

Riveting. Electrifying. Sobering. *Death by "Gun Control"* is a wake-up call to all who love liberty. It should be required reading in every home and school.

> Richard Poe
> Author, *The Seven Myths of Gun Control*
> Editor, *FrontPageMagazine.com*

Death by "Gun Control" explains the fundamentals in such a lucid, accessible way that you could give the book to your middle schooler as a first primer on the value of an armed citizenry. At the same time, it's so packed with well-organized information that experienced gun-rights activists and researchers should keep it close at hand for intellectual ammunition. I thought I'd read a lot on this topic; but Aaron and Richard taught me things I'd never known and gave me new ways of looking at familiar concepts. This is a seriously valuable book.

> Claire Wolfe
> Author of *101 Things to Do 'Til the Revolution* and
> co-author of *The State vs. the People*

Zelman and Stevens tell the story we all must know—how successful twentieth century tyrants knew they had to disarm their people before they could torture and kill them. The power of their story makes clear our imperative—to preserve at all costs the natural right of self defense and its corollary, the right to keep and bear arms.

> Timothy Wheeler, MD
> Director, Doctors for Responsible Gun
> Ownership, a Project of The Claremont Institute

George Santayana wrote: "Those who cannot remember the past are condemned to repeat it." In the 20th Century, nuclear weapons were used by government to kill a few hundred thousand people, whereas "gun control" was used by governments to pave the way for killing over 100,000,000 people. Read this book to understand how and why we must help prevent the 21st century from repeating the government destruction of life and liberty of the past century—we cannot afford another like it.

> Durk Pearson and Sandy Shaw
> Scientists and authors of the No. 1 bestseller
> *Life Extension, A Practical Scientific Approach*

Mazel Freedom Press, Inc.
P.O. Box 270014
Hartford, WI 53027

ISBN 0-9602304-6-1

Distributed by:
Jews for the Preservation of
Firearms Ownership, Inc.
P.O. Box 270143
Hartford, WI 53027
262-673-9745 — Fax 262-673-9746
www.jpfo.org

Cover art by Turner Type & Design, Lacey, WA.

DEATH *by* "GUN CONTROL"

THE HUMAN COST
OF VICTIM DISARMAMENT

by Aaron Zelman
and Richard W. Stevens
ATTORNEY AT LAW

We dedicate this book *to all the people
who have ever fought against oppression,
against slavery, and against the ideology
of victim disarmament.*

With profound sadness *we also recall
the millions of unarmed and defenseless men,
women and children who suffered and died
at the hands of civilian and government aggression.*

We sincerely thank the contributors *James Bovard,
Stephen P. Halbrook, Jacob G. Hornberger,
and Larry Pratt for consenting
to include their excellent works in this book.
We gratefully appreciate the ideas, research, support,
insights and help provided by Ken Holder, Garn Turner,
Claire Wolfe, and by our wives Nancy and Connie.*

We salute the members *of
Jews for the Preservation of Firearms Ownership,
who truly have made this book possible.*

Introduction

By James Bovard

Not every firearms regulation leads inexorably to genocide. But, as this sweeping historical study shows, supposedly "reasonable measures" such as licensing and registration of gun owners have been followed too many times in recent history by government atrocities. The issue is not the supposed good intention of reformers who seek to reduce private gun ownership. The issue is the nature of political power.

Aaron Zelman and Richard Stevens's book vividly reviews and analyzes the slaughter of disarmed populaces from the Turkish slaughter of the Armenians to Stalin's slaughter of the peasantry to the Guatemalan slaughter of Indians. The book goes in-depth into the bloodbath that was the Third Reich, as well as the Khmer Rouge urban renewal experiments, Mao's depredations, and other atrocities. The book also recounts the abuse that Blacks suffered in the United States after laws were passed to disarm them — for the convenience of the Klan and other marauders.

Governments around the world have stripped hundreds of millions of people of their right to own weapons and then left them to be robbed, raped, and slaughtered.

Sober American Skeptics

Some people may try to dismiss Zelman and Stevens's distrust of government officials as un-American. But the distrust of government's grabbing guns has a long and honorable history in this country. The American revolutionaries were concerned about the potential for unlimited power inherent in British laws and policies. The initial conflicts at Lexington and Concord occurred because British regiments were marching out to confiscate the colonists' arms caches. The British assumed that seizing the weapons would quell resistance to the expansion of their power. George Mason, the father of the Bill of Rights, later declared that the British decided that "to disarm the people ...was the best and most effectual way to enslave them." If the colonists reasoned like some contemporary Americans, they would have interpreted the British troops' attempt to seize their guns as proof of how much they "cared about the children."

Many proponents of restrictions on firearms ownership insist that the specific measure they champion can have little or no adverse impact on people's freedom. Americans of the Revolutionary Era recognized that the passage of a law does not signal the end of a political onslaught. Instead, it is merely the starting point for a push to further extend government in the same direction—to pursue the "logic" of a new act to its conclusion. As James Madison wrote in 1787, "The sober people of America...have seen that one legislative interference is but the first link of a long chain of repetitions, every subsequent interference being naturally produced by the effects of the preceding." Unfortunately, most Americans today seem naively unconcerned about politicians planting their flag on new turf.

Dangerous Masters

Politicians continually complain about "loopholes" in existing gun laws as a pretext to enact new gun laws. But the ultimate loophole is freedom: the principle that citizens should not be forced to depend on often lackadaisical government employees for their own safety and survival. Every restriction on citizens' rights to acquire and carry firearms means increasing citizens' subordination to government employees who are authorized to carry such weapons.

Broad restrictions on private gun ownership produce one main result: The vast increase in the power of politicians. But political tyranny has destroyed far more lives in the last century than have abusive private gun owners. Unfortunately, gun control advocates offer no solution to the problem of political tyranny — almost as if the problem will disappear if we all pretend government is our friend.

On gun control, we have to judge politicians as a class by their records, not by empty promises that can never be enforced after citizens have been disarmed. Gun control laws ultimately rest on the trustworthiness of the political ruling class. The only way that firearms could be less vital to defending freedom now than in the past is if politicians were no longer dangerous. But there is no trigger guard on political ambition.

James Bovard is the author of Lost Rights: The Destruction of American Liberty, Freedom in Chains: The Rise of the State and the Demise of the Citizen, *and most recently* Feeling Your Pain: The Explosion and Abuse of Government Power in the Clinton-Gore Years.

Table of Contents

Directory of Tables

Chapter One
The Idea That Kills

Death by "Gun Control" is not just about "gun control" laws. This book is about "gun control" as an ***idea***. The "gun control" idea outcrops in many forms, but it boils down to these two fundamental beliefs:

(1) Only a government has any *right* to have and use firearms.

(2) Citizens have no *right* to use armed force for defense against aggression (i.e. crime, invasion, repression, violence, etc.).

The "gun control" idea, as explained in this book, means training decent non-violent citizens to:

- Hate, fear and avoid guns as objects
- Shun and ostracize civilian gun owners
- Favor laws that restrict or prohibit firearms possession and use
- Accept as normal that citizens should be powerless to overthrow an oppressive government
- Applaud government's using armed force to achieve foreign and domestic policy goals
- Depend upon government agencies to protect individuals from aggression and crime

The "gun control" idea implants hatred and fear into the hearts and minds of people. The "gun control" idea breeds attitudes, slogans, policies and laws that *kill*.

This book shows exactly how "gun control" means *victim disarmament* — and how victim disarmament leaves millions of innocent people vulnerable to aggression: abuse, rape, robbery, murder, and government-made genocide.

To save millions of innocent lives, we must not merely modify or repeal certain "gun control" laws. This book shows why there can be no compromise. We must destroy the very *idea* of "gun control."

The Human Cost of "Gun Control" Ideas

Government	Dates	Targets	Civilians Killed	"Gun Control" Laws	Features of Over-all "Gun Control" Scheme
Ottoman Turkey	1915-1917	Armenians (mostly Christians)	1 – 1.5 million	Art. 166, Pen. Code, 1866 & 1911 Proclamation, 1915	• Permits required • Government list of owners • Ban on possession
Soviet Union	1929-1945	Political opponents; farming communities	20 million	Resolutions, 1918 Decree, July 12, 1920 Art. 59 & 182, Pen. code, 1926	• Licensing of owners • Ban on possession • Severe penalties
Nazi Germany & Occupied Europe	1933-1945	Political opponents; Jews; Gypsies; critics; "examples"	20 million	Law on Firearms & Ammun., 1928 Weapon Law, March 18, 1938 Regulations against Jews, 1938	• Registration & Licensing • Stricter handgun laws • Ban on possession
China, Nationalist	1927-1949	Political opponents; army conscripts; others	10 million	Art. 205, Crim. Code, 1914 Art. 186-87, Crim. Code, 1935	• Government permit system • Ban on private ownership
China, Red	1949-52 1957-60 1966-76	Political opponents; Rural populations Enemies of the state	20 – 35 million	Act of Feb. 20, 1951 Act of Oct. 22, 1957	• Prison or death to "counter-revolutionary criminals" and anyone resisting any government program • Death penalty for supplying guns to such "criminals"
Guatemala	1960-81	Mayans & other Indians; political enemies	100,000-200,000	Decree 36, 1871 • Act of 1932 Decree 386, 1947 Decree 283, 1964	• Register guns & owners • Licensing with high fees • Prohibit carrying guns • Bans on guns, sharp tools • Confiscation powers
Uganda	1971-79	Christians; political enemies	300,000	Firearms Ordinance, 1955 Firearms Act, 1970	• Register all guns & owners • Licenses for transactions • Warrantless searches • Confiscation powers
Cambodia (Khmer Rouge)	1975-79	Educated persons; political enemies	2 million	Art. 322-328, Penal Code Royal Ordinance 55, 1938	• Licenses for guns, owners, ammunition & transactions • Photo ID with fingerprints • License inspected quarterly
Rwanda	1994	Tutsi people	800,000	Decree-Law No. 12, 1979	• Register guns, owners, ammunition • Owners must justify need • Concealable guns illegal • Confiscating powers

3

Chapter Two:
What Do These People Have in Common?

Four boys, ages 5 and 6, suspended from school for pointing their fingers at other children and saying "bang."

Two second-graders, charged by police for the crime of making "terrorist threats" by threatening fellow students with a paper gun.

A teenage girl who witnessed the pitchfork murder of two young siblings.

Black men and women, who "insulted" a white person, die by mob torture and lynching.

Women, children and old folks ordered by the hundreds from their towns, marched to distant camps, and starved or butchered on the way.

Whole villages of people searched for weapons and then massacred.

An entire city of people subjected to unrestrained rape, degradation, mutilation, mass killings and grisly "games" of creative murder.

What do these people have in common?

All were victims of "gun control" ideas.

Chapter Three:
You Have the Power

> Man is deeply vulnerable when faced with overwhelming evil. Instead of consolidating his energy to fight it, he wastes valuable time and effort puzzling over it, insisting it is not, cannot possibly be, what it seems.
>
> — Konnilyn G. Feig[1]

Imagine 17 people standing in your living room. Multiply that by **10**: 170 people in ten living rooms. Multiply that by **100**: 170,000 people in one thousand homes. Can you still imagine the number? Multiply that by **100** again: **17,000,000** people in one hundred thousand homes.

That's a huge number, maybe too large to think about. A number larger than the populations of most American states. In your mind's eye you have been seeing fully clothed people standing comfortably, maybe chatting, maybe snacking, maybe dancing, maybe children playing.

Hold the number — change the picture. They aren't standing. They're crouched, crumpled, strewn about, sprawled, stacked in piles. They are grandpas and grandmas, babies, men, women, teens, children. They're sliced, strangled, gassed, stabbed, tortured, hacked, burned, starved, mutilated, shot.

Now multiply the number by 10 again: *170,000,000 people. The victims of genocide by government in the 20th Century.*

Imagine you were there. In each home. You saw it all. It will happen again.

You **can prevent it. This book shows you how.**

First, you learn about the **Genocide Formula** and its three elements. How it inflicted its horror around the world. Even in

7

America.

You learn that you can stop genocide. You and fellow decent people can prevent the killing of innocents, whether by government or by criminals. You have that power — if you will use it.

You will also see how "gun control" stands against your preventing the deaths. This book shows exactly how "gun control" clears the way for crime and murder at all levels: home invasions, school attacks, death squads, death camps.

Read this book. Stop the crime. Stop the torture. Stop the killing. ***Now.***

End Notes

[1]Feig, Konnilyn G. 1979. *Hitler's Death Camps: The Sanity of Madness.* New York: Holmes & Meier Publishers, p. 444.

Chapter Four:
What is "Gun Control"?

The term "gun control" does not have a clear definition. To discuss things or ideas, such as neutrons or negligence, we could first define them by consulting dictionaries and encyclopedias. "Gun control" is not definable because it is a "buzz word" or slogan.

When people discuss important ideas by using slogans, the meaning drains out of their conversation. Imagine asking a person, "do you favor gun control?" If the person answers "yes," then what exactly does that person actually favor? If the person answers "no," then what does that person actually oppose? You just do not know without asking more specific questions.

"Gun control" is a slogan, and it is loaded. It carries certain unspoken ideas and emotions within it. For starters, the term focuses attention on the "gun", not on human beings. It also implies that guns ought to be controlled.

The word "gun" itself is one of those gut-level Anglo-Saxon rooted words that drive their meanings straight into the mind of the listener. But like so many of the three- and four-letter Anglo-Saxon rooted words, such as "back" and "life" and "dog," the word "gun" has a series of both distinct and overlapping meanings, and those meanings conjure various mental images.

Add the word "control" and what do you have? The term "gun control" suggests the action of "controlling", but there are no details. Who or what does the "controlling?" How does one actually perform "gun control"? The term leaves the listener clueless — and that gives the term propaganda power.

By using the term "gun control," people unconsciously accept (1) that "guns" can be "controlled", (2) that the controlling can occur without costs or side-effects, and (3) that once installed, a system of "gun control" operates constantly with little additional effort required. With "gun control," things will be "under control."

The term "gun control" does not contain the seeds of doubt; it suggests a problem solved once and for all. The term does not describe anything about who would control or how the control would be done. It does not even limit itself to any *type* of "gun."

Minds Numbed by Newspeak

"Gun control" is Newspeak. In the appendix to his novel *1984*, George Orwell described Newspeak, the language of the book's totalitarian socialist world. Newspeak was designed "to provide a medium of expression for the world-view and mental habits" of the ruling class, and "to make all other modes of thought impossible."[1]

Newspeak category "B" words "consisted of words which had been deliberately constructed for political purposes: words that not only had in every case a political implication, but were intended to impose a desirable mental attitude upon the person using them."[2] These Newspeak words were difficult to translate into ordinary English because they "were a sort of verbal shorthand, often packing whole ranges of ideas into a few syllables."[3] These "B words" were always compound words, a noun-verb combination welded together and easy to pronounce.[4]

The term "gun control", although still a two-word phrase, fits Orwell's definition of Newspeak "B words": Noun-verb, easy to pronounce, implying a wide range of concepts, molded to fit a distinct world-view, and crafted to minimize questions about it.

Snappy Slogan – Disarming Details

So there is no single clear definition of "gun control." Rather, the term serves as the advertising slogan for ideas and government policies that affect people who own or use firearms. "Gun control" ideas can be implemented as government "gun control" policies. Table 4A describes many of these government policies:

Table 4A: What "Gun Control" Means

Government "gun control" policy	Effect / Implementation
Gun Registration	Collect information about firearms and owners.
Gun Licensing	Collect information about firearms and owners; give permission for ownership and use of firearms.
Taxes & Fees on guns / ammunition	Increase costs of legal transactions and use of firearms.
Waiting Periods for gun sales	Delay legal transactions in firearms; impose financial costs on dealers.
Limits on number of gun purchases	Delay legal transactions in firearms; impose financial costs on dealers.
Restrictions on possession or sales of certain types of guns	Make it unlawful for citizens to have or use certain firearms.
Restrictions on possession of certain types of ammunition	Make it unlawful for citizens to have or use certain types of ammunition.
Restrictions on who can own or possess a gun	Deny the right of armed self-defense to certain classes of people.
Restrictions on carrying concealed weapons	Deny the right of armed self-defense to certain classes of people.
Permit systems for carrying concealed weapons	Collect data about firearms owners and firearms; impose financial costs and delays on individuals seeking a permit; deny the right of armed self-defense to certain classes of people or certain individuals.
Background Checks on gun buyers	Collect data about firearms buyers; detect when a prohibited person attempts to buy a firearm; delay lawful transactions in firearms; inhibit sales of firearms to prohibited persons.
"Gun Free Zones"	Impose legal penalties on citizens who possess a firearm in specified locations or within a certain distance of certain kinds of locations; deter citizens from transporting or carrying firearms.
Mandatory "safe storage" laws	Create barriers to rapid retrieval and use of firearms in emergencies.
Limits on magazine / clip ammunition capacity	Limits function of firearm.

Each one of the "gun control" laws listed above in Table 4A tend to discourage law-abiding citizens from owning, practicing and using firearms. How? By making it

- more difficult or inconvenient
- more expensive
- more embarrassing or humiliating
- more legally risky

for private citizens lawfully to own and use firearms.

Every type of "gun control" law discourages private firearms ownership in one or more of these four ways. It is undeniably true that whenever the cost of some activity goes up, all other things being equal, the number of people doing the activity tends to go down. So "gun control" tends to decrease the number of law-abiding people who own and use firearms. Table 4B shows how each type of "gun control" policy impacts the citizens.

Raising the costs of firearms ownership does not much affect criminals and others for whom having a gun is a high priority even if it is illegal. In Japan where private possession of handguns is outlawed, organized criminals import the guns they need or have them fabricated in the underground market.[5] After England enacted a ban on private possession of handguns, the underground market in unlawfully imported firearms is thriving; criminals get all the guns they want.[6] In an interview with a CBS-TV reporter, an American convicted criminal explained how he had *rented* a gun for "$150 just for this particular job... The more money you make on a job, the more you pay for this pistol."[7] Guns are tools of the trade for criminals, so the cost of the gun (including the risk of being caught and punished) is factored in as a business expense.

Disarming By Paper Chase

When pressed hard, advocates will admit that "gun control" schemes are designed to discourage private firearms ownership -- and thereby disarm the citizens. Way back in 1965, Leonard E. Reisman, then Deputy Commissioner of the New York City Police Department, frankly admitted this purpose of the harsh New York "gun control" laws when he testified before the House Ways and Means Committee:

Senator Thompson: Commissioner, if a householder in

New York wanted a pistol to keep in the house for protection of his home, how much trouble would it be for him to get it, or could he get it?

Mr. Reisman: He could get it. It would be a fair amount of trouble for him to get it. He would have to make application, be fingerprinted, have persons vouch for his good character, and his house, his premises, would be checked to see if they are reasonably secure for the possession of such weapons. We do issue some. We do not issue many.

Senator Thompson: You, in other words, discourage the ownership of a pistol under any conditions?

Mr. Reisman: Yes, we do.[8]

Table 4B: Effects of "Gun Control" Policies on Private Firearms Ownership

Government "gun control" policy	Discourages Firearms Ownership by
Gun Registration / Licensing	Increased cost, inconvenience, humiliation, risk of penalties or criminal prosecution for paperwork violations.
Taxes & Fees on guns / ammunition	Increased costs of lawful gun transactions and use of firearms.
Waiting Periods for gun sales	Impaired self-defense, humiliation, dealers' costs of storage and risk of penalties or prosecution for paperwork violations.
Limits on number of gun purchases	Inconvenience and humiliation.
Restrictions on possession or sales of certain types of guns and ammunition	Inconvenience, humiliation, legal risk in innocent purchase or inheritance of firearms without knowledge of the law.
Restrictions on who can own or possess a gun	Inconvenience, humiliation, risk of penalties or prosecution for innocent use or possession of firearms by accident or for defense (or for allowing a restricted person access to a firearm, even if no one is hurt).
Restrictions on carrying concealed weapons; permit requirements for concealed carry.	Inconvenience, expense, humiliation, risk of penalties or prosecution for carrying firearms for immediate self defense.

Table 4B: (continued) Effects of "Gun Control" Policies on Private Firearms Ownership	
Government "gun control" policy	Discourages Firearms Ownership by
Background Checks on gun buyers	Inconvenience, embarrassment or humiliation, particularly if the background check incorrectly flags buyer as prohibited from buying firearms.
"Gun Free Zones"	Impaired self-defense, embarrassment or humiliation, legal risk of penalties or prosecution for accidentally possessing a firearm within a zone without knowledge of the zone or the law.
Mandatory "safe storage" laws	Inconvenience, expense, risk of penalties or prosecution for violation that harms no one.
Limits on magazine / clip ammunition capacity	Impaired self-defense, risk of penalties or prosecution for violations that harm no one.

Psyching Out the Victims

As listed above, "gun control" laws work in four main ways to discourage firearms ownership and the culture of self-defense:

(1) increase the difficulty,

(2) increase the financial cost,

(3) increase the psychic cost (embarrass or humiliate), and

(4) increase the legal risk.

Least understood among these four ways is the psychic cost. Most people won't admit it when something embarrasses them. If a person feels uncomfortable being pushed into singing at a karaoke bar, or gets too much attention when he or she slips on a banana peel, or feels scorned by a practical joke, that person likely won't walk around telling people about feeling embarrassed or humiliated. Instead, and quite silently, that person will work overtime to avoid getting into that situation again.

There is an expression: "fool me once, shame on you; fool me twice, shame on me." It captures the idea that a person expects to feel personally responsible for being embarrassed — at least when that person knows how to avoid the embarrassing situation.

Many "gun control" laws and policies operate to raise the

psychic cost of firearms ownership. There are six main ways to raise psychic cost:

(1) Raise interpersonal tension
(2) Create an awkward scene
(3) Force the need to beg or apologize
(4) Draw unwanted public attention
(5) Construct an unfavorable stereotype
(6) Reduce to a cliché

Raise the cost of a product, and fewer people will buy it. Raise the psychic cost of an activity — make it less easy or pleasant — and fewer people will do it. That is an elementary fact of human action.[9] If the psychic costs of firearms ownership are raised, fewer people will own firearms. The "gun control" strategy to raise psychic costs is perhaps the most dangerous because it is unspoken by its advocates, and never admitted by its victims.

How do "gun control" laws and policies raise psychic costs in these six ways? Table 4C summarizes the cost-raising effects of several common "gun control" laws.

"Gun control" ideas and policies, even if they fall short of being actual laws, work to instill a culture of civilian disarmament. For example, after several highly-publicized cases of students killing fellow students in schools, some school districts devised "zero tolerance" policies against guns. It makes sense to forbid children from carrying firearms unless they are authorized to do so, but these "zero tolerance" policies have been enforced to embarrass and humiliate students who even think about a gun.

The Wall Street Journal has created an archive containing dozens of "zero tolerance" cases from all across the nation.[10] Consider these examples:

Sayreville, New Jersey: School authorities suspended four kindergarten students for "frightening other pupils by using their fingers as guns in a game of cops and robbers." All four boys, aged 5 and 6, received a three day suspension because they pointed their fingers at people and shouted words like "bang." One boy said "I have a bazooka and I'm going to shoot you."[11]

Pacoima, California: When a substitute teacher looked into a student's book bag and saw pictures showing a firearms practice session, the teacher confiscated the photos and reported the boy

15

to the school principal. The boy, aged 9, was sent to the principal's office where the school nurse questioned him about the pictures. The principal's secretary telephoned the boy's mother and threatened to call the police unless the mother came to the school at once. The school administrators proposed to suspend the boy, but the Los Angeles Unified School District officials overruled the suspension and eventually returned the photos to the boy's home.

What did the photos show? Scenes from a session at the shooting range, where the boy and his brother were learning firearms skills from their aunt, a certified police weapons instructor.[12]

Green Bay, Wisconsin: A third grader was suspended from school because he had a key chain with a small replica of a gun.[13]

Atlanta, Georgia: School administrators suspended an 11-year-old girl from school because a chain attached to a "Tweety Bird" wallet was too long and might be used as a weapon.[14]

Holland, Michigan: Officials at Harbor Lights Middle School flagged an academically-advanced 12-year-old boy as potentially dangerous because of comments he made during a classroom discussion. The boy had offered his opinion that he would feel safer in school if some of the adults at the school were trained and allowed to carry firearms. School officials flagged the boy as a potential violence risk and referred him and his parents to the school's "Hazard and Risk Assessment Team." The boy had previously stood out from the crowd by strongly favoring First and Second Amendment rights. He had refused to sign a "vow of peace" which called for students to renounce the right to self-defense and to never use a firearm or other weapon. He had also violated the school's "zero tolerance" violence policy by fighting in self-defense against three schoolyard attackers.[15]

Jonesboro, Arkansas: An 8-year-old boy was disciplined by his elementary school principal for "pointing a breaded chicken finger at a teacher and saying, 'Pow, pow, pow.'" The boy's conduct violated the "zero tolerance" policy against weapons, so he was suspended for three days. The principal defended the punishment for the boy's threat of violence: "[It] depends on the tone, the demeanor, and in some manner you judge the intent. It's not the object in the hand, it's the thought in the mind. Is a plastic fork worse than a metal fork? Is a pencil a weapon?"[16]

Irvington, New Jersey: "Two second-graders playing cops and robbers with a paper gun were charged with making terrorist threats." According to the *Washington Post* story, each boy had pointed the same paper gun at classmates and said, "I'm going to kill you all." Under the school district's "zero tolerance" policy, the two boys were suspended and the police notified. The boys' parents said that the matter should have been handled by the school principal, but police charged both boys with the crime.[17]

These examples show how a "zero tolerance" policy can be turned to embarrass, humiliate and punish people for any thought about or contact with anything that even suggests a weapon. Are the school officials overreacting and irrational? No — they are carrying out the policy to the letter.

In those cases where the children pretended to threaten violence, it was the mock *gun* that triggered the serious punishment — not the suggestion of killing. That these school officials ignored the hint of *violence* is no surprise, given the numbers of assaults and murders that are daily played out on television and in movies.

The purpose of the "zero tolerance" policy becomes clear by its implementation: to make public examples by punishing a few children, so that everyone learns to avoid and hate weapons of any type, regardless of their potentially lifesaving uses.

We know the "zero tolerance" policies have an anti-gun propaganda purpose precisely because they are "zero tolerance." A policy designed to promote nonviolence would not be "zero tolerance." A good nonviolence policy would provide exceptions for:
- righteous self-defense
- lack of wrongful intent
- high improbability of injury based on type or condition of "weapon"
- freedom of speech and expression

The "zero tolerance" anti-weapons policies do more than punish the occasional student. They teach youngsters that it is proper for government to make laws to punish innocent conduct.

"Sensible" Gun Law?[18]

A teacher in Manassas, Virginia, obtained a state-issued permit to carry a concealed weapon, and did carry her sidearm for protection at night. On March 6, 2000, she accidentally and unknowingly brought the loaded sidearm onto school property in her closed purse. Another teacher came upon the purse left unattended, opened it, and discovered the gun.

Nobody had been endangered and the dedicated teacher had no history of violence whatsoever. Nevertheless, she was charged and convicted of the felony crime of bringing a loaded handgun onto school property. It didn't matter that it was an accident. It didn't matter that she had no criminal intent.

The jury recommended a 12 month prison term with a $2,500 fine. The judge suspended the prison term and reduced the fine slightly. The teacher lost her job, probably permanently.

Virginia's "sensible" gun law snared this teacher for a mistake that hurt nobody. The same law would never stop a school attacker — but the armed teacher could stop that attacker.

The anti-self-defense ("gun control") lobby did not protest this senselessly severe application of that "sensible" law. Do those lobbyists actually prefer schools full of unarmed potential victims? Are innocent teachers the real targets of their laws?

Punishment as Persecution

Punishing innocent conduct means the destruction of fundamental rights. For centuries the Common Law of England, imported and sustained in America, declared that there could be no crime without intent.[19] In modern times that principle has been whittled away. Time and again judges lately have held that society can punish a person for a "crime," when that the person had no evil or criminal intent and did not know the conduct was unlawful.[20] The schools' "zero tolerance" policies transmit this unjust notion to the very young.

School rules and schoolyard behavior powerfully affect the minds of children. Where those rules and behavior reflect national policy, the results can be horrifying. When the National Socialist Workers Party (Nazis) took over Germany in 1933, they began a policy of identifying Jews as filthy and dangerous to society. During the same pre-World War II period, anti-Jewish policy extended to ostracize Jewish pupils in elementary grades.[21] The policy aimed to embarrass and humiliate Jewish children, as part of a larger plan to expel them from mainstream society.

The policy worked, as Richard L. Miller has reported:

• When a Jewish boy returned to school after a period of being out sick, he was surprised by a new ritual. At the beginning of class, the teacher shouted, "Heil Hitler!" and the class echoed the shout. The teacher smilingly informed the boy:"The Jewish boys are excused from giving the Hitler salute."[22]

• One Jewish girl felt "awkward and embarrassed" each morning when she had to remain seated and quiet while Aryan pupils began the day by standing with the patriotic shout, "Heil Hitler!"[23]

• One Jewish boy who wanted to play in sports "was forced to stand before the class and repeat aloud, 'I don't want to play.'"[24]

• In 1935 the Bavarian Education Authority decreed: "Non-Aryan pupils, whether boys or girls, must not be taken on school outings. During the break period of their own class they must attend lessons in some other class selected by the headmaster."[25]

• During games played in kindergarten, each pupil would be given some animal to play. Frequently Jewish children had to play pigs. After being made a pig day after day, one six-year-old Jewish girl refused to go to the school any more.[26]

Laws That Serve the State

What is the purpose of law? Does the law provide a framework of neutral rules, known in advance, that keep the peace among individuals by punishing aggression and fraud? Or does the law exist to protect the state, and to serve the state by "educating" the people about how to act?

In a nation comprised of free individuals, the law provides the neutral rules. Friedrich Hayek described that system as liberty under the rule of law: "Within the known rules of the game the individual is free to pursue his personal ends and desires, certain that the powers of government will not be used deliberately to frustrate his efforts."[27] The legal system builds a framework to protect individuals in their pursuit of happiness.

In a totalitarian or police state, the law protects the state. The law "educates" the citizenry by allowing judges to punish people for acts which deserve punishment. The law forms the foundation

Table 4C:
Psychological Costs of "Gun Control" Strategy

"Gun Control" Law	Psychological Cost Event	Typical Scenes / Comments
Gun registration/ licensing	interpersonal tension awkward scene need to beg or apologize unwanted public attention unfavorable stereotype cliché fear of government intrusion	"You don't have the right documents." "This ID is expired" "Is this a photo of you?" "We can't accept this form of ID" "You have to prove your citizenship" "Seems to be a problem with your background check" "Police need to know exactly who has guns" "Need to be able to trace crime guns to their owners" "Sir, you'll have to show your license or we'll have to confiscate all the guns"
Waiting period/ one gun per month	interpersonal tension awkward scene unwanted public attention unfavorable stereotype cliché	"Sorry, you'll have to leave it here" "We can't let you walk out of here with it now" "You have to come back next Monday" "You'll just have to reschedule your hunting trip, I can't let you have the gun today" "Otherwise, people will amass huge arsenals"
Restrictions on open carry of firearms	interpersonal tension awkward scene need to beg or apologize unwanted public attention	"Sir, can you show me your identification?" "Honest, officer, I was just bringing it home from the range" "Hey, you're scaring my kids by carrying that gun around"
Federal bans of selected types of firearms and magazine	need to beg or apologize unfavorable stereotype cliché	"Only a real nut thinks he needs that kind of gun" "It's the criminals' gun of choice" "What, you gonna hunt ducks with an assault rifle?" "Too much firepower for sporting or self-defense" "They're only good for killing people"
"Gun Free Zones"	fear for safety need to beg or apologize unwanted public attention unfavorable stereotype cliché	"Yes, I have a felony conviction — for having an unloaded gun in my trunk" "Sorry, you can't get this job because of your criminal record" "Keep dangerous weapons away from our kids"

for finding guilt and sets the lower limits of punishment. Judges are encouraged to show their dedication to the state by punishing as much anti-social behavior as possible, and by showing no mercy.

Nazi laws and policies followed the service-to-state model. The legal philosophy was "no crime without punishment." Statutes in the 1935 Nazi criminal code put the philosophy into black and white. Article 2 of that code required prosecutors and judges to look for ways to punish people, even when there was no specific law violation:

> Whoever commits an act which the law declares as pun-
> ishable or which deserves punishment according to the
> fundamental idea of a penal law or the sound sentiment
> of the people, shall be punished. If no specific penal law
> can be directly applied to the act, it shall be punished
> according to the law whose underlying principle can be
> most readily applied to the act.[28]

When the law aims to serve the state and educate the people, then officials can do almost anything that could be viewed as pro-moting the public good. An official or judge would be violating his civic duty if he were lenient or imposed lesser penalties upon wrongdoers than called for by law.[29]

When school officials exert themselves to sternly punish grade schoolers for having pictures of guns or pretending to "shoot" a chicken strip, these officials follow the pattern of Nazi law. Taking these seemingly ridiculous, extreme interpretations of the "zero tolerance" policies shows an intent to "educate" children to serve the will of people in authority. Punishing people as though they were criminals, when there is no evidence of criminal intent, runs contrary to justice in a free society. These "zero tolerance" policy attitudes have no place in the educational system of a nation of lim-ited government, neutral laws and individual rights.

End Notes

[1]Orwell, George. 1949. *Nineteen Eighty-Four.* New York: New American Library, Inc., p. 246.

[2]*Ibid.,* 249.

[3]*Ibid.*

[4]*Ibid.,* 249-250.

[5]Kopel, David B. 1992. *The Samurai, The Mountie, and The Cowboy.* Buffalo, NY: Prometheus Books, pp.21-22.

[6]Ungoed-Thomas, Jon. 2000. Killings rise as 3M illegal guns flood Britain. *The Sunday Times.* January 16. *(www.sunday-times.co.uk)*

[7]Kukla, Robert J. 1973. *Gun Control.* Harrisburg, PA: Stackpole Books, p. 66 (quoting CBS-TV transcript).

[8]Kukla 1973, p. 310 (quoting transcript of hearings).

[9]Mises, Ludwig von. 1966. *Human Action.* Third Edition. Chicago: Henry Regnery Co., pp. 97, 119-120, 240-242.

[10]Taranto, James. 2001. "Zero Tolerance Makes Zero Sense." *The Wall Street Journal.* May 18, P. A-15. *(www.opinionjournal.com,* linking to archive.)

[11]Dumenigo, Argelio. 2000. Kindergarten penalty spurs parents to sue. *Star-Ledger* (New Jersey). Jun. 2. (www.nj.com/news/ledger)

[12]Rubush, Scott. 2000. Public Schools Are "Clueless" About Guns. *FrontPageMagazine.com.* December 7. (www.frontpagemag.com)

[13]Rubush, Dec. 7, 2000.

[14]Rubush, Dec. 7, 2000.

[15]Dougherty, Jon E. 2000. Sixth Grader targeted for pro-gun remarks: "A" student defends 2nd Amendment, flagged as violence risk. *WorldNetDaily.* March 30. (www.worldnetdaily.com)

[16]Boy Suspended for Pointing Chicken. Associated Press. Jan. 31, 2001. (dailynews.yahoo.com)

[17]N.J. Boys Charged After Playing with Paper Gun. *The Washington Post.* March 22, 2001, p. A9.

[18]Honawar, Vaishali. 2001. Gun-toting teacher gets fine and probation. *The Washington Times.* Jan. 5, p. C-1.

[19]Roberts, Paul Craig and Lawrence M. Stratton. 2000. *The Tyranny of Good Intentions.* Roseville, Calif: Prima Publishing, pp. 11, 61-2, 64.

[20]See *United States v. Balint,* 258 U.S. 250, 251 (1922)("where the emphasis of the statute is evidently upon achievement of some social betterment rather than the punishment of crimes," a citizen may be found guilty even when the citizen had no intent to commit a crime); *United States v. Dotterweich,* 320 U.S. 277, 280-81, 285-86 (1943)(corporate president convicted of crime when he was unaware of the activity and had no criminal intent); compare *Morissette v. United States,* 342 U.S. 246, 250-65 (1952)(extended discussion of history and importance of requiring

proof of intent before imposing criminal liability).

[21]Miller, Richard Lawrence. 1995. *Nazi Justiz: Law of the Holocaust.* Westport, Conn: Praeger Publishers, p. 70.

[22]Miller 1995, p. 70, citing Zeller, Frederic. 1989. *When Time Ran Out: Coming of Age in the Third Reich.* Sag Harbor, New York: The Permanent Press, p. 28.

[23]Miller 1995, p. 70, citing Henry, Frances. 1984. *Victims and Neighbors: A Small Town in Nazi Germany Remembered.* South Hadley, Mass: Bergin & Garvey Publishers, p. 61.

[24]Miller 1995, p. 70, citing *New York Times,* March 5, 1934, p. 10.

[25]Miller 1995, p. 70, citing *The Yellow Spot: The Outlawing of Half a Million Human Beings: A Collection of Facts and Documents Relating to Three Years' Persecution of German Jews, Derived Chiefly from National Socialist Sources, Very Carefully Assembled by a Group of Investigators.* New York: Knight Publications, 1989, 247.

[26]Miller 1995, p. 70, citing *Manchester Guardian,* October 9, 1933.

[27]Hayek, Friedrich A. 1944. *The Road to Serfdom.* Chicago: University of Chicago Press, p. 73.

[28]Miller 1995, p. 49 (quoting source).

[29]Miller 1995, p. 50.

Chapter Five:
The Genocide Formula

This book shows the Genocide Formula in action in several countries around the world.[1] Simply stated, the formula is:

Hatred + Government + Disarmed Civilians = Genocide

Each term in the formula has a specific meaning:

Hatred:　　Fear, loathing, disgust, or malicious disregard for the life and well-being of a human being. The state of mind that would order, encourage or permit the intentional killing of innocent people.

Hatred appears in many forms. It can be racism: the belief that one's race is superior to another, to the point that members of the inferior race can be degraded, victimized and killed. It can be ideology, as with Marxism and Communism: the belief that members of an economic class are parasites or traitors, and thus must be eliminated. It can be a doctrine of aggression: the demonization of designated enemies to make it acceptable, easy, routine, even "fun" to kill them. It can be personal resentment and desire for revenge. It can be the extreme desire for wealth and power that will tolerate no resistance.

Government:　　An organization that considers itself morally authorized to impose force and violence against persons in the name of religion or the greater good of the nation, race or humanity. The social apparatus that possesses the means to compel and coerce persons over whom it claims to rule.

25

Government includes popularly elected leaders, hereditary kings and princes, military regimes, and those regimes established by invasion, conquest or rebellion. For the Genocide Formula, the key factors of Government are: the mechanisms to set goals, make rules and determine programs for people to live under and carry out, combined with the physical power to force those people to comply (or die). Thus, the term Government does not refer so much to a written system of laws and organization, as it refers to using Power to achieve chosen goals for society. Government exerts its Power via individuals and groups obeying orders or following expectations, typically military, police, judicial and other agencies selected by Government leaders.

Disarmed Civilians: Persons over whom Government exercises Power, but who are not considered or acting as part of the Government, and who have no lawful or no physical way to obtain self-defense weapons such as firearms (pistols, rifles, shotguns, etc.) These are persons whose chief defense against aggression is using hand combat, wielding small knives or sticks, or running away.

The difference between a Disarmed Civilian and an unarmed person is not large. The term Disarmed Civilian refers to a person who, except for government law, cultural norms or other social pressures, would have been free to possess firearms and other substantial defense tools. The unarmed person is simply that: a person who does not have a defense tool (such as a firearm) at the time it is needed, for whatever reason.

Genocide: Causing the destruction of any group of people identifiable by their national, ethnic, racial, religious, regional or economic background, whether by direct or indirect means.

The term "genocide" typically refers to a plan and practice of killing members of certain identifiable groups, such as when the Nazis tried to exterminate the Jews, or the Turkish government tried to exterminate the Armenians. In this book, Genocide refers to such group extermination, but it also includes the killing of people to achieve political or economic goals, even if those people do not neatly fit into a target group.[2] The killings might be done by governments in place or by outside groups either advancing the cause of the government or seeking to become the government. In place of "genocide" we would happily use the word coined by Professor R. J. Rummel, "democide," except that as yet most Americans do not know or use that term.[3]

Government & Power

Ludwig von Mises, the Austrian economist, concisely explained it: "State or government is the social apparatus of compulsion and coercion."[4] Thomas Paine, senior commando in the Idea campaign of the American Revolutionary War, saw danger built into the very essence of any such social apparatus, declaring "government, even in its best state, is but a necessary evil; in its worst state, an intolerable one."[5] James Bovard, nationally recognized author and columnist, pithily observed that, "Government is ourselves — armed with clubs."[6]

Professor Rummel concisely states the connection between Government and Power: "The more power a government has, the more it can act arbitrarily according to the whims and desires of the elite, and the more it will make war on others and murder its foreign and domestic subjects."[7] Professor Rummel's work, *Death by Government,* proves his point beyond dispute.

Perhaps the most famous phrasing of the point is Lord Acton's dictum: "Power corrupts; absolute Power corrupts absolutely."[8]

Powerful Government stands guilty of the most heinous destruction of 169,000,000 innocents in the 20th Century.[9] This fact proves that the citizens, the people, even if they initially vote for a government, cannot always control it. Certainly the people lack direct control when the government obtains power by rebellion, coup d'etat, or conquest. The people might not be able to directly control the formation of Hatred and Government.

But the people can control the third element of the Genocide Formula. The people can retain the ability to stop governments that turn tyrannical or evil. The people keep their authority over government by remaining armed.

It didn't take the 20th Century experience to teach this lesson.

The American Founders knew it well from earlier world history. As just one example, Noah Webster, an influential Federalist who argued for the adoption of the U.S. Constitution, explained how government can oppress only when it can overwhelm the people:

> Another source of power in government is a military force. But this, to be efficient, must be superior to any force that exists among the people, or which they can command; for otherwise this force would be annihilated, on the first exercise of acts of oppression.

For oppression to prevail, disarmed civilians are needed, as Webster continued:

> Before a standing army can rule, the people must be disarmed; as they are in almost every kingdom in Europe. The supreme power in America cannot enforce unjust laws by the sword; because the whole body of the people are armed, and constitute a force superior to any band of regular troops that can be, on any pretense, raised in the United States.

By design of the Constitution, an armed civilian population stops tyranny in America, as Webster concluded:

> A military force, at the command of Congress, can execute no laws, but such as the people perceive to be just and constitutional; for they will possess the power, and jealously will instantly inspire the inclination, to resist the execution of a law which appears to them unjust and oppressive.[10]

What the Founders like Noah Webster knew, so also have modern Americans, such as Hubert H. Humphrey, long-time U.S. Senator from Minnesota, Vice-President under President Lyndon Johnson, and 1968 Democratic candidate for President. Mr. Humphrey wrote in 1960:

> Certainly one of the chief guarantees of freedom under any government, no matter how popular and respected is the right of the citizen to keep and bear arms. This is not to say that firearms should not be very carefully used and that definite rules of precaution should not be taught and enforced. But the right of the citizen to bear arms is just one more safeguard against a tyranny which now appears remote in America, but which historically has proved to be always possible.[11]

For an Armed Citizenry: John F. Kennedy

While running for president in 1960, then-Senator John F. Kennedy gave an interview to *Guns* magazine about his position on the right to keep and bear arms as set forth in the Second Amendment to the U.S. Constitution. Mr. Kennedy, who himself owned and enjoyed shooting high-powered rifles and shotguns, spoke about the relevance of the Second Amendment to America in the nuclear age:

> By calling attention to a well-regulated militia for the security of the Nation, and the right of each citizen to keep and bear arms, our Founding Fathers recognized the essentially civilian nature of our economy. Although it is extremely unlikely that the fears of governmental tyranny, which gave rise to the second amendment, will ever be a major danger to our Nation, the amendment still remains an important declaration of our basic military-civilian relationships, in which every citizen must be ready to participate in the defense of his country. For that reason I believe the second amendment will always be important.[12]

Mr. Kennedy thus recognized the importance of an armed citizenry, both as a check on governmental tyranny and as a vital component of national defense. On the occasion of Patriots Day, March 20, 1961, President Kennedy accepted with appreciation a Life Membership in the National Rifle Association.[13]

The "Gun Control" – Genocide Connection

How does "gun control" relate to genocide? As explained in this book, "gun control" schemes try to make it unpopular and then relatively rare for private citizens to own and use firearms. Anti-gun laws make it more costly and risky to have guns. Anti-gun rhetoric weakens the spirit of people to be armed.

Licensing, registration and safety-inspection laws do more than discourage firearms ownership. By enforcing these laws the government creates a list of people who could possibly resist tyranny and oppression. As shown in this book, evil governments use such lists to locate, disarm, and eliminate firearms owners from the population.

When the firearms are confiscated and the defense-minded people gone, only the defenseless unarmed people remain. The third element of the Genocide Formula — the only one that the people can directly control — is in place.[14]

Bottom Line: *Preventing genocide is the duty of the people; only armed people can do it.*

End Notes

[1]The Genocide Formula was earlier (and first) stated as Hatred + Government + "Gun Control" = Genocide. Simkin, Jay, Aaron Zelman and Alan M. Rice. 1994. *Lethal Laws*. Milwaukee, WI: Jews for the Preservation of Firearms Ownership, pp. 9-11. Here, the revised definition replaces "gun control" with "disarmed civilians."

[2]Polsby, Daniel D. and Don B. Kates, Jr.. 1997. *Of Holocausts and Gun Control*. Wash. Univ. Law Qtly. Vol 75, p. 1237 (using the term "genocide" in a similar broad fashion).

[3]Rummel, R. J. 1994. *Death by Government*. New Brunswick, NJ: Transaction Publishers, pp. 32-38.

[4]Mises, Ludwig von. 1963. *Human Action*. Third Edition. Chicago: Henry Regnery Co., p 149.

[5]Paine, Thomas. 1995 [1760]. *Common Sense*. New York: Barnes & Noble. Ch. 1, p. 1.

[6]Bovard, James. 1999. *Freedom in Chains: The Rise of the State and Demise of the Citizen*. New York: St. Martin's Press, p. 262.

[7]Rummel 1994, pp. 1-2.

[8]Rummel 1994, p. 1, citing Lord Acton's letter to Bishop Creighton.

[9]Rummel 1994, p. 27.

[10]Webster, Noah. [1787] An Examination in the Leading Principles of the Federal Constitution, in Ford, P., ed. 1888. *Pamphlets on the Constitution of the United States,* p. 56 (quoted in Halbrook, Stephen P. 1984. *That Every Man Be Armed*. San Francisco: Liberty Tree Press, p. 68).

[11]Humphrey, Hubert H. 1960. Know Your Lawmakers. *Guns*. Feb., p. 4.

[12]Kukla 1973, p. 33 (quoting article in *Guns* magazine, April 1960, inserted into the record of congressional hearings in 1963-1964).

[13]Kukla 1973, p. 33 (quoting letter of President Kennedy to NRA Executive Vice President Franklin L. Orth, inserted into the record of congressional hearings in 1967.)

[14]"[O]ver the long run, the risk to life from criminal governments is overwhelmingly larger than the risk to life from lone criminals. Gun control measures which substantially reduce the possibility of resistance to genocide, but which offer little commensurate increase in lives saved, might thus be considered to endanger rather than enhance public safety." Kopel, David B. 1995. Lethal Laws. (Book review). *New York Law School Journal of International and Comparative Law.* Vol. 15, pp. 355, 389.

Genocide Formula:
By The Nations

Chapter Six:
Cambodia

Out of Cambodia's 1970 population of about 7,100,000, governments and those seeking control of government power murdered 2,035,000 men, women and children.[1]

Over one quarter of the population — 29% — every fourth individual — killed in the span of 1970 to 1980. The Genocide Formula at work. The common factor: victims who had no means to resist.

Brief History of "Gun Control" in Cambodia

Although Cambodia had existed as a kingdom for centuries, France effectively ruled the land as a protectorate from 1864 until withdrawing in 1954. Anti-colonial agitation and violence shook Southeast Asia in the 1920's and 1930's, and in the 1930's Cambodia suffered from bands of criminals robbing and terrorizing villages all over the nation.

Likely designed to combat the banditry and to deter armed uprisings against the colonial government, a new "gun control" law, Cambodian Royal Ordinance No. 55, was issued on March 28, 1938.[2] Pre-existing laws had regulated the carrying of weapons and air-rifles, but this new Ordinance established a more comprehensive "gun control" scheme of licensing.

Cambodia's "modern" program of restrictions on firearms ownership and possession thus began in 1938 and remained in force, with supplements and amendments, until at least 1970. The Cambodian Penal Code retained the "gun control" laws after the French left.

Most Cambodian people were poor and likely not able to afford many firearms. Those who could have afforded firearms were discouraged from doing so by the "gun control" laws. Combining these facts with the people's generally Buddhist beliefs in nonviolence, the result was a population of defenseless civilians, unfamiliar with the defensive tools necessary to deter or resist armed aggression.

Even were the Cambodians inclined to band together to obtain firearms for defense of a community rather than individually, the "gun control" laws made that nearly impossible. The licenses for firearms had to be issued to individuals; sharing firearms would subject the participants to criminal penalties. Table 6A summarizes the "gun control" laws of Cambodia.

The Khmer Rouge apparently enacted no laws (except their initial constitution) and had little use for legal processes and paperwork.[3] Thus, the Khmer Rouge "gun control" program was essentially a firearms confiscation program. People who were forced out of cities were typically searched for weapons and foreign currency.[4] Khmer Rouge troops that came into villages were known to have conducted house-to-house searches for weapons.[5]

Given that there was a civil war between 1970 and 1975, firearms were available illegally from military and rebel sources. Apparently, few non-partisan Cambodians (regular citizens) obtained firearms. Thus they were mostly defenseless against any armed aggressors, large or small.

Massacres I: Norodom Sihanouk Regime

Between 1967 and 1979, three killer governments came to power and inflicted death on the Cambodian people. The first and least deadly arose during the period from 1967 to 1970 when former Prince Norodom Sihanouk ruled. A powerful ruler who had been crowned King in 1941, Sihanouk gave up the throne in 1955 to be more directly active in implementing his vision as Premier. Sihanouk ruled with "a light authoritarian hand" and was immensely popular with the Cambodian people.[6]

When there was protest or rebellion, however, Sihanouk responded harshly. When the Sihanouk government in 1966 took private land in Battambang province without paying compensation, local villagers were outraged. In 1967, the government deployed troops to collect taxes from the people in the region, and villagers attacked and killed two soldiers in a detachment.

The government responded by sending in paratroopers and national police. To pacify the region, soldiers employed maximum force and were promised bounties for each severed head they sent to headquarters.[7] By June, 1967, 4,000 people had left the Battambang province, yet the government repression grew more brutal. Villages were bombed, strafed, and in several cases, totally destroyed. Sometimes the army would surround a town and massacre all the inhabitants. Heads of victims were sent by truckload to headquarters.[8]

Unrest spread to other provinces. Fifty villages were burned, villagers clubbed to death and beheaded. Thousands of people, including many teachers and students, fled into the forests to escape the killings.

Meanwhile, rebellions arose in other areas. Sihanouk blamed communists and foreign agents for instigating the uprisings, and launched a hunt for suspected communists. Provincial officials were ordered to kill peasants who were guilty of living in areas that harbored communists. Sihanouk ordered 40 school teachers to be thrown off a cliff because of suspected anti-government activity. Prisoners from communist-influenced regions had their guts cut open and were tied to trees to die slowly in agony. Rebel villages were destroyed, their inhabitants wiped out.[9]

A low estimate of outright killings of civilians by the Sihanouk regime places the number at about 12,000 dead.[10] That was just the beginning.

Massacres II: Lon Nol Regime

As political tensions increased and economic conditions worsened, Prince Sihanouk increasingly lost support. Not surprisingly, while Sihanouk was abroad, Premier and Chief General Lon Nol, backed by the Acting Prime Minister, took over the government by force in April, 1970. Under military guard, the Cambodian National Assembly voted unanimously to unseat the prince. Lon Nol became prime minister, head of state, and commander in chief.

Lon Nol sported a history of ugly violence. As an army general, he had commanded the troops who had so mercilessly put down rebellions in 1967-1968 (see above). In earlier operations, Lon Nol's troops reportedly had typically moved into villages, killed all the adult men and women, and then held strength contests in which soldiers would grasp babies by the legs and pull them apart.[11]

Although he professed to be pro-American and anti-communist, Lon Nol also was fiercely racist. Dedicated to rebuilding the Khmer people as an ethnic group, Lon Nol's regime targeted and murdered in cold blood Catholics and ethnic Vietnamese. The genocide count under Lon Nol came to about 15,000 dead.[12]

Communist North Vietnamese, native communist Cambodians (Khmer Rouge), and forces still loyal to Prince Sihanouk, joined forces for a time to drive Lon Nol out. The anti-Lon Nol fighters exacted retribution, invading towns and killing people suspected of supporting the Lon Nol coup.[13] The megamurder was about to begin.

Megamurderers: The Khmer Rouge

The Khmer Rouge ("Red Khmers") were the Cambodian Communists. Pol Pot had headed the Khmer Rouge since 1962.[14] Pol Pot and the communist Khmer Rouge, between 1975 and 1979, *murdered Cambodian citizens at an annual rate eight times that of Nazi Germany.* The Khmer Rouge wiped out about one-third of the nation's population in four years.

Before they toppled Lon Nol in April, 1975, the Khmer Rouge had linked with the Vietnamese communists and elements of Prince Sihanouk's supporters. Once the Lon Nol regime was weakened and on the defensive, the Khmer Rouge built itself up by recruitment and training.[15] By 1973, the Khmer Rouge had virtually disconnected from the other groups, and had purged (by killing) from their organization and troops anyone who had been trained in Hanoi or had served with Vietnamese communists or who held "incorrect" beliefs. Whole families, whom the Khmer Rouge believed had sheltered communist Vietnamese troops, were massacred.[16]

In regions where the Khmer Rouge obtained control, they literally emptied whole towns and cities, sending the people into the countryside to live as farmers and peasants. Khmer Rouge cadres outlawed all free speech, travel, and any expression of religion. Money was eliminated, all farming was collectivized, and the Khmer Rouge cadres had absolute command over the life and death of every person. Typically, people worked from morning until after dark. The smallest violation of any rule resulted in death.[17]

Food shortages and hunger spread under this communist system. People who stole food to eat were executed; the others scrambled to find banana leaves, roots and weeds to eat. Meanwhile, all persons over age 16 were drafted into the Khmer Rouge; refusal usually meant death.

As the Khmer Rouge took over more territory, their methods only became more brutal. For example, when the Khmer Rouge occupied the former capital of Oudong, they forced the entire population out into the jungle. They burned houses everywhere and destroyed the town. The Khmer Rouge split people into groups, executed any uniformed Lon Nol troops on the spot, and killed all the school teachers and government officials they could identify.[18]

The rule by terror under the Khmer Rouge, and the resulting forced labor and starvation, caused thousands of Cambodians to flee. The U.S. bombing campaign had destroyed many towns and farming areas, driving even more people to leave. A large number of the refugees went to Phnom Penh, the capital, and swelled its population to more than two million.[19]

After steadily surrounding and laying siege on the capital city for years, a Khmer Rouge army of 68,000 troops captured Phnom Penh in April, 1975. Almost immediately, the Khmer Rouge ordered every person out of the city. No exceptions.

Other cities in Cambodia were emptied in the same way at the same time. Including the population of Phnom Penh, over 4,000,000 million people were ordered out of the nation's cities. No exceptions. It did not matter if the person was actually undergoing surgery or having a baby, he or she had to leave at once.

The millions of defenseless civilians left, any way they could. They drove, pedaled, or walked. Ill, crippled, sick, it did not matter. A British journalist reported that he had personally watched as the Khmer Rouge were

> Tipping out patients [from the hospitals] like garbage in the streets. ... Bandaged men and women hobble by the embassy. Wives push wounded soldier husbands on hospital beds on wheels, some with serum drips still attached. In five years of war, this is the greatest caravan of human misery I have seen.[20]

Fear of death made it happen. Any person among the masses of refugees would be instantly killed if he failed to obey any order of the Khmer Rouge regime and troops.[21] The troops had the guns. The citizens did not.

The huge masses of city dwellers were force marched, for days or weeks, wearing only what they had on their backs. In short order the very young and old, the sick, injured and infirm, died on the roads and trails. The people had brought very little food or water, because they had no time to prepare and because the Khmer Rouge had said the evacuation of the cities would be temporary.[22]

Pol Pot later admitted that the massive evacuation of the cities was part of a plan, not a spur-of-the-moment security precaution. Along the evacuation routes there were troops at checkpoints already established. The underlying objective was to destroy the old order of things and rebuild Cambodia by placing everyone who survived in a collectivized forced-labor farm.[23]

To destroy the old order, however, required destroying as many educated people as might pose any threat whatsoever. That meant any person who was "rich," all college students, teachers, police officers, and former government officials. Doctors, lawyers, anyone who could speak English or French, anyone with an education over the seventh grade, anyone who wore glasses. These all were tortured and either killed outright or worked to death.[24]

Rebuilding Cambodia meant operating a nation-sized concentration camp, divided into sections and run with maximum cruelty. There were no personal rights, no freedoms of any sort, no religions permitted, no courts, judges or laws. Nobody could receive mail, telephone calls, skilled medical care, books, periodicals or any schooling. Everyone ate in groups, nobody could grow, raise, cook or eat food privately. Nobody could use their personal names, and there were no holidays. There was no sexual freedom, no private conversation, no independent family life.[25]

Everyone over age 5 had to work. Laughing or crying was punishable, sometimes by death. Saying a kind word to a loved one would result in interrogation, sometimes brutal torture. Showing sadness at the death of one's child would get a person killed on the spot.[26]

The forced workday in communist Cambodia typically started before dawn and sometimes extended late into the night.

Exhausted and often starving, the victims were mostly too weak to resist or revolt. They also had no weapons; their captors were well armed and ruthless.[27]

Terror and extermination were the constant work of the Khmer Rouge. As the communists extended and deepened their control, they located suspected former military men, government officials, businessmen and religious leaders. These victims they often viciously tortured and then murdered, along with their whole families.[28]

In one case, the Khmer Rouge came to believe that the people of the small village of Kauk Lon were all former Lon Nol regime employees. Communist troops forced all 360 villagers, men, women and children, to march into a forest. Every one of the villagers was cut down by waiting machine gunners.[29]

In the massacre at Mongkol Borei, the communist commander ordered ten civil servants and their families to be bound and trucked to a banana plantation. Going family by family, the communists pulled out the men, methodically stabbed each one, and then dragged the horrified family members next to the dying men and stabbed the wives also by bayonet thrusts. The children and babies were stabbed last.[30]

Not only were educated people the immediate targets of the communist death squads. The Khmer Rouge targeted specific ethnic and religious groups.

Buddhism, the religion of 90 percent of the people, was to be extinguished. About 95% of all monks were defrocked and many killed: Of the 40,000 to 60,000 Buddhist monks, only an estimated 1,000 survived the Pol Pot era. About 95% of all Buddhist temples in the country were destroyed; the rest turned to other uses.[31]

Islam, and the Muslim minority called the Cham, were slated for extermination as well. Starting in 1973, the Khmer Rouge had persecuted this minority by suppressing all Islamic practices and killing Cham religious and community leaders. To humiliate and degrade the Cham further, the Khmer Rouge often forced them to eat pork, and then required they be buried upside down (not facing Mecca as their religion requires).[32] Top Islamic clergymen were tortured and murdered (boiled alive, beaten to death, disemboweled, starved). Cham villages were destroyed, and their people massacred or dispersed. In one district alone, five towns were leveled and 20,000

Cham people were killed. Half the total Cham population of Cambodia was killed.[33]

The genocide also aimed at people of Chinese, Vietnamese, Thai or Lao ancestry. Approximately 541,000 persons of these ethnic minority backgrounds, including thousands of Catholic and Protestant Christians, were murdered by the Khmer Rouge.[34]

Perhaps the least "innocent" victims of the Khmer Rouge were the members of the Khmer Rouge who themselves were "purged" by Pol Pot. Based on a fear and loathing of the ancient enemy, Viet Nam, any communist who was suspected of being pro-Vietnamese was imprisoned, tortured and killed. Nearly 20,000 men, women and children were questioned, tortured and murdered in just one place, the infamous Tuol Seng facility located in a former high school in Phnom Penh.[35]

In 1978, Pol Pot tried to purge the whole region that bordered Vietnam by killing all officials, party members, village leaders and innocent civilians.[36] Many of these victims had access to weapons, so they rebelled against the purge. Although the fighting was fierce, the communist government troops won and exterminated as many in the region as possible. The death toll was at least 100,000 people.[37]

There were several rebellions and coup attempts instigated by Khmer Rouge troops in 1976-1977. All of these uprising were suppressed, with whole units of rebels executed.[38]

Downfall of the Khmer Rouge

Killing Vietnamese people, part of the Khmer Rouge's overall race hate and ethnic cleansing program, ultimately caused the downfall of the communist regime. Starting in earnest in March 1977, the Khmer Rouge began crossing the border and attacking Vietnamese troops and civilians.[39]

For example, in September 1977 a Khmer Rouge brigade charged across the border into the Vietnam's Tay Ninh province in Vietnam. The Cambodian troops massacred nearly 300 Vietnamese civilians. Attacks like this continued, sometimes involving battles with Vietnamese military units. In a period just over a year, the Khmer Rouge murdered an estimated 30,000 Vietnamese people in cross-border attacks.

While Pol Pot was purging (murdering) his own people along the Vietnamese border, the Hanoi government on December 25,

1978, launched a full scale invasion of Cambodia. Between 60,000 and 200,000 Vietnamese troops, supported by heavy weapons, helicopter gun ships and tanks, easily overcame the Khmer Rouge defenders. Local villagers liberated by the Vietnamese helped throw off the communists. Within a month, the Vietnamese occupied Phnom Penh.[40]

Violence and killing did not instantly end in Cambodia, as Khmer Rouge guerrillas harassed the Vietnamese occupation force. The puppet government in Phnom Penh may itself have killed another quarter million people.[41] Nevertheless, the Khmer Rouge death state was gone.

Why Kill Millions?

What had motivated the Khmer Rouge guerrillas and government to kill so many Cambodians? Scholars suggest these reasons:[42]

- Insecurity and paranoia among Khmer Rouge leaders who desperately feared one another, foreign agents, and loss of control over the country.

- Virulent racism of the Khmer Rouge, who believed in the superiority of ethnic dark-skinned Khmer over all others.

- Numbness of the Khmer Rouge troops, who had suffered much deprivation before coming to power. Many of them were trained as children to be cruel and unemotional about hurting and killing. (They had practiced doing so on monkeys, dogs, cats and other animals during training.)

- Fanatical communism: the desire to destroy all vestiges of anything foreign, capitalist, or religious; the vision of an entirely socialized, collectivized, and pure communist nation, where the communist party would indoctrinate the children and direct all activity for the greater good.

- The express goal to kill off millions of Cambodians, except for about 1 million, and make Cambodia entirely self-sufficient; subject the survivors to forced labor day and night, seven days a week, to build infrastructure, expand agriculture, and develop an industrial base rapidly.

- Nationalism with purification: the desire to resurrect the ancient glorious Khmer Kingdom, which involved extinguishing all the influences of Western culture and city life by returning the people to a simple life of hard labor on communal farms.

Hatred + Government + Disarmed Civilians = Genocide

Ugly images and horrific events from the Cambodian genocide teach mankind a lesson. People who:

- lose the power to affect government policy,
- lack a culture of self-defense against tyranny,
- have little or no familiarity with firearms, and
- cannot feasibly and legally obtain firearms

become defenseless victims when their government turns evil.

Table 6A
Summary of Cambodian "Gun Control" Laws
(Source: Penal Code and Penal Laws, 1956[43])

Laws & Ordinances	Regulation / Prohibition
Penal Code Art. 322	Prohibits making, importing, dealing in, or distribution of firearms, air-rifles, and ammunition.
Penal Code Art. 323	Prohibits making, importing, distributing "steel weapons of the same type used in the military" and of "concealable offensive weapons" such as daggers, switchblades, brass knuckles, truncheons.
Penal Code Art. 324	Prohibits acquiring, possessing, carrying, and storage of firearms, air-rifles and ammunition, unless holding a permit to do so.
Penal Code Art. 324	Prohibits persons who hold a valid permit from selling, lending, renting or otherwise transferring possession of any weapons or ammunition to a person who lacks a permit.
Penal Code Art. 325	Prohibits possession and transportation of "offensive or concealed steel weapons," such as truncheons and brass knuckles, without a "legitimate reason."

Table 6A (continued)
Summary of Cambodian "Gun Control" Laws

(Source: Penal Code and Penal Laws, 1956[43])

Laws & Ordinances	Regulation / Prohibition
Penal Code Art. 326	Prohibits permit holder from buying or obtaining ammunition, and from selling or exchanging weapons, without prior authorization.
Penal Code Art. 327	Violations of these regulations are punishable as criminal offenses and by revocation of weapons permits.
Penal Code Art. 328	Keeping a weapon more than eight days after revocation or suspension of the permit, or possessing several weapons on a single-weapon permit, or possessing more ammunition than authorized by a permit, is punishable as a criminal offense and by revocation of permits.
Royal Ord. 55, Art. 1	Permit system installed for hunting rifles, specified carbines, and small caliber air rifles.
Royal Ord. 55 Art. 2	Permits must have photographs and fingerprints of the holder. Permit holder must present the permit for inspection every three months. Permit may be renewed during the December inspection visit only.
Royal Ord. 55 Art. 3	Permit is valid for five years.
Royal Ord. 55 Art. 4	If permit and/or weapon is lost, holder in Phnom Penh must report it within 24 hours; elsewhere must report it within 8 days.
Royal Ord. 55 Art. 5	Prohibits possession of more than one weapon at a time "except in exceptional cases."
Royal Ord. 55 Art. 6	Princes, sons and grandsons of the King, ministers and their deputies, and approved government officials, employees and agents, are entitled to no-fee, non-expiring permits to carry military and hunting weapons.
Royal Ord. 55 Art. 7	Permit holders must get a permit to buy ammunition, and must present their permit to do so to the seller.
Royal Ord. 55 Art. 8	Permits may be revoked by order of the Mayor of Phnom Penh or any provincial governor, "for reasons of ensuring public safety."
Royal Ord. 55 Art. 9	Weapons permits are "strictly personal." Prohibits permit holder from entrusting a weapon to another person, and from selling a weapon unless the permit has been transferred to the buyer. Prohibits permit holder from carrying or possessing any weapon or ammunition that is not authorized by the permit.
Royal Ord. 55 Art. 10	Violations of this Ordinance are punishable as crimes.

End Notes

[1]Rummel, R.J. 1996. *Death by Government*. New Brunswick, NJ: Transaction Publishers, p. 160, subtracting out the estimates of 60,000 killed by the massive U.S. bombing in 1973, and the killings of 35,000 Vietnamese nationals and other non-Cambodians.

[2]Simkin, Jay, Aaron Zelman, and Alan M. Rice. 1994. *Lethal Laws*. Milwaukee, WI: Jews for the Preservation of Firearms Ownership ("LL"), pp. 304-305.

[3]Rummel 1996, p. 181; LL, p. 306.

[4]LL 306, citing Yathay, Pin. 1987. *Stay Alive, My Son*. New York: Simon & Schuster, p. 42.

[5]LL 306, citing Wilkinson, Alec. 1994. *A Changed Vision of God*. The New Yorker. Jan. 24, pp. 54-55.

[6]Rummel 1996, p. 162.

[7]Rummel 1996, p. 163.

[8]Rummel 1996, pp. 163-64.

[9]Rummel 1996, p. 164.

[10]Rummel 1996, p. 165.

[11]Rummel 1996, p. 168.

[12]Rummel 1996, p. 165.

[13]Rummel 1996, pp. 170-71.

[14]LL, p. 303.

[15]LL, p. 312.

[16]Rummel 1996, pp. 173, 177.

[17]Ibid., p. 173.

[18]Ibid., p. 175.

[19]LL, p. 312; Rummel 1996, p. 175.

[20]Rummel 1996, p.178, quoting Barron, John and Anthony Paul. 1977. *Peace with Horror: The Untold Story of Communist Genocide in Cambodia*. London: Hodder and Stoughton. American edition titled *Murder of a Gentle Land* (New York: Readers' Digest Press - Thomas Y. Crowell), pp. 19-20.

[21]Rummel 1996, p. 178.

[22]Ibid., p. 179.

[23]LL, p. 312; Rummel 1996, p. 180.

[24]Rummel 1996, pp. 181-190.

[25]Ibid., p. 183.

[26]Ibid., pp. 183-185.

[27]LL, pp. 313-314.

[28]Rummel 1996, p. 184.

[29]Ibid., p. 184.

30 Rummel 1996, p. 185, quoting Barron and Paul 1977, pp. 82-83.

31Rummel 1996, p. 187.

32LL 314, quoting Hawk, David. *The Photographic Record,* in Jackson, Karl D, ed. 1989. *Cambodia, 1975-1978: Rendezvous with Death.* Princeton, NJ: Princeton University Press, pp. 212-213.

33Rummel 1996, p. 188.

34Ibid.

35LL, pp. 314-15, citing and quoting Chandler, David. 1992. *Brother Number One: A Political Biography of Pol Pot.* Boulder CO: Westview Press, p. 130.

36Rummel 1996, p. 190.

37Ibid.

38Ibid.

39Ibid., p. 191.

40Ibid.

41Ibid., p. 165.

42Ibid., pp. 194-199.

43LL, pp. 317-323.

Chapter Seven:
China: Empire of Genocide

Professor R. J. Rummel summarized Chinese history in the 20th Century: "no other people in this century except Soviet citizens have suffered so much mass killing in cold blood as have the Chinese."[1] The Chinese example offers perhaps the clearest proof of the Genocide Formula:

Hatred + Government + Disarmed Civilians = Genocide

In the Chinese experience, government power and civilian disarmament are directly linked, and have been for centuries. Briefly visiting the history of Chinese political theory helps show why.

Seeking and exercising political power has recurred as a theme in the thousands of years of history in China. The earliest ruling dynasty dates from about 2100 B.C.E. An emperor of the Qin dynasty is credited with unifying, by military force, a large portion of China in 221 B.C.E. The Chinese view of their history "is the idea of a unified state with a strong central government led by a single ruler exerting control over subordinate, weaker local governments and neighboring states."[2]

Confucius (551-479 B.C.E.) and his followers assembled and developed the body of thought that has most enduringly affected Chinese thought for 2,500 years. Confucius's teachings specified a system of ethics and proper behavior.[3] Confucianism sees human society as a "web of human relationships" involving "mutual responsibilities: the subordinate was obliged to obey, the superior to provide a moral example, and if all went well, laws, rewards, and penalties would be superfluous."[4]

In Confucius's view, governmental functions and the social system were facts of life that should be sustained by ethical values. A highly influential disciple of Confucius, Xun Zi, taught that mankind is innately selfish and evil. His ideas formed a school of thought called Legalism, which argues that government must be strong enough to command the subjects to fulfill their ethical duties.[5]

Under centuries-old tradition, the Chinese citizen serves family, society and state. Contrary to Western civilization's philosophical grounding on the rights of individuals, "the concept on which Chinese culture is based is the primacy of the family and the society, and the emphasis in that tradition is on individual obligations, not rights or freedoms. The individual has obligations to the family, and the family has obligations to the society. The ruler's task is to ensure that these obligations are fulfilled."[6]

As one Chinese scholar has put it, "Both in the Imperial period and the PRC era the Chinese social order has been characterized by a state-society relationship in which society is almost totally subordinated to the state."[7] In the thousands of years of Chinese imperial rule, five elements appear consistently:[8]

1. State imposed official ideology.
2. Power concentrated in the hands of one person or a small few, unrestrained by institutions or political traditions.
3. State control over all aspects of social life and the economy.
4. Law used as a tool to govern, while the rulers are above the law.
5. Private citizens serve as subjects and possessions of the state.

Thus, just as in police states of Western civilization, government in Chinese tradition had the duty to control and regulate as many aspects of individual citizens' lives as necessary to achieve the rulers' vision of a better society.[9]

In China, power traditionally was delegated from the central authority to regional and local authorities. "State bureaucrats held a monopoly on political power within each local community."[10] China has never truly followed the Western notion of the "rule of law," where the government is subject to specific limitations, and everyone knows the rules of the game. Rather, "China's political system is rooted in the concept of the rule of men (in recent years expanded in a limited way to include some women), and the individual officeholder stands above the law and serves as the arbiter to whom disputes are referred."[11]

Local rulers, authorized by the central government to exercise a monopoly of political power, unchecked by an objective system of laws: these might be called "warlords." The citizens: pawns.

Twentieth Century "Gun Control" in China

For centuries in China, the people have served the society and state. The early "gun control" laws of the Republic of China (founded in 1912 to replace the empire) would likely have roused practically no public resistance at all. Article 205 of the Chinese criminal code in 1914 thus forbade citizens from possessing rifles and cannon without government permission:

> Whoever — without having received an official order, permit or authority — manufactures, possesses, or imports from abroad, rifles or cannons with military uses, … will be punished by [prison, detention, or a fine].[12]

Most private Chinese citizens at that time could not afford to buy and own firearms. Article 205 operated mainly to authorize the new government to disarm private armies maintained by various anti-government "warlords" still holding power in local areas of China.[13]

In the early years of the Republic, the Communist Party and the non-communist Nationalist Party had unified to drive out the incursions of the Japanese Empire and other foreign influences. In 1925, the Nationalists under Chiang Kaishek formed an army and drove north to pacify the warlords and unite them into the Nationalist movement. In 1927, the Nationalists turned against the Communists and drove them far to the northwest of the country.[14]

In 1935, the Nationalist-controlled government enacted another "gun control" law, Article 186 of the revised Criminal Code. This law was similar to the Article 205 law, in that it prohibited making, transporting and possessing any weapons, such as guns, ammunition, cannons, and explosives, designed "for military use."[15] Article 186 prescribed punishments of fine or imprisonment for violations, regardless of the person's reason or intent.[16] A companion law, Article 187, mandated imprisonment for a much longer period for the same offense if the convicted person did have criminal intent.[17]

Killing by Nationalist Government

Was life under Nationalist rule serene and peaceful when "gun control" was in place? No, not for the more than 10,000,000 citizens who were killed by their Nationalist government. Lethal features of the Nationalist regime included:

1927-28:   Wave of terror massacres that extended to every village, town, and city; soldiers unleashed to loot, rape and murder at will.[18]

1933-34:   Campaign to exterminate all communists, killing any left behind from Mao's famous Long March retreat, and attacking and destroying whole populations suspected of any communist sympathy or support.[19]

1938:   As part of a plan to slow the Japanese military incursion, the Nationalist army dynamited the Yellow River dikes in two places, intentionally causing massive flood, destroying over 4,000 villages, wrecking vital crops, displacing millions of people and killing over 800,000 Chinese citizens.[20]

1942-44:   Government and army aggravated famines by extorting grain from farmers, pressing the starving people for taxes, confiscating whole harvests. Over 4,000,000 died of starvation and related causes; likely half of these directly because of government policies.[21]

1945-46:   Soldiers and officers returning to villages after the war against Japan, took opportunity to murder or officially prosecute and then kill personal enemies or suspected communists.[22]

1937-49:   During the Sino-Japanese war, and the following civil war, Nationalist government forcibly drafted civilian men into services. Civilians were paid bounties for captured men sold to the army. Those who resisted conscription were killed or mutilated; those who could not keep up, or tried to escape, or disobeyed orders, often were shot. Many conscripts, chained in gangs as they marched, starved to death on the way to army camps; the sick were left by the road to die. The death toll exceeded 4,000,000.[23]

1947:   After strafing and bombing Chinese workers trying to protect their lands, Nationalists again dynamited dikes of the Yellow River, causing a flood that inundated 500 villages, displacing hundreds of thousands of people, destroying crops, and killing at least 6,000 people. This was done to advance the civil war against the communists.[24]

1947-49: After invading Formosa (now Taiwan) and imposing tyranny upon the Formosans, Nationalists launched a bloody campaign of repression, murdering between 10,000 and 40,000 people.[25]

Defenseless people killed by Nationalist government and army: 10,214,000.[26]

Nanking: Defenseless Against Brutal Invaders

What single fact, seen in the world's reaction to the Rape of Nanking, condemns mankind to repeat the Genocide Formula? It is

the frightening ease with which the mind can accept genocide, turning us all into passive spectators to the unthinkable. The Rape of Nanking was front-page news across the world, yet most of the world stood by and did nothing while an entire city was butchered.[27]

What single fact made possible the Rape of Nanking? Disarmament of the defenders and civilians.

Parts of China were attacked, subdued and occupied by forces of the Japanese Empire starting in 1931. The Japanese occupied Manchuria and installed a puppet emperor of China in that year. The Chinese Communists and Nationalists (temporarily) united to resist the takeover.[28]

Air raids began the Japanese Imperial Army's siege of Nanking, China on August 15, 1937, and continued intermittently for months. Open war in China had already started in the summer of 1937, with three months of fierce fighting especially in Shanghai where the Chinese lost 300,000 troops.[29] The Japanese eventually took Shanghai in November of that year, and started marching toward Nanking.[30]

The Japanese forces did not merely move toward Nanking; they burned, looted, raped and murdered whole towns and cities on the way. An estimated 300,000 or more mostly non-combatant Chinese were killed.[31]

On December 5, 1937, the Japanese force of 225,000 soldiers

was surrounding 300,000 Chinese troops near Nanking when the initial order was given to Japanese commanders to kill all captives.[32] As the Japanese troops closed in upon Nanking in the next few days, many Chinese soldiers literally threw away their firearms and other weapons as they attempted to flee the city.[33] On December 12, 1937, the Chinese army leaders decided to retreat and give up the city of Nanking to the invaders. The Japanese army shelled the city, causing huge fires.

Then began a terror-driven rush of soldiers trying to escape in any possible way out of the city and across the Yangtze River. Blocking the path of the retreating men were huge quantities, literally heaps, of military equipment dropped and ditched near the gate of the city: machine guns, hand grenades, helmets, vehicles, uniforms, everything.[34]

The advancing Japanese troops faced almost no resistance at all, and thousands of Chinese troops surrendered peacefully. One Japanese military commander was astonished by the wholesale surrender of the Chinese, given that even unarmed the 7,000 Chinese men could have overwhelmed their armed captors. Instead of fighting, the surrendered men clung to white flags for protection.[35] The first to be systematically murdered in Nanking were the surrendered disarmed Chinese troops, divided into small groups and dispatched rapidly, by orders given on December 13 and December 17.[36] Iris Chang, who has documented the events, has noted:

> Those who remained after the [Chinese] soldiers departed tended to be the most defenseless: children, the elderly, and all those either too poor or physically weak to secure passage out of the city. Without protection, without personal resources, without a plan, all these people had was hope that the Japanese would treat them well.[37]

What took place in Nanking under Japanese occupation, December 1937- February 1938, was "so sickening " that "even the Nazis in the city were horrified."[38] For those readers who need more gruesome details to be convinced, there is Iris Chang's monumental book *The Rape of Nanking: The Forgotten Holocaust of World War II* (1997). For those readers who need to see pictures, there is *The Rape of Nanking: An Undeniable History in Photographs* by Shi Young and James Yin (Second edition, 1997).

If it is possible to summarize the Japanese atrocities committed during the Rape of Nanking, then these are the documented facts. The Imperial Japanese Army, at the direction and with the participation of its officers, murdered between 200,000 and 350,000 unarmed defenseless Chinese people in Nanking in about seven weeks.[39]

In addition to shootings, either random or methodical, the occupation troops:

- Raped, tortured and murdered up to 80,000 women
- Used Chinese men for bayonet practice and decapitation contests
- Buried people alive
- Carved out organs and roasted people alive
- Hanged people by their tongues on iron hooks
- Watched dogs tear apart people buried up to their waist
- Committed sadistic sex-related tortures and unprintable barbarities
- Shoved bound groups of people into pits to burn alive
- Forced naked people onto the Yangtze ice to freeze to death

Author Iris Chang herself confirmed two of the three elements of the Genocide Formula: Hate & Government.[41]

Had the civilians possessed firearms with ammunition and the familiarity to use them, would the outcome at Nanking been different? There is no certain answer, of course. Iris Chang did consider whether it would have been better for the Chinese troops to stay and fight to the death to defend Nanking, and observed:

> Head-to-head combat would certainly not have worked. The Japanese were much better armed and trained and would surely have overcome the Chinese forces sooner or later.[42]

Ms. Chang's argument overlooks the possibility that *the citizens themselves can form an army of resistance*. There were over 600,000 Chinese people in Nanking when it fell to the Japanese army.[43] There had been an additional 300,000 Chinese troops in the area. If only half of the civilians had owned and been trained in using firearms, then the number of Chinese fighters and guns opposing the Japanese would have totaled 600,000 — over twice the number of the invaders.

Ms. Chang suggested how the Chinese army could have resisted the attack:

> But a lengthy, drawn-out struggle using guerrilla-style tactics might have demoralized the Japanese and elevated the Chinese. If nothing else, many more Japanese soldiers would have died fighting the Chinese and their arrogance toward the Chinese soldier would have been muted by a fierce resistance.[44]

Ms. Chang evidently did not imagine the effectiveness of guerrilla tactics when every able-bodied man, woman and teenager is armed to help. Compare the civilian defense of the Ghetto in Warsaw, Poland, from April 19 to May 16, 1943. At the beginning of their urban guerrilla defense action, the Jewish resistance fighters at the Warsaw Ghetto numbered about 1,000 men and women, including youths. Using firearms and a few grenades that were smuggled in or taken from dead Nazis, the defenders inflicted hundreds of casualties and stalled for 28 days the Nazi force of nearly 10,000 men who had aircraft and artillery support.[45]

The Warsaw Ghetto resistance fighters were outnumbered by about 10 to 1, but were able to hold off the Nazi war machine using urban guerrilla tactics. It seems likely that 600,000 armed citizens and soldiers, who actually outnumbered the Japanese invaders by at least 2 to 1, would have achieved at least as much success. At the very least, widespread armed civilian resistance would have cost the Imperial Japanese Army and slowed its advance.[46]

A culture of civilian disarmament, and "gun control" laws that further discouraged firearms ownership and training, produced the ironic plight of Nanking: awash in armaments, yet unable to defend herself against vicious invaders. More evil and megadeath would befall the unarmed Chinese, however, at the hands of their own government.

Communists

At the end of World War II, warring resumed between the Communists under Mao Zedong and the Nationalists under Chiang Kai-shek. Ultimately, the Communists conquered China by driving out the Nationalists in 1949. Little changed in the way political power was used.

The government planned to destroy the traditional social and political system of China, and replace it with a socialist "dictatorship of the proletariat."[47] During the 1950's and 1960's, **millions** of landowners, bureaucrats, dissenters, intellectuals and Party members were stripped of wealth and power, sentenced to years of hard labor or put to death, all without employing the laws or the legal systems.[48] In addition, forced collectivization of agriculture to achieve socialist visions caused the world's largest known famine and the starvation of 27,000,000 people.[49]

Consider the "Great Leap Forward" (1957-1960), the government program that promised to immediately advance China's economic standing. During that period there were increased arrests, prosecutions and convictions as police dispensed justice "on the spot" with executions or long imprisonment of people for even minor offenses.[50] Predictably, the socialist program was a great flop. Some 10,000,000 to 30,000,000 Chinese people died from starvation, malnutrition and disease, the results of the government's policies causing massive famine.[51] Some scholars view the "Great Leap Forward" as the single most murderous program in modern Chinese history.[52]

In total, from 1949 to 1987, the Communist government of China worked to death, starved, and executed 35,236,000 citizens — with some estimates ranging over 100,000,000. What is more, the Chinese government admitted to many thousands of these deaths and killings.[53]

Did "Gun Control" Laws Even Matter?

The laws of the Republic of China and the Nationalist regime were abolished by the Communists in 1949.[54] Starting in 1950, the government moved to suppress "counter revolutionaries" — that meant killing or sending to forced labor millions of civilians, such as landowners, scientists, scholars, intellectuals, "spies," "bad elements," and their families, including their children.[55] Few cases came to any court. Instead, local administrative agencies and local police conducted mass trials, executed hundreds of thousands, and sentenced many more to prison camps.[56]

The Chinese Communists did introduce new legal codes in the 1950's, modeled after the Soviet Union. The Communist Chinese legal system contained three main institutions: the Ministry of Public Security (national police); a "procuracy" at each level of government to prosecute crimes reported to the Supreme People's Procuracy; and courts at each level of government which heard and decided cases and set punishments.[57]

These state organs of compulsion operated to advance Communist ideology, however, not to apply the rule of law. "Written law, courts, judges, and the whole paraphernalia of a functioning legal system," served the Communist government as "expedient political tools to construct a communist society, liquidate bad classes, and punish opposition."[58] Indeed, the founding dictator Mao Zedong reportedly said, "We don't really know what is meant by law, because we have never paid any attention to it!"[59]

Did "gun control" laws directly give rise to the Chinese government's killing of 35,000,000 citizens? Not really, because actual "gun control" laws under the Communist regime scarcely existed. What continued to exist, as it has for centuries, was *a culture of millions of unarmed civilians following the dictates of the government*. Confucian attitudes about the relationship of government and citizen have persisted, including: "authoritarianism, unthinking obedience to leaders, deprecation of expert knowledge, lack of appreciation for law, and the failure to apply laws to leaders."[60]

Marxism married with Confucianism only continued the ideology of rule by rulers, not the rule of law:

> Marxism and Confucianism share the same elitist bias and advocate the rule of man instead of the rule of law. For Confucianism, the rule of man is realized by the Sage sovereign leading a group of scholar officials. For official Marxism, the new social order is directed by the party leader and his corps of the "most advanced and progressive elements of the proletariat." Both Marxism and Confucianism denigrated the role of law and neglected institutional constraints on political power. ...The traditional imperial effort of the emperor and his state to "rectify" people's minds, especially since the Ming dynasty, was revived in new form.[61]

"Gun control" laws are just part of a system to strip citizens of the power to resist tyranny. Having a culture that prepares its people to worship leaders and follow orders is another direct route to a powerless citizenry. Either way, if the citizens cannot resist, then the tyrants can rule.

When the tyrants rule, then the citizens have no legal protections. If the written laws simply authorize the tyrants to act, then the laws strengthen the tyrants. If the tyrants do not follow or apply laws, then the laws do not matter.

Such has been the case in Communist China. The written laws, adapted from the Soviet Union's codes, gave written authority to the tyrants. Table 7A sets forth some examples.

Citizens of free nations under the rule of law might find it hard to understand a Communist government. In a nation of laws, the rules of society apply to ordinary citizens as well as to the government and government officials. The rules are supposed to make it easier for free people to get along, do business and live safely.

Under the Communist Chinese regime, the laws are political devices. The laws demand punishment of people who commit "counter-revolutionary" activities — with the term "counter-revolutionary" being a political term that can apply to anyone or anything that is targeted. A "gun control" law in such a system supplies just another excuse to arrest, imprison and execute people. But when the regime is all powerful and the people obey, then "gun control" is not required. The tyrant has already everything he needs.

The Communist Chinese laws against undermining the regime cover much more territory than "gun control" laws. If, without any proper trial or due process, government agencies can imprison or execute a person for anything deemed "anti-government," then the government doesn't need "gun control" laws to kill people who have guns.

Founding dictator Mao Zedong quite clearly understood how firearms — guns — were and are the key to the balance of power between the citizens and the government. Mao said:

> Political power flows out of the barrel of a gun, [but] our principle is that the Party commands the gun and the gun must never be allowed to command the Party.[60]

Final Thought

Defenseless Chinese people in the 20th Century suffered immensely at the hands of their own government, domestic forces seeking power, and foreign invaders. Americans who advocate "gun control" say that people are safer if all guns are controlled by the police and the military. **Were the Chinese victims really safer because only police and military forces had firearms? Were the people really safer because they were unarmed and unprepared — physically and culturally — to resist oppression?**

Table 7A
Selected Laws of the People's Republic of China[63]

Law	Source	Notes
Counter-revolutionary criminals who intend to overthrow or to undermine the regime, are to be punished.	Act of Feb. 20, 1951, Article 2	Targets anyone labeled "counter-revolutionary"; punishes actions that "undermine" the regime.
"Supplying domestic or foreign enemies with weapons, ammunition, or other war material" is punishable.	(Same), Article 6	Penalty is death or life imprisonment for giving a firearm to someone dubbed a "domestic enemy." "Minor" cases punished by at least 5 years in prison.
Attacking, injuring or killing government employees, or "stealing from or destroying any "important public or private property" is punishable.	(Same), Article 9	Penalty is death or life imprisonment, if crime committed with "counter-revolutionary intent." "Minor" cases punished by at least 5 years in prison.
"Inciting the masses to resist or to evade" any government order or program, is punishable.	(Same), Article 10(1)	Penalty is at least 3 years in prison; if crime is "major," then life imprisonment or death.
"Inciting strife" between groups or between the people and the government, or "carrying out counter-revolutionary propaganda and agitation," or spreading rumors, is punishable.	(Same), Article 10 (2) - (3)	Penalty is at least 3 years in prison; if crime is "major," then life imprisonment or death.
Punishments may be reduced for those who willingly surrender and sincerely repent, or who repent and reform themselves after being accused.	(Same), Article 14	The penalty for all crimes in this act depend upon the judge's determination about whether the accused was contrite and "sincerely" repentant.
Anyone who commits any crime, with "counter-revolutionary intent," can be punished in a manner that is "comparable" to crimes listed in this Act.	(Same), Article 16	Allows judge to decide whether the accused has "counter-revolutionary intent" and then increase the penalties based on a comparison with a listed crime.
Anyone convicted of listed counter-revolutionary crimes may lose "political rights" and some or all of their property.	(Same), Article 17	Allows judge to compound the penalty by confiscating property of convicted person.

Table 7A (continued)
Selected Laws of the People's Republic of China[63]

Law	Source	Notes
Provisions of the Act apply retroactively to "counter-revolutionary criminals."	(Same) Article 18	The laws apply ex post facto, to punish people for something they did before the law was enacted.
Fishing and hunting where these are prohibited, constitutes "disrupting public order."	Act of Oct. 22, 1957, Article 7(1)	Implicit "gun control" law; penalty is a fine or jail up to 15 days.
Taking photographs where it is prohibited, is punishable.	(Same), Article 7(2)	Penalty is a fine or jail up to 15 days.
"Unauthorized entry into districts into which entry is banned," is punishable.	(Same), Article 7(3)	Penalty is a fine or jail up to 15 days.
Failing to register the household with the government, or making a false registration report, is punishable.	(Same), Article 14	Penalty is fine or jail up to 5 days.

End Notes

[1]Rummel, R.J. 1996. *Death by Government.* New Brunswick, NJ: Transaction Publishers, p. 91.

[2]Starr, John Bryan. 1997. *Understanding China : a guide to China's economy, history, and political structure.* New York : Hill & Wang, p. 43.

[3]Worden, Robert L., et. al, eds. 1988. *China, a country study.* Washington, D.C.: Federal Research Division, Library of Congress. ("Country Study"), p. 8.

[4]*Country Study,* pp. 198-199.

[5]Ibid. p. 8.

[6]Ibid., p.198.

[7]Fu, Zhengyuan. 1993. *Autocratic Tradition and Chinese Politics.* New York: Cambridge University Press, pp. 5-6, quoted in Caplan, Bryan. 2000. Autocratic Ghosts and Chinese Hunger. *The Independent Review,* Vol. 4, No. 3, pp. 431-438, at 434.

[8]Caplan 2000, p. 435, citing Fu 1993, p. 2.

[9]See Chapman, Brian. 1970. *Police State.* London: Pall Mall., pp. 16-20, 37-39, 82.

[10]Starr 1997, p. 49.

[11]Ibid., pp. 197-98.

[12]Simkin, Jay, Aaron Zelman, and Alan M. Rice. 1994. *Lethal Laws*. Milwaukee, WI: Jews for the Preservation of Firearms Ownership ("LL"), p. 188.

[13]Ibid., p. 188; Country Study, pp. 30-31.

[14]LL, pp. 188-189.

[15]Ibid., pp. 189.

[16]Ibid., p.195.

[17]Ibid.

[18]Rummel 1996, p. 124.

[19]Ibid., p. 125.

[20]Ibid., pp. 131-32.

[21]Ibid., pp. 133-34.

[22]Ibid., pp. 126, 127.

[23]Ibid., pp. 129-30.

[24]Ibid., p. 132.

[25]Ibid., p.125.

[26]Ibid., p. 137.

[27]Chang, Iris. 1997. *The Rape of Nanking*. New York: Basic Books, p. 221.

[28]Chang 1997, p. 29.

[29]Young, Shi and James Yin. 1997. *The Rape of Nanking: An Undeniable History in Photographs*. Second Edition. Chicago: Innovative Publishing, Inc.("Young & Yin"), p. 9.

[30]Chang 1997, pp. 33-34.

[31]Ibid., pp. 37-38.

[32]Chang 1997, p. 40; Young & Yin, p. 21.

[33]Chang 1997, p. 42.

[34]Chang 1997, pp. 74-77; Young & Yin, p. 44.

[35]Chang 1997, p. 43.

[36]Chang 1997, pp. 40-41,44-45; Young & Yin, pp. 52-54.

[37]Chang 1997, p. 81.

[38]Ibid., p. 6.

[39]Chang 1997, pp. 5-6, 102-103; Young & Yin, p. 242 (citing sources).

[40]Chang 1997, pp. 6, 81-99; Rummel 1996, pp. 145-46.

[41]Chang 1997, pp. 218, 220.

[42]Ibid., p. 104.

[43]Ibid., p. 139.

[44]Ibid., p. 104.

[45]Guttman, Jon. 2000. Genocide Delayed. *World War II Magazine.* March 2000. (www.thehistorynet.com/WorldWarII), reprinted in *The Bill of Rights Sentinel,* Hartford Wisconsin: Jews for the Preservation of Firearms Ownership, Fall 2000, pp. 15-19.

[46]Polsby, Daniel D. and Don B. Kates, Jr.. 1997. Of Holocausts and Gun Control. *Wash. Univ. Law Qtly.* Vol 75, p. 1237 (analyzing practicality of armed civilian defense against genocide, concludes that resistance at least raises the aggressor's costs and likely deters some aggression).

[47]Rummel 1996, p. 97.

[48]Starr 1997, p. 200.

[49]Rummel 1996, p. 97.

[50]Country Study, p. 515.

[51]LL 187, quoting Fairbank, John King. 1992. *China: A New History.* Cambridge, MA: Harvard University Press, p. 368, and quoting Shalom, Stephen. 1984. *Deaths Due to Communism in China.* Tempe, AZ: Arizona State University, p. 61.

[52]Caplan 2000, pp. 431-32, citing Becker, Jasper. 1996. *Hungry Ghosts: Mao's Secret Famine.* New York: Free Press.

[53]Rummel 1996, pp. 98-107.

[54]Country Study, p. 511.

[55]Rummel 1996, p. 98.

[56]Country Study, p. 512.

[57]Starr 1997, p. 200.

[58]Rummel 1996, p. 105.

[59]Ibid.

[60]Country Study, pp. 105-106.

[61]Caplan 2000, p. 437, quoting Fu 1993, p. 172.

[62]Quoted in Starr 1997, p. 73.

[63]Chinese original text with full English translation are set forth in LL, at 193-227.

Chapter Eight:
Guatemala: The Textbook Case

Hatred + Government + Disarmed Civilians = Genocide

Guatemala's history shows all three elements of the Genocide Formula in deadly interplay, with civilian disarmament laws and policies playing a key role to set up the mass murder of Indians[1] (mostly Mayans) between 1960 and the 1980's. World authorities deem this mass murder a genocide.[2]

The first element, Hatred, has arisen in a number of ways. During the 300 years of Spanish rule over Guatemala, from 1523 to 1821, the Indians who spoke Maya (or other native languages) were systematically oppressed and enslaved. Landowners could actually rent slaves from the Spanish Crown.[3] Even after the withdrawal of Spanish rule in 1821, the Indian peoples have lived as second-class citizens to the more wealthy, Spanish-speaking, European-influenced society.[4] Centuries of insecurity, resentment and fear between the two cultures forms one clear basis for hatred.

Other factors helped divide Guatemalan society and pit one segment against another. The government of Guatemala repeatedly has been upset, overthrown and replaced by political intrigue, assassination, and military coup d'etat. The more "stable" governments survived with dictators at their helm.[5]

Poorer Indians suffered economically as a class for decades. A system of debt-slavery was recognized and enforced by the government, whereby people sold themselves into slavery for a period to pay a debt. Children of debt-slaves inherited the debts of their parents.[6] Landowners legally exercised nearly absolute power over their plantations, and had the authority to punish persons who committed crimes on their lands.[7] Society was thus divided as landowners and their lieutenants tried to maintain control of large numbers of low-paid agricultural workers and debt-slaves.

The second element, powerful Government, added into the mix. The government of Guatemala has frequently been headed by a dictator, and at many times has oppressed the Indian population. Examples of economic oppression abound. Indians were required to perform forced labor until 1878. The government early allowed debt-slavery, and then fully recognized debt-slavery by law in 1894. Under the regime of General Jorge Ubico that began in 1931, the Vagrancy Law was enforced. That law required all Indians to work at least 150 days per year. All male citizens were required to carry a work card that would show the number of days worked in the past year — those who had too few hours were effectively forced to work on plantations to make up their hours. The government also required Indians to give two weeks of unpaid labor to build or maintain highways.[8]

The oppression of the Indians created opportunities for anti-government ideas and groups to gain supporters among the oppressed. Movements advocating socialism, "land reform," and communism found followings among the Indians. Demonstrations and uprisings occurred, some of them violent.[9]

In 1944, Juan Jose Arevalo was elected by a huge majority to be President. Arevalo did close down the secret police, repeal the Vagrancy Law, and encouraged the drafting of a new constitution that would guarantee civil rights.[10] Arevalo did not abolish "gun control," however, although he simplified the law. His successor, Jacobo Arbenz, was elected in 1951 and instituted "land reform" by which the government bought unused farm land and turned it over to landless families.[11]

Large corporate landowners, including the United Fruit Company, opposed the "land reform" program. United States Secretary of State John Foster Dulles declared that Arbenz's regime was communist.[12] Then began a program where the U.S. Central Intelligence Agency (CIA) trained insurgents to attack and bring down the Guatemalan government. Although Arbenz wanted to distribute firearms to citizens to help defend the government, the Army of Guatemala refused to follow his orders. Arbenz resigned.[13]

A series of military and civilian regimes followed. The reforms of Arevalo and Arbenz were reversed.[14] Meanwhile, anti-government revolutionary and guerrilla movements formed, and a civil war began in 1962 that did not fully end until the 1990's. The United States generally supported the ruling regimes because they were "anti-communist."

Guatemala was nothing like a free country during this period. The UN-sponsored Commission for Historical Clarification (CEH) prepared and delivered in 1999 an extensive report on human rights violations and genocide in Guatemala.[15]

The CEH report observed the history and practice of Guatemala's government, and among other things, noted these factors:

- Long-standing racism against Mayans and other Indians.[16]
- Authoritarian nature of government since inception.[17]
- Since 1962, an underground system of repression, directed by the military, became the government's main means of social control.[18]
- Judicial system historically supported or ignored government repression and failed to protect individual rights.[19]
- Since 1952, government has repressed opposition political parties.[20]
- Government developed notion of an "internal enemy", i.e. communists, rebels and any other opposition, which had to be rooted out and destroyed.[21]
- As resistance to government repression grew in the 1960's, the government deployed military and national security forces to intimidate and annihilate the opposition.[22]
- Beginning in the 1960's, police forces and security forces were "militarized," i.e. placed under Army control.[23]
- The Army trained a special anti-guerrilla force, Los Kaibiles, using extremely cruel and desensitizing techniques, such as killing animals and eating them raw, to produce "killing machines."[24]
- Targets of destruction between 1962 and 1970 were small farmers, farmworker organizers, teachers, students, and anti-government guerrilla sympathizers.[25]
- Starting in 1981, the Army created Civil Patrols. Civilians, many of them Mayan teenage males, were drafted to serve

the Civil Patrols, and hundreds were forced at gun point to rape, torture, mutilate corpses and kill. The aim was to break down social cohesion among the Mayans.[26]

- The most violent and bloody period of repression (1978-1985) involved military operations in principally Mayan areas.[27] Mayans as a group were deemed to be guerrilla allies and targeted.[28]

- Government forces perpetrated massacres, scorched earth operations, "disappearances" and executions, against Mayan communities even where proof of pro-guerrilla action was lacking.[29] Observers concluded that the brutality of these military operations were motivated in large part by racism.

Opposing the government were armed rebels (guerrillas or "counter insurgents"). The anti-government forces were actively supported by Cuba to provoke an armed takeover of the government. Cuba's objective was to empower Marxist revolutionaries in Guatemala to ascend to power there.[30] The anti-government Marxist guerrillas themselves targeted non-combatants as enemies, and have been credited with human rights violations, calculated violence against men, women and children, arbitrary executions and forced "disappearances."[31]

The CEH reported that these guerrillas employed terrorism to intimidate the people, often committing "violent and extremely cruel acts" against victims in front of their families and neighbors. These actions "accentuated the already prevalent climate of fear, arbitrariness and defencelessness."[32]

Systematically Disarmed Civilian Victims

Over and again the reports indicate the oppressing and killing of "defenseless" victims in Guatemala. Three factors of history suggest why the people were so defenseless. First, for the hundreds of years the Indian peoples were slaves or serfs of Spanish rulers and various landowners. In bondage the people likely developed few ideas about a right to self-defense.

Second, since Guatemala's independence, the common people have never had any legally-protected right to keep and bear arms. Many of the people remained debt-slaves or working at subsistence. No tradition of an armed citizenry arose.

Third, starting with a "gun control" law in 1871, many of

Guatemala's regimes reacted to displays of opposition or fear of revolution by increasing costs and legal restrictions on civilian ownership and carrying of firearms. Table 8A below summarizes the key features of the "gun control" laws that discouraged people from developing private armed self-defense.

Over time and increasingly restrictive, these laws banned private ownership of some guns and ammunition, licensed owners, registered guns, imposed high fees, traced every private firearms transaction, and even banned carrying "sharp-pointed" tools. Broad vaguely-worded laws about "public order" empowered government agents to seize firearms. All of these same laws carved huge exceptions to allow the government and its agents, employees, officials and military, to maintain a monopoly of weapons and force.

When the government became tyrannical, the people had neither a culture of armed resistance nor the tools (weapons) necessary to overthrow that government. Government entities and officials, the military, and the (nationalized) police were always fully armed. Groups wanting to seize the power from the regime would gather armed forces (often from the rebellious military units), and if they won, they would install a new autocratic government. Marxism and socialism inspired some of the people to organize in protest against their government, and Cuban communists supplied these people with resources, weapons and training as guerrillas. In the civil war starting in 1962 between the Cuban-backed guerrillas and the government, the common people suffered — because both factions terrorized and murdered noncombatant civilians for political ends. ***Unarmed, lacking a shared culture that upholds fundamental human rights, and untrained to resist killers, the common people were robbed, raped, tortured and slaughtered.***

Displacement and Death

What was the human cost of the Guatemalan genocide? Estimates range from 100,000[33] to 200,000.[34] The vast majority of the victims were Indians (Mayans).[35] About 93% of all the killings are attributable to the government, military, and Civil Patrols; about 7% attributable to Cuban-backed anti-government guerillas.[36]

The estimated number of persons driven by terror to flee their homes ranges from 500,000 to 1,500,000.[37] The numbers of those who died in flight is not accurately known.

The CEH summarized the motivations that spurred the genocidal reign of terror in Guatemala:

> The Army's perception of Mayan communities as natural allies of the guerillas contributed to increasing and aggravating the human rights violations perpetrated against them, demonstrating an aggressive racist component of extreme cruelty that led to the extermination en masse, of defenceless Mayan communities purportedly linked to the guerillas — including children, women and the elderly — through methods whose cruelty has outraged the moral conscience of the civilized world.[38]

> These massacres and the so-called scorched earth operations, as planned by the State, resulted in the complete extermination of many Mayan communities, along with their homes, cattle, crops and other elements essential to survival. The CEH registered 626 massacres attributable to these forces.[39]

> The CEH has noted particularly serious cruelty in many acts committed by agents of the State, especially members of the Army, in their operations against Mayan communities. ... Acts such as the killing of defenceless children, often by beating them against walls or throwing them alive into pits where the corpses of adults were later thrown; the amputation of limbs; the impaling of victims; the killing of persons by covering them in petrol and burning them alive; the extraction, in the presence of others, of the viscera of victims who were still alive....[40]

Message from Guatemala

The lesson from Guatemala is clear. When people are:
- Second-class citizens or targets of hate
- Lacking a culture of individual rights and self-defense
- Unarmed and untrained in resisting killers
- Ruled by an unrestrained government that turns bad

then the defenseless people will suffer and die in very large numbers.

Table 8A
History of "Gun Control" Laws in Guatemala

(Source: *Lethal Laws*,[3] pp. 229-269)

Date	Substance of Law	Decree / Section	Apparent Purpose
Nov. 25, 1871	"New models of firearms" are "dangerous by their nature" and should be possessed only by "well-known persons."	No. 36, Preamble[41]	Enacted by insurgents who had overthrown previous elected government after a two year war, to consolidate power.
"	All persons who have "any new model firearm" must "register himself" with the commanding general, and must indicate how many cartridges possessed.	No. 36, Art. 1	Identify the owners of modern firearms, such as rifles and carbines.
"	Citizens may not trade such arms or possess them "in large numbers."	No. 36, Art. 2	Restrict ability of citizens to acquire arms to resist or overthrow government.
"	Registered firearms owner must notify the commanding general of the person to whom a firearm is sold.	No. 36, Art. 3	Track owners and their firearms.
"	Registered owners of firearms must turn them over to government (for temporary safekeeping) "if public order is disturbed in the smallest degree."	No. 36, Art. 4	Empower government to seize firearms upon nearly any circumstance deemed a public disturbance.
"	Violation of this Decree "will result in the loss of the arms."	No. 36, Art. 5	Empower government to confiscate firearms.
May 17, 1873	Prohibits importation and sale of all firearms.	No. 98, Art. 1[42]	Ban sales of firearms to rebels (country deemed in a "state of war").
"	Police chiefs and military commanders must enforce law requiring firearms dealers to store their entire stock with a government agency within 3 days.	No. 98, Articles 2 and 4	Seize and detain supplies of firearms from dealers, until "tranquility shall be restored."
April 18, 1876	Prohibits importation and exportation of firearms, ammunition, military munitions and military clothing from or to El Salvador	No. 156	Prevent the supply of firearms to or from El Salvador, during war between the two nations.

69

Table 8A (continued)
History of "Gun Control" Laws in Guatemala
(Source: *Lethal Laws,* pp. 229-269)

Date	Substance of Law	Decree / Section	Apparent Purpose
Aug. 24, 1923	Bans importation of most firearms; bans carrying firearms in towns (except for government officials); bans private ownership of firearms of military calibers; requires licenses to carry a firearm on roads and railways; license requires proof of "honesty"; imposes high fees for carry licenses.	No. 834, Art. 1, 3, 4, 5, 19, 20[44]	Maintain control of population after military coup had overthrown civilian government.
June 14, 1930	Similar to Decree No. 834 above. Carry permit license fee set to several weeks' wages for average Guatemalan worker.	No. 1661[45]	Maintain control of population under new ruler.
May 20, 1931	Bans importation of cartridges (by repealing part of prior law).	Legislative Decree[46]	Protect new regime that had just taken power.
May 31, 1932	Replaces Decree No. 1661 with more restrictive "gun control" law.	Legislative Act[47]	Maintain government and military monopoly on firearms possession.
June 27, 1940	Bans carrying of firearms, except for hunting firearms, and except for government officials and licensed land owners on their own land.	No. 2395[48]	Impose higher risks and costs on unauthorized firearms use. Protect government system under which Indians were forced to work on highways and on plantations (where plantation owners were authorized to punish anyone committing crimes on their land).
May 19, 1947	Consolidates the law; licenses required to carry private firearms (except for government officials and their agents).	No. 386, Art. 1-3[49]	Maintain monopoly of force in government and military hands.
"	Prohibits carrying firearms in towns (does not apply to government officials).	No. 386, Art. 10	
"	Imposes annual fees for owning revolvers and shotguns.	No. 386, Art. 8	

Table 8A (continued)
History of "Gun Control" Laws in Guatemala
(Source: *Lethal Laws,* pp. 229-269)

Date	Substance of Law	Decree / Section	Apparent Purpose
May 19, 1947	Requires license applicants to obtain written character testimonials "from two persons of known honesty."	No. 386, Art. 6	Maintain monopoly of force in government and military hands.
"	Government maintains registry of license holders.	No. 386, Art. 4	
Aug. 3, 1949	Declares that carrying truncheons, sharp-pointed tools or firearms without a license, is punishable by confiscation of weapon and 30 days in jail — except for guns and tools used for hunting, fishing and farm implements.	No. 147,[50] Art. 40 (amended by No. 653)	Solve problem of farm workers being punished under "weapon control" law for carrying ordinary sharp-pointed farm tools.
July 2, 1958	Declares "that the ownership and carrying of arms is exclusive to the Army of Guatemala."	No. 1239,[51] Preamble	Establish the government monopoly of force in Guatemala.
"	"It is forbidden to own and to carry arms and all types of military supplies, of which the Guatemalan Army is the sole user."	No. 1239, Art. 1	Outlaw civilian ownership and possession of "military" weapons and "supplies."
"	Military weapons include larger caliber handguns, rifles, ammunition, grenades, and combat-style knives and swords.	No. 1239, Art. 2	Tilt scales of firepower in favor of government and military.
Oct. 27, 1964	Carries out "the State's obligation to regulate" the importation, transportation, sale and carrying of non-military arms.	No. 283, Preamble and Art. 1	"To ensure internal security and public order."
"	Permits citizens to possess smaller caliber firearms "in private homes for personal defense."	No. 283, Art. 2	"To ensure internal security and public order."
"	Only licensed dealers and gun clubs may sell firearms and ammunition. Detailed records of transactions must be maintained. Private transfer are allowed only by government approval.	No. 283, Art. 14, 15; 44, 49	Maintain central government surveillance of firearms location and ownership.
"	All sales of firearms and ammunition (except lighter shotgun loads) must be reported to Ministry of National Defense.	No. 283, Art. 16 & 19	<same>

Table 8A (continued)
History of "Gun Control" Laws in Guatemala
(Source: *Lethal Laws,* pp. 229-269)

Date	Substance of Law	Decree / Section	Apparent Purpose
Oct. 27, 1964	License (with high fee) required to carry firearms. All carrying must be concealed.	No. 283, Art. 20-22	Maintain central government surveillance of firearms location and ownership.
"	No license to carry is required for high level government officials, judges, mayors, active duty military and law enforcement personnel.	No. 283, Art. 26	Maintain wide division between government officials and civilians; place government agents practically aove the law.
"	Prohibits carrying daggers, swords, brass knuckles, truncheons, and "any kind of sharp-pointed or club-like tool or farming implement outside of a town." Pen knives with 2 inch blades are allowed.	No. 283, Art. 27-28	Impose "knife control" and "tool control;" give legal grounds to authorities to arrest and punish non-violent citizens as though they endanger the public order.
"	Allows only the Ministry of National Defense to manufacture firearms and ammunition.	No. 283, Art. 46	Confer monopoly of firearms industry upon government.
"	Hunting rifles with telescopic sights, and the sights themselves, must be registered with the government.	No. 283, Art. 54	
"	All prohibited firearms and ammunition possessed by citizens must be surrendered within 60 days of the date of this law.	No. 283, Art. 58	

End Notes

[1] We use the term "Indian" to refer to the indigenous peoples of Guatemala not of European descent, as the term has been used for centuries. We do not use the term "Indian" to denigrate any group or person.

[2] Commission for Historical Clarification. 1999. Guatemala: Memory of Silence. ("CEH Report") Conclusions, ¶¶ 108-123. The entire report is available from the American Association for the Advancement of Science, http://hrdata.aaas.org/ceh.

[3] Simkin, Jay, Aaron Zelman, and Alan M. Rice. 1994. *Lethal Laws.* Milwaukee, WI: Jews for the Preservation of Firearms Ownership ("LL"), p. 231. (This book also contains side-by-side Spanish text with English translations

for many of the laws cited.)

4LL, p. 229.

5LL, pp. 229-233.

6LL, p. 231, citing Calvert, Peter. 1985. *Guatemala: A Nation in Turmoil.* Boulder, CO: Westview Profiles, p. 145, and Dombrowski, John et al. 1983. *Guatemala: A Country Study.* Washington, D.C.: U.S. Gov't Printing Office, p. 27.

7LL, p. 232, quoting Dombrowski 1983, pp. 32-33.

8LL, pp. 231-232.

9LL, p. 232, citing Calvert 1985, p. 75.

10Ibid., p. 232, citing Calvert 1985, p. 75.

11Ibid., p. 232, citing Calvert 1985, pp. 77-78.

12LL, p. 233, citing Calvert 1985, p. 79.

13Ibid., p. 233, citing Calvert 1985, p. 79.

14LL, p. 233.

15The tone and analysis of the CEH Report indicates a decidedly Leftist bias, but its factual observations have not been seriously questioned.

16CEH Report, Conclusions, ¶3.

17Ibid.

18Ibid., ¶ 9.

19Ibid., ¶ 10.

20Ibid., ¶ 11.

21Ibid., ¶¶ 15, 25.

22Ibid., ¶ 25.

23Ibid., ¶ 43.

24Ibid., ¶ 42.

25Ibid., ¶ 26.

26Ibid., ¶ 50.

27Ibid., ¶ 27.

28Ibid., ¶ 31.

29Ibid., ¶ 32.

30Ibid., ¶ 18.

31Ibid., ¶ 21.

32Ibid., ¶ 45.

33LL, p. 229, citing Jonas, Susanne. 1991. *The Battle for Guatemala.* Boulder, CO: Westview Press, p. 149.

34CEH Report, Conclusions, ¶ 2.

35Ibid., ¶ 1.

36Ibid., ¶¶ 15, 21, 82.

[37]Ibid., ¶ 66.

[38]Ibid., ¶ 85.

[39]Ibid., ¶ 86.

[40]Ibid., ¶ 87.

[41]*Recopilacion de Las Leyes emitidas de la Republica de Guatemala.* June 3, 1871- June 30, 1881. Volume 1.

[42]*Recopilacion de Las Leyes emitidas de la Republica de Guatemala.* June 3, 1871- June 30, 1881. Volume 1.

[43]*Recopilacion de Las Leyes emitidas de la Republica de Guatemala.* June 3, 1871- June 30, 1881. Volume 1.

[44]*Recopilacion de Las Leyes de la Republica de Guatemala.* 1926-1927. Volume 45.

[45]*Recopilacion de Las Leyes de la Republica de Guatemala.* 1930-1931. Volume 49.

[46]*Recopilacion de Las Leyes de la Republica de Guatemala.* 1931-1932. Volume 50.

[47]*Recopilacion de Las Leyes de la Republica de Guatemala.* 1932-1933. Volume 51.

[48]*Recopilacion de Las Leyes de la Republica de Guatemala.* 1940-1941. Volume 56.

[49]*Recopilacion de Las Leyes de la Republica de Guatemala.* 1947-1948. Volume 66.

[50]*Recopilacion de Las Leyes de la Republica de Guatemala.* 1949-1950. Volume 68.

[51]*Recopilacion de Las Leyes de la Republica de Guatemala.* 1958-1959. Volume 77.

[52]*Recopilacion de Las Leyes de la Republica de Guatemala.* 1964-1965. Volume 83.

Chapter Nine:
Nazi Firearms Law and the Disarming of the German Jews

by Stephen P. Halbrook*

> We are in danger of forgetting that the Bill of Rights reflects experience with police excesses. It is not only under Nazi rule that police excesses are inimical to freedom. It is easy to make light of insistence on scrupulous regard for the safeguards of civil liberties when invoked on behalf of the unworthy. It is too easy. History bears testimony that by such disregard are the rights of liberty extinguished, heedlessly at first, then stealthily, and brazenly in the end.
>
> Justice Felix Frankfurter[1]

> The most foolish mistake we could possibly make would be to allow the subject races to possess arms. History shows that all conquerors who have allowed their subject races to carry arms have prepared their own downfall by so doing.
>
> Adolph Hitler[2]

Gun control laws are depicted as benign and historically progressive.[3] However, German firearm laws and hysteria created against Jewish firearm owners played a major role in laying the groundwork for the eradication of German Jewry in the Holocaust. Disarming political opponents was a categorical imperative of the Nazi regime.[4] The Second Amendment to the U.S. Constitution declares: "A well regulated militia, being necessary to the security of a free state, the right of the people to keep and bear arms, shall not be infringed."[5] This right, which reflects a universal and historical power of the people in a republic to resist tyranny,[6] was not recognized in the German Reich.

This article addresses German firearms laws and Nazi policies and practices to disarm German citizens, particularly political opponents and Jews. It begins with an account of post-World War I chaos, which led to the enactment in 1928 by the liberal Weimar republic of Germany's first comprehensive gun control law. Next, the Nazi seizure of power in 1933 was consolidated by massive searches and seizures of firearms from political opponents, who were invariably described as "communists." After five years of repression and eradication of dissidents, Hitler signed a new gun control law in 1938, which benefitted Nazi party members and entities, but denied firearm ownership to enemies of the state. Later that year, in *Reichskristallnacht* (the Night of the Broken Glass), in one fell swoop, the Nazi regime disarmed Germany's Jews. Without any ability to defend themselves, the Jewish population could easily be sent to concentration camps for the Final Solution. After World War II began, Nazi authorities continued to register and mistrust civilian firearm owners, and German resistence to the Nazi regime was unsuccessful.[7]

The above topic has never been the subject of a comprehensive account in the legal literature.[8] This article is based on never before used sources from archives in Germany, German firearms laws and regulations, German and American newspapers from the period, and historical literature. It contributes to the debate concerning firearms ownership in a democracy and presents the first scholarly analysis of the use of gun control laws and policies to establish the Hitler regime and to render political opponents and especially German Jews defenseless.

I. A Liberal Republic Enacts Gun Control

Germany's defeat in World War I heralded the demise of the Second Reich and the birth of the Weimar republic. For several years thereafter, civil unrest and chaos ensued. Government forces, buttressed by unofficial *Freikorps* (Free Corps), battled Communists in the streets.[9] The most spectacular event was the crushing of the Spartacist revolt in Berlin and other cities in January 1919, when *Freikorps* members captured and murdered the Communist leaders Rosa Luxemburg and Karl Liebknecht.[10] This coincided with the passage of the *Verordnung des Rates der Volksbeauftragten über*

Waffenbesitz (Regulations of the Council of the People's Delegates on Weapons Possession), which provided: "All firearms, as well as all kinds of firearms ammunition, are to be surrendered immediately."[11] Whoever kept a firearm or ammunition was subject to imprisonment for five years and a fine of 100,000 marks.[12] That decree would remain in force until repealed in 1928.[13]

When Spartacists attacked a Berlin police station in March, Reich Minister of Defense Gustav Noske declared that "any person who bears arms against government troops will be shot on the spot."[14] A Social Democrat, Noske was known as the "Bloodhound of the Revolution".[15] Another order was issued that anyone in mere possession of arms would be shot with no trial.[16] Under these orders, hundreds of Berliners were killed.[17]

An inept April 1919 Communist uprising in Bavaria fared no better.[18] Lieutenant Rudolf Mann, a regimental adjutant in the *Freikorps*, was humored by the "mopping-up operations" against the Reds:

> The supreme commander tacked proclamations to the walls: "Warning! All arms are to be surrendered immediately. Whoever is caught with arms in his possession will be shot on the spot!" What could the poor citizen of average intelligence do? Surrender — but how? If he took his rifle under his arm to take it to the place were arms were collected, he would be shot on the steps of his house by a passing patrol. If he came to the door and opened it, we all took shots at him because he was armed. If he got as far as the street, we would put him up against the wall. If he stuck his rifle under his coat it was still worse . . . I suggested that they tie their rifles on a long string and drag them behind them. I would have laughed myself sick if I had seen them go down the street doing it.[19]

Armed conflict continued into 1920 when Communists called a general strike in the Ruhr, attacked the Freikorps, and then were defeated.[20] A young *Freikorps* member wrote about the counteroffensive:

> Our battalion has had two deaths; the Reds 200-300. Anyone who falls into our hands first gets the rifle butt and then is finished off with a bullet... We even shot 10 Red Cross nurses *(Rotkreuzschwestern)* on sight because they were carrying pistols. We shot those little ladies

with pleasure—how they cried and pleaded with us to save their lives. Nothing doing! Anybody with a gun is our enemy....[21]

While the government officially proclaimed that it would no longer rely on the services of the *Freikorps*, the latter continued obtaining financial support and arms from the government, often by theft or fraud.[22] *Freikorps* members would go on to become part of the backbone of National Socialism.[23]

The *Gesetz über die Entwaffnung der Bevölkerung* (Law on the Disarmament of the People), passed on August 7, 1920, provided for a Reichskommissar for Disarmament of the Civil Population.[24] He was empowered to define which weapons were "military weapons" and thus subject to seizure.[25] The bolt action Mauser rifles Models 1888/98, which had 5-shot magazines, were put in the same class as hand grenades.[26] Persons with knowledge of unlawful arms caches were required to inform the Disarmament Commission.[27]

Civil disorders would continue off and on, particularly the Hamburg uprising of 1923. This revolt was instigated by Communists who attacked a few police stations and seized arms, only to be suppressed.[28] Under Communist ideology, arms were to be obtained in the course of the revolution itself.[29] Whatever the support or lack of support of members of the "working class" for Communism, the lack of arms in their hands would in later years prevent them from creating armed resistance to the Nazi regime.

By 1928, the Weimar republic was ready to enact a comprehensive firearms law. The *Gesetz über Schußwaffen und Munition* (Law on Firearms and Ammunition)[30] required a license to manufacture, assemble, or repair firearms and ammunition, or even to reload cartridges.[31] A license was also required to sell firearms as a trade.[32] Trade in firearms was prohibited at annual fairs, shooting competitions, and other events.[33]

Acquisition of a firearm or ammunition required a *Waffen-oder Munitionserwerbsschein* (license to obtain a weapon or ammunition) from the police.[34] The requirement applied to both commercial sales and private transfers. It did not apply to transfer of a firearm or ammunition to a shooting range licensed by the police for sole use at the range.[35] Exempt were "authorities of the Reich" and various government entities.[36]

Carrying a firearm required a *Waffenschein* (license to carry a weapon). The issuing authority had complete discretion to limit its validity to a specific occasion or locality.[37] "Licenses to obtain or to carry firearms shall only be issued to persons whose reliability is not in doubt, and only after proving a need for them."[38] Licenses were automatically denied to "gypsies, and to persons wandering around like gypsies"; persons with convictions under various listed laws, including this law (i.e., the 1928 *Gesetz*) and the 1920 Law on the Disarming of the Population; and "persons for whom police surveillance has been declared admissible, or upon whom the loss of civil rights has been imposed, for the duration of the police surveillance or the loss of civil rights."[39]

The above categories of persons who were disqualified from obtaining an acquisition or carry license were prohibited from possession of a firearm or ammunition. Persons not entitled to possess firearms were ordered to surrender them immediately.[40] Further, a license was required to possess a firearms or ammunition "arsenal," which was defined as more than five firearms of the same type or more than 100 cartridges.[41] (These quantities would have been very low for collectors or target competitors.) Also included in the definition was more than ten hunting arms or more than 1000 hunting cartridges.[42] Licenses were available only to "persons of unquestioned trustworthiness."[43] It was forbidden to manufacture or possess firearms which are adapted for "rapid disassembly beyond the generally usual extent for hunting and sporting purposes."[44] Firearms with silencers or spotlights were prohibited.[45]

The penalty for willfully or negligently violating the provisions of the law related to the carrying of a firearm was up to three-years imprisonment and a fine.[46] The same penalty applied to anyone who inherited a firearm or ammunition from a deceased person and failed to report it in a timely manner.[47] Three years imprisonment was also the penalty for whoever deliberately or negligently failed to prevent a violation of the law by a member of his household under 20 years of age.[48] Other violations of the law or implementing regulations were punishable with fines and unspecified terms of imprisonment.[49]

The new law was passed on April 12, but did not take effect until October 1, 1928. On the effective date, the 1919 law requiring immediate surrender of all firearms and ammunition would be repealed.[50] That would allow over six months for compliance with the new law while leaving the more draconian but widely ignored law on the books for the same period.

The bill was sent to the Reichstag in 1928, and "the parties unanimously considered the swift settlement of this matter as so urgent that the law passed immediately in the plenary session, without consultation in the committee . . . and was adopted in all three readings without a debate."[51]

> Thus, the law required a permit for the manufacturing of firearms and ammunition, although, Reichskommissar Kuenzer commented, "it is important to note that the permit may not be made contingent on an examination of the applicant."[52] Firearms sold commercially must bear the name or stamp of the manufacturer or dealer "in the interest of solving criminal acts committed with firearms."[53]

> Unlike the 1919 regulation that required immediate surrender of all firearms and ammunition and punished disobedience with five years imprisonment, the 1928 law allowed possession of firearms in the home.[54] The 1928 law was seen as deregulatory to a point but enforceable, in contrast to a far more restrictive albeit unenforceable order. Less regulation meant fewer "denunciations," although it was unrealistic to anticipate that the odious practice of "denunciations" would end. This would be seen when the Nazis came to power in 1933 and disarmed all political opponents.

The law prohibited possession of firearms by "adolescents, incapacitated persons, gypsies and persons traveling around like gypsies, as well as persons who are considered unreliable because of criminal convictions."[55] Kuenzer added: "This will certainly be welcomed by the general public."[56]

To "facilitate the shooting sport," the 1928 law did not require a license to acquire or use a firearm at a range with a police permit. Further, "special provisions were adopted for hunters":

> When hunting, conducting game protection or practicing shooting, or on their way to or from those activities, owners of a hunting permit of a German State may carry hunting weapons and a handgun without needing a special weapons permit.[57]

Implementing regulations adopted in 1928[58] provided that, unless otherwise specified, the firearms acquisition permit entitled a citizen to acquire only one firearm, and the ammunition acquisition permit entitled the holder to acquire only 50 jacketed or ball cartridges.[59] When the firearm(s) authorized by the acquisition permit was obtained, the transferor (whether a dealer or a non-dealer) was required to submit the permit to the police.[60] Dealers kept acquisition and disposition books which were subject to police inspection on demand.[61]

Within a decade, Germany had gone from a brutal firearms seizure policy which, in times of unrest, entailed selective yet immediate execution for mere possession of a firearm, to a modern, comprehensive gun control law. Passed by a liberal republic, this law ensured that the police had records of all firearms acquisitions (or at least all lawful ones) and that the keeping and bearing of arms were subject to police approval. This firearms control regime was quite useful to the new government that came to power a half decade later.

II. 1933: The Nazis Seize Power

Adolph Hitler was named Chancellor of Germany on January 30, 1933. The Nazi regime immediately began a campaign to disarm and obliterate all enemies of the state, who were invariably designated "Communists." The following describes this process from contemporaneous sources.

On February 1, in the Charlottenburg area of Berlin, a large police detachment arrived to investigate the alleged shooting deaths of two National Socialist officers by "Communists" the night before. "The police closed off the street to all traffic while at the same time criminal detectives conducted extensive raids in the houses. Each individual apartment was searched for weapons. The raid lasted several hours."[62] Countless reports of this type would appear in the coming months.

It took about a month for the Nazi party to consolidate its power over the central government. On February 28, the Hitler regime persuaded President Paul von Hindenburg to issue an emergency decree, based on Article XLVIII of the Constitution (a provision passed by the Weimar republic), suspending constitutional guarantees and authorizing the Reich to seize executive power in any State which failed to take "the necessary measures for the restoration of law and order."[63] The official explanation was that evidence of "imminent Communist terrorism" was discovered in a search of the Karl Liebnecht House, Berlin's Communist headquarters, and that Communists were responsible for the Reichstag (German Parliament) fire of the night before. The decree was adopted after Hermann Göring, Minister without Portfolio and chief of the Prussian Interior Ministry, reported on the Reichstag fire and plans for Communist terror. It was claimed that, on the coming Sunday election day, the Communists intended to attack Nazi party members and "to disarm the police by force."[64] It is widely believed that the Nazis themselves set the Reichstag fire in order to justify the repressive measures which followed.[65]

The decree authorized the government to suspend the constitutional guarantees of personal liberty, free expression of opinion, freedom of the press, and the rights to assemble and to form associations. Secrecy of postal and telephonic communication was suspended, and the government was authorized to conduct search and seizure operations of homes.[66] It provided that whoever commits the offenses defined in the Penal Code as "severe rioting" or "severe breach of public peace" by "using weapons or in conscious and intentional cooperation with an armed person ...shall be sentenced to death or, if the offense was not previously punishable more severely, to the penitentiary for life or to the penitentiary for up to 15 years."[67] Since the terms "riot" and "breach of peace" could be applied to a protest march by political opponents, the mere keeping or bearing of a weapon might have become a capital offense.

It was reported that measures to suppress "subversive activities" took place throughout Germany. Hamburg, Dresden, Hanover, Stuttgart, and numerous other cities "reported bans on Communist activities and the searching of houses for Communist literature and illegal weapons."[68] Police were put on constant alert until after the election.[69] As Communist members of the Reichstag fled, a government spokesman noted that votes for Communists would not be counted because they were "non-German."[70]

Meanwhile, non-Nazis throughout Germany were disarmed as "Communists." "Party headquarters throughout the country were raided and subversive literature and weapons were seized."[71] At the same time, even more Nazis were armed by the government.

"Throughout Prussia some 60,000 Nazi storm troopers and members of the Stahlhelm have been enrolled as auxiliary police and have been armed with revolvers and truncheons."[72] The outcome of the "election" could not be in doubt.

German news reports indicated the use of the "Communist gun owner" bogeyman as a propaganda tool, the extensive searches and seizures being conducted by the police to confiscate firearms and arrest their owners, and the use of the Firearms Law against Nazi opponents. It is clear that firearms were being seized from persons of all types, not just "Communists."

Not surprisingly, the Nazis won the election, leaving the Hitler regime with executive power in all the German States.[73] The repression continued unabated. Anti-Semitic actions began to be reported. One account noted, "The Produce Exchange in Breslau was entered today by Nazi storm troops, who searched the place for arms and ousted the occupants. Several Jewish-owned department stores there were forcibly closed, and the storm troopers ejected Jewish judges and lawyers from the courts."[74]

In another incident, six Nazi storm troopers raided the apartment of the widow of former President Friedrich Ebert.[75] They demanded her "mustard flag," the Nazi term for the republican black, red, and gold emblem.[76] When her son protested that they had no flag on the premises, they conferred among themselves on whether to search the apartment anyway.[77] "They decided finally to look for hidden arms, but found only a revolver belonging to Herr Ebert, which he handed to them together with a permit that had expired. With these the Nazis marched off."[78]

By this point in time the Nazis had foisted a totalitarian regime over all of Germany. Not only had the Socialist and Communist presses been shut down, but also Centrist and neutral presses were subject to immediate suppression should anything objectionable to the regime be published.[79] Germans were forbidden to reveal any information to foreigners. To enforce this repression, telephones were tapped and informants lingered in cafes.[80] The police and the courts were instruments of the dictatorship. Jews were fleeing persecution.[81]

Despite the repression, foreign presses continued to report the news. The following *New York Times* account demonstrates that the Nazi drive to seize arms was in part a ruse to conduct searches and seizures and to harass selected persons:

NAZIS HUNT ARMS IN EINSTEIN HOME
Only a Bread Knife Rewards Brown Shirts'
Search for Alleged Huge Cache
OUSTING OF JEWS GOES ON . . . .

BERLIN, March 20. - Charging that Professor Albert Einstein had a huge quantity of arms and ammunition stored in his secluded home in Caputh, the National Socialists sent Brown Shirt men and policemen to search it today, but the nearest thing to arms they found was a bread knife.

Professor Einstein's home, which for the present is empty, the professor being on his way back to Europe from the United States, was surrounded on all sides and one of the most perfect raids of recent German history was carried out. The outcome was a disappointment to those who have always regarded Professor Einstein's pacifist utterances as a mere pose.[82]

If one could find humor in the above, the reality was not humorous. The above report also described the elimination of Jews from the professions. Jewish physicians were being dismissed from the hospitals, Jewish judges in criminal court were removed and placed in civil court, and Jewish prosecutors were terminated.[83]

On March 23, the Reichstag passed, by a vote of 441 to 94, the enabling act that permitted the Cabinet to make laws without consulting that body and without action by the President. The Reichstag then dissolved *sine die*. The Cabinet of eleven members included three Nazis: Chancellor Hitler, Dr. Wilhelm F. Frick, and Hermann Göring.[84] The others were Nationalists and appointees of President von Hindenburg.[85]

The enabling act made the Hitler cabinet a dictatorship through three simple provisions. Article I provided: "Federal laws may be enacted by the government [the cabinet] outside of the procedure provided in the Constitution . . . ."[86] Article II stated: "The laws decreed by the government may deviate from the Constitution . . . ."[87] And Article III provided: "The laws decreed by the government are to be drafted by the Chancellor [Hitler] and announced in the *Reichsgesetzblatt*."[88]

The above accounts concern Nazi policy to seize all arms from political opponents. Nazi policy also mandated the prohibition of possession of "military" firearms by citizens at large. An SA *Oberführer* warned about an ordinance issued by the provisional Bavarian Minister of the Interior:

> The deadline set by § 4 of the Ordinance for the Surrender of Weapons will expire on March 31, 1933. I therefore request the immediate surrender of all arms from former army stores to the local stations of the Gendarmie.
>
> Pursuant to § 3 of the ordinance, individuals may be permitted to keep a handgun together with proper ammunition for the protection of house and farm. Well-founded requests in this regard may be submitted to the local Gendarmerie stations by way of the mayor.
>
> The units of the national revolution, SA, SS, and Stahlhelm, offer every German man with a good reputation the opportunity to join their ranks for the fight. Therefore, whoever does not belong to one of these named units and nevertheless keeps his weapon without authorization or even hides it, must be viewed as an enemy of the national government and will be held responsible without hesitation and with the utmost severity.[89]

In other words, anyone who possessed a military rifle or handgun was a public enemy unless he or she was a member of a Nazi-approved organization. Of the three listed organizations, the SS (*Schutzstaffeln*) or Elite Guard of the National Socialist Party, headed by Heinrich Himmler, emerged as the most powerful Nazi police organization.[90] The SA (*Sturmabteilung*) or storm troopers were appointed as an auxiliary police force which carried out many of the excesses of the Nazi revolution until its leadership, headed by Ernst Roehm, were eliminated in the "night of the long knives" in 1934.[91] The *Stahlhelm* or Steel Helmets, a veterans' organization,[92] had as its honorary commander President Hindenburg, whose death in 1934 would complete Hitler's consolidation of absolute power[93] and doubtlessly eliminated this organization's special privileges.

On March 28, the State Ministry of the Interior headed by Frick issued a secret directive to the government units, police, municipal commissars, and special commissioners of the highest SA leaders regarding the execution of the ordinance on the surrender of military weapons. It began: "Despite all of the measures taken so far, parts of the population opposed to the national government and the national movement behind it are still in possession of military weapons and military ammunition."[94] It ordered the police "immediately to order the population to surrender any military weapons in a timely manner to the special commissars listed in the official gazettes as well as in the local press."[95] Weapons to be surrendered included not just heavy weapons but also "military rifles" (which were bolt actions) and "army revolvers."[96] The directive continued:

> [T]he Special Commissar of the Highest SA Leader may exempt members of the SA, SS, and Stahlhelm units as well as members of veterans' associations by confidential order to the pertinent leaders of those units/associations. Under no circumstances may the public, especially the press, be informed about this exemption, given the fact that the provisions on disarmament of the Versailles Treaty are still in effect. Further, upon request, the Special Commissar may allow reliable persons to keep a rifle together with the necessary ammunition for the protection of house and farm. The same applies to army revolvers that are the personal property of the owner. Only such persons can be considered reliable from whom a loyal attitude toward the national government can be expected. These approved exceptions must also be treated as confidential.[97]

The surrendered arms were to be stored with the SA, SS, and Stahlhelm.[98] These groups in turn would assist the police "to conduct weapons searches in places where military weapons and military ammunition are still suspected."[99]

A terse newspaper announcement about the above began: "We would like to point out one more time that all military weapons and ammunition in private possession have to be surrendered by March 31, 1933... ."[100] It warned: "If we find military weapons or ammunition after 31 March 1933, we will be forced to proceed ruthlessly . . . ."[101]

Having disarmed and mopped up the "Communists," at times a euphemism for citizens who were not National Socialists, and having prohibited possession of "military" firearms to citizens who were not members of Nazi-approved organizations, the Nazis now turned their attention more toward the Jews. Apparently hoping to depict Jews as subversive by proving them to be in possession of illegal firearms, search and seizure operations were executed on April 4, 1933.[102] The *New York Times* reported:

Raid on Jewish Quarter

A large force of police assisted by Nazi auxiliaries raided a Jewish quarter in Eastern Berlin, searching everywhere for weapons and papers. Streets were closed and pedestrians were halted. Worshipers leaving synagogues were searched and those not carrying double identification cards were arrested. Even flower boxes were overturned in the search through houses and some printed matter and a few weapons were seized.[103]

The Völkische Beobachter contained a revealing account of the raid on the Jewish quarter under the headline: "The Time of the Ghetto Has Come; Massive Raid in the Scheunenviertel;[104] Numerous Discoveries of Weapons— Confiscation of Subversive Material; Numerous Arrests of 'Immigrants' from East Galicia."[105] The article included a dramatic and lengthy description of how the police, supported by the SS and criminal detectives, approached the Scheunenviertel ("Barn District") of Berlin and searched the houses and basements of the Jewish inhabitants. It reported:

During the very extensive search, the search details found a whole range of weapons. Further, a large amount of subversive printed material was confiscated. 14 persons who did not have proper identification were detained. Most of them were Jews from Poland and Galicia who were staying in Berlin without being registered.[106]

Despite the headlines, the article does not state how many or what types of arms were seized or whether they were even unlicenced or otherwise illegal. Prohibition of Jewish possession of firearms was enacted later in 1938. The article does expand on the "subversive material" discovered. It includes two illustrations: first, the assemblage of SS and police on the street, and second, a pathetic picture of an elderly Jewish man in front of a microphone explaining to Nazi radio broadcasters on the scene that he did not know why he was being searched. *Beobachter* readers were apparently supposed to "get it," but the picture and statement evokes sympathy for the old man.

Nazi repressive measures against Jewish firearms owners were facilitated by the 1928 Weimar gun control law, which banned firearms from "untrustworthy" persons and allowed the police to keep records on who acquired or carried firearms.[107] As the *New York Times* reported:

> *Permission to Possess Arms Withdrawn From Breslau Jews*
>
> Breslau, April 21. The Police President of the city has decreed that "all persons now or formerly of the Jewish faith who hold permits to carry arms or shooting licenses must surrender them forthwith to the police authorities."
>
> The order is justified officially on the grounds that Jewish citizens have allegedly used their weapons for unlawful attacks on members of the Nazi organization and the police.
>
> Inasmuch as the Jewish population "cannot be regarded as trustworthy," it is stated, permits to carry arms will not in the future be issued to any member thereof.[108]

Meanwhile, Wilhelm Frick, the Reich Minister of the Interior, wrote to Hermann Göring, Minister of the Interior of Prussia and head of the police of that state, that pistol imports had increased tenfold, and that "for reasons of public security we cannot tolerate the unrestrained import of such huge amounts of weapons." While the 1928 law already restricted firearm acquisitions, "the rules will not be observed by all of the weapons dealers, [and] that unauthorized persons will obtain foreign weapons flowing into the country . . . ."[109] Accordingly, on June 12, Frick decreed a prohibition on the importation of handguns.[110] Handgun ownership by German citizens, including Jews and political opponents, was apparently subversive to the Nazi regime.

Historians of the period have shown little or no interest in the above phenomena, with the exception of William Allen, whose *The Nazi Seizure of Power* is based on the experiences of the town of Northeim in Lower Saxony. This work demonstrates the Nazi's manipulative hysteria about firearms owners in 1933.[111] As Allen demonstrates, the town's citizens found "that it was extremely unhealthy to have any sort of weapon around the house."[112] Discovery of firearms by the police "was a first-class justification for the repeated police raids and arrests."[113]

Allen observes that the town's Reichsbanner (armed section of the Social Democratic party) awaited orders from party headquarters in Berlin to fight the Nazis, but the order never came. "Had it been given, Northeimer's *Reichsbanner* members would have carried out the tested plan they had worked on so long—to obtain and distribute weapons and to crush the Nazis."[114] Social Democrats were "the only defenders of democracy in Germany, the men who should have been gathering guns and calling the general strike," but instead their homes were being raided in midnight arms searches and they were being hauled off to concentration camps.[115]

In any event, the Nazi seizure of power was complete. It remained to consolidate this power for the aims of National Socialism.

III. Hitler's Gun Control Act of 1938

On seizing power, as the above demonstrates, the Nazis were well served by the 1928 Firearms Law. Discussions about possible amendments were held over a five-year period among the highest Nazi leadership.[116] The result was the Nazi *Waffengesetz* (Weapons Law) of March 18, 1938.[117] It was decreed and signed by Adolph Hitler and Reich Minister Frick under the Enabling Act passed in 1933.

The 1928 Weimar firearms law that was still in place empowered the police with discretion to issue or refuse to issue permits to acquire or carry firearms. As the following 1936 memorandum from the Bavarian Political Police to all subordinate police reveals, in late 1935 the Gestapo had ordered that no weapons permits would be issued to Jews without Gestapo approval:

> Pursuant to an order of the Political Police Commander of the States [Länder] of December 16, 1935, No. I G - 352/35, the police authorities always have to obtain the opinion of the Geheimen Staatspolizei [Gestapo or Secret State Police] authorities on the political reliability of the individual requestor, before any permits to carry weapons are issued to any Jews.
>
> Requests by Jews for the issuance of weapons permits therefore have to be sent to the Bavarian Political Police, II/1 for special disposal, so that it can state its

> opinion about the political reliability of the requestor.
>
> In general, the following has to be taken into account with regard to the issuance of weapons permits to Jews:
>
> In principle, there will be very few occasions where concerns will not be raised regarding the issuance of weapons permits to Jews. As a rule, we have to assume that firearms in the hands of the Jews represent a considerable danger for the German people. Therefore, in the future, an extreme measure of scrutiny will have to be applied to the question of political reliability of the requestor in all cases where an opinion needs to be given about the issuance of weapons permits to Jews. Only in this way will we be able to prevent numerous Jews from obtaining firearms and causing danger to the German population.
>
> Most likely, the forwarding of applications will come into consideration only in special cases.[118]

In short, before the 1938 Weapons law was decreed, the legal and police tools were already in place to disarm whatever group the Nazis disfavored.

As adopted, the 1938 (Hitler-Frick) weapons law combined many elements of the 1928 law with National Socialist innovations. A license was required to manufacture, assemble, or repair firearms and ammunition, or even to reload cartridges. "A license shall not be granted if the applicant, or the persons intended to become the commercial or technical managers of the operation of the trade, or any one of them, is a Jew."[119] Firms with licenses under the 1928 law had to comply with this provision within a year or the license would be revoked.[120]

A license was also required to sell firearms as a trade. Again, Jews were excluded.[121] Trade in firearms was prohibited at annual fairs, shooting competitions, and other events.[122] This would have included traditionally-popular events as shooting festivals and gun shows.

Acquisition of a handgun required a *Waffenerwerbschein* (license to obtain a weapon).[123] That did not apply to transfer of a handgun to a shooting range licensed by the police for sole use at the range. Exempt were "authorities of the Reich," various government entities, and "departments and their subdivisions of the

National Socialist German Workers' Party designated by the deputy of the Führer."[124]

Carrying a firearm required a *Waffenschein* (license to carry a weapon). The issuing authority had complete discretion to limit its validity to a specific occasion or locality.[125] The decree further provided:

1. Licenses to obtain or to carry firearms shall only be issued to persons whose reliability is not in doubt, and only after proving a need for them.

2. Issuance shall especially be denied to:...

3. gypsies, and to persons wandering around like gypsies;

4. persons for whom police surveillance has been declared admissible, or upon whom the loss of civil rights has been imposed, for the duration of the police surveillance or the loss of civil rights;

5. persons who have been convicted of treason or high treason, or against whom facts are under consideration which justify the assumption that they are acting in a manner inimical to the state...

6. persons who have received final sentence to a punishment of deprivation of liberty for more than two weeks...for resistance to the authorities of the state.[126]

Notably, on the face of the law, Jews were not named as automatically disqualified. Gypsies were the only ethnic group which did not qualify. It could be that the Nazi leadership did not feel confident of the support of enough Germans to disarm Jews at this time. Many Jewish men had fought in the Great War and retained their side arms.[127] This reluctance would change later that year.

For officially-supplied firearms, a license to acquire or carry firearms was not required of members of the armed forces, the police, "members of the SS reserve groups and the SS skull and cross-bones units [*Totenkopfverbände*],"[128] and lower echelon Nazi and Hitler Youth leaders. [129]

Possession of any kind of weapon could be prohibited where "in individual cases a person who has acted in an inimical manner toward the state, or it is to be feared that he will endanger the public security."[130] This could include any opponent of Nazism or simply any disfavored person.

It was forbidden to manufacture or possess "firearms which are adapted for folding or telescoping, shortening, or rapid disassembly beyond the generally usual extent for hunting and sporting purposes."[131] Firearms with silencers or spotlights were prohibited.[132] Finally, .22 caliber rimfire cartridges with hollow point bullets were outlawed.[133]

The penalty for willfully or negligently violating the provisions of the law related to the carrying of a firearm was up to three-years imprisonment and a fine.[134] A fine and indeterminate imprisonment was imposed on anyone who violated other provisions of the law or implementing regulations.[135]

The primary Hitler-Frick innovations to the 1928 Weimar law were the exclusion of Jews from firearms businesses and the extension of the exceptions to the requirements for licenses to obtain and to carry firearms to include various National Socialist entities, including party members and military and police organizations. Although the 1938 law no longer required an acquisition license for rifles and shotguns, but only for handguns, any person could be prohibited from possession of any firearm based on the broad discretion of authorities to determine that a person was "acting in a manner inimical to the state," had been sentenced "for resistance to the authorities of the state,"[136] or "it is to be feared that he will endanger the public security."[137] An innovation of the 1938 law was to ban .22 caliber rimfire cartridges with hollow point bullets, which were mostly used for small game hunting but which could be lethal to humans.

The major features of the 1928 law were retained as particularly suitable for Nazism's goals:

- the requirement of licenses to make and sell firearms, including recordkeeping on transferees and police powers to inspect such records;
- the requirements of licenses to obtain and to carry weapons, and the retention by police of the identities of and information on such licensees;
- the provision that "licenses to obtain or to carry firearms shall only be issued to persons whose reliability is not in doubt, and only after proving a need for them";
- the denial of licenses to "persons for whom police surveillance

has been declared admissible," or who presumably "are acting in a manner inimical to the state";

- the prohibition on possession of any weapon by a person "who has acted in an inimical manner toward the state, or it is to be feared that he will endanger the public security"; and
- the prohibition on firearms with certain features not generally used "for hunting and sporting purposes."

Again following the 1928 law, the 1938 law directed that the Reich Minister of the Interior shall issue implementing regulations.[138] Exercising that power, on March 19, 1938, Frick issued extensive regulations governing the manufacture, sale, acquisition, and carrying of firearms.[139] The regulations began by entrusting the higher administrative authority in the hands of the presidents of the governments or highest officials in the various States, except that in Berlin the power was in the hands of the Police Chief.[140]

Extensive recordkeeping was required. A manufacturer, which included not only the original producer but also a person who assembled firearms in his shop from parts made by others, was required to keep a book with each firearm identified and its disposition. A handgun seller was obliged to keep books on the acquisition and disposition of each handgun. Once a year, the book for the previous year was submitted to the police authorities for certification. All records were subject to police inspection on demand. The records were to be kept for ten years except that, on discontinuance of business, they were required to be turned over to the police.[141]

Licenses to obtain or carry firearms, the form of which was prescribed, were issued by the district police authority of the residence of the applicant. A firearm acquisition permit was valid for one year, and a license to carry a specific firearm was valid for three years.[142] When a person obtained the handgun authorized by an acquisition permit, the transferor, whether dealer or private person, submitted the permit showing the acquisition to the police.[143] Muzzle loading pistols and revolvers, and blank and gas firearms, were exempt.[144] "Individual exceptions" were now permitted to the 1933 ban on importation of handguns.[145] Apparently because the law itself covered the subject in detail, the regulations did not mention the prohibition on Jews being licensed as manufacturers or sellers or the numerous exceptions for government and National Socialist party members.

In short, under the 1938 law the police decided who could and who could not possess firearms. Aryans who were good Nazis could acquire firearms with relative ease. Any possession of firearms by a person considered "undesirable" by the police was prohibited. The Nazis thereby imposed on the German people a firearms law based on totalitarianism and police-state principles.

IV. *Reichskristallnacht*: The Disarming of the Jews

On November 7, 1938, Herschel Grynszpan, a 17-year old German Jewish refugee whose father had been deported to Poland, went to the German Embassy in Paris intending to shoot the ambassador. Instead he shot and mortally wounded Ernst vom Rath, the third secretary in the Embassy, who ironically was being watched by the Gestapo because he opposed anti-Semitism and Nazism.[146] As the following demonstrates, the Nazi hierarchy recognized the incident as creating a favorable opportunity to disarm Germany's Jewish population.

On the morning of November 9, German newspaper headlines reported variously "Police Raid on Jewish Weapons,"[147] "Armed Jews,"[148] "Berlin's Jews were Disarmed,"[149] "Disarming the Berlin Jews,"[150] and "Surrender of Weapons by Jews in Berlin, A Measure by the Police President."[151] The articles all contained substantially the same text as follows:

> In view of the Jewish assassination attempt in the German Embassy in Paris, Berlin's Police President made known publicly the provisional results so far achieved, of a general disarming of Berlin's Jews by the police, which has been carried out in recent weeks.
>
> The Police President, in order to maintain public security and order in the national capital, and prompted by a few individual incidents, felt compelled to disarm Berlin's Jewish population. This measure was recently made known to Jews by police stations, whereupon—apart from a few exceptions, in which the explicit nature of the ban on possession of weapons had to be articulated— weapons until now found by the police to be in the possession of Jews who have no weapons permit were voluntarily surrendered.
>
> The provisional results clearly show what a large amount of weapons have been found with Berlin's Jews and are still to be found with them. To date, the campaign led to

the taking into custody of 2,569 stabbing and cutting weapons, 1,702 firearms, and about 20,000 rounds of ammunition.

Upon completion of the weapons campaign, if a Jew in Berlin is found still to possess a weapon without having a valid weapons permit, the Police President will, in every single case, proceed with the greatest severity.[152]

The Berlin Police President, Count Wolf Heinrich von Helldorf, apparently announced the above results the day before.[153] As noted, the disarming had been carried out in "recent weeks" and had been "prompted by a few individual incidents" which were not specified. Was the disarming an attempt to control any resistance to the repressive measures currently underway which motivated Grynszpan? Or was it in anticipation of a major pogrom against Jews just waiting for the proper incident to exploit, which now existed from the shooting at the Paris embassy? The disarming meant that Jews could not protect themselves from attacks.[154]

The *New York Times* reported from Berlin that "Nazis Ask Reprisal in Attack on Envoy," and that "Berlin Police Head Announces 'Disarming' of Jews—Victim of Shots in Critical State."[155] Its account repeated the above statistics from Police President von Helldorf of weapons seized and the announcement that "any Jews still found in possession of weapons without valid licenses are threatened with the severest punishment."[156]

The attempted assassination was called "a new plot of the Jewish world conspiracy against National Socialist Germany," and the German press called for retaliation. Recalling David Frankfurter's shooting in 1936 of Nazi leader Wilhelm Gustloff in Switzerland, the *Börsen Zeitung* declared: "International Jewry and foreign Jews living in Germany as well will soon feel the consequences that the Reich will draw from the fact that for the second time in three years 'a Jew has shot.'" The Angriff asked for "the sharpest measures against Jews."[157]

Vom Rath died on the 9th, which by coincidence was the *"Tag der Bewegung"* (Day of the Movement), the anniversary of Hitler's failed 1923 Beer Hall Putsch in Munich. Hitler gave his annual speech in the *Bürgerbräukeller* to commemorate and remember the "fallen heroes" who died in the shootout with the police.[158] Vom Rath's death was reported to Hitler early that evening while dining at Munich's town hall chamber. Hitler turned and spoke quietly to Propaganda Minister Joseph Goebbels.[159] Mentioning localized anti-Jewish riots the night before, the Führer stated that the Nazi party was not to initiate such demonstrations, but would not intervene to halt "spontaneous" pogroms.[160] Hitler was also overheard to say that "the SA should be allowed to have a fling."[161] Goebbels gave a speech calling for revenge with such vehemence that the party and police leaders would discern that they should take an active role.[162]

The telephone orders between chief of staff of the SA Group *Nordsee*, Roempagel, and his superior, were included in a secret SS report prepared the following year.[163] Among the instructions Roempagel received were: "All Jewish stores are to be destroyed immediately by SA men in uniform"; "Jewish synagogues are to be set on fire immediately, Jewish symbols are to be safeguarded"; "the police must not intervene. The Führer wishes that the police does not intervene." The following instruction would ensure the success of the attacks as well as achieve an ultimate goal: "All Jews are to be disarmed. In the event of resistance they are to be shot immediately."[164]

After 11:55 p.m. on November 9, SS *Standartenführer* (Colonel) Heinrich Müller sent an urgent teleprinter message from Gestapo Headquarters in Berlin to every state police bureau in the Reich, alerting them that "demonstrations against the Jews, and particularly their synagogues, will take place very shortly." The Gestapo was not to interfere, but was to cooperate with the regular police to prevent looting and other excesses.[165] The last paragraph of Müller's message read:

> If, during the actions about to take place, Jews are found in possession of weapons the most severe measures are to be applied. The special task units of the SS as well as the general SS may be employed for all phases of the operation. Suitable measures are to be taken to ensure that the Gestapo remains in control of the actions under all circumstances.[166]

On the morning of November 10, the following decree appeared in newspapers throughout Germany:

Jews Forbidden to Possess Weapons
By Order of SS Reichsführer Himmler
Munich, November 10 [1938]
The SS Reichsführer and German Police Chief has issued

the following Order:

Persons who, according to the Nürnberg law, are regarded as Jews, are forbidden to possess any weapon. Violaters will be condemned to a concentration camp and imprisoned for a period of up to 20 years.[167]

All hell broke loose. The *New York Times* reported: "Nazis Smash, Loot and Burn Jewish Shops and Temples Until Goebbels Calls Halt."[168] In Berlin and throughout Germany, thousands of Jewish men, particularly prominent leaders, were taken from their homes and arrested.[169] *The Angriff*, Goebbel's organ, implored that, "For every suffering, every crime and every injury that this criminal [the Jewish community] inflicts on a German anywhere, every individual Jew will be held responsible."[170] The Times account reported the arms prohibition as follows:

Possession of Weapons Barred

One of the first legal measures issued was an order by Heinrich Himmler, commander of all German police, forbidding Jews to possess any weapons whatever and imposing a penalty of twenty years confinement in a concentration camp upon every Jew found in possession of a weapon hereafter.[171]

The destruction was carried out by *Rollkommandos* (wrecking crews) under the protection of uniformed Nazis or police.[172] However, the people at large generally did not participate, and most appeared to be gravely disturbed by the attacks.[173] Some members of the public helped Jews leave their stores unmolested, but citizens who protested against the attacks on Jews were threatened and silenced by the *Rollkommandos*.[174]

The anti-Jewish pogrom extended into Austria, which Germany had annexed earlier that year. Arson was committed against Vienna's temples, and Nazis attacked Jewish businesses. The *New York Times* reported: "Thousands of Jews had their dwellings searched for concealed arms, documents and money. The police claim to have found quantities of them..."[175]

On November 11, Interior Minister Frick issued the *Verordnung gegen den Waffenbesitz der Juden* (Regulation Against Jews' Possession of Weapons).[176] Its preamble recites that it was issued pursuant to § 31 of the 1938 Weapons Law, which in turn empowered the Interior Minister to issue "the necessary legal and administrative regulations for the implementation and

Death by Gun Control

fulfillment of this Law." § 1 of the new regulation provided:

> Jews...are prohibited from acquiring, possession, and carrying firearms and ammunition, as well as cutting or stabbing weapons. Those now having in their possession weapons and ammunition must at once surrender them to the local police authority.[177]

Foreign Jews could be exempted by the Interior Minister or delegate.[178]

Section 2 of the regulation stated: "Weapons and ammunition found in a Jew's possession will be forfeited to the Reich without compensation." Concerning any person in violation, § 4 provided: "Whoever willfully or negligently violates the provisions of § 1 shall be punished with imprisonment and a fine. In especially severe cases of deliberate violations, the punishment is imprisonment in a penitentiary for up to five years." The regulation was applicable in Germany, Austria, and the Sudetenland.[179]

There were about 550,000 Jews in those jurisdictions. The number of Jews arrested during the rampage was approximately 30,000 males aged 16-80.[180]

The American Consulate in Stuttgart reported to U.S. Ambassador Hugh R. Wilson in Berlin on November 12 that "the Jews of Southwest Germany have suffered vicissitudes during the last three days which would seem unreal to one living in an enlightened country during the twentieth century...." The Consulate's office was flooded with Jews begging for visas or immigration assistance for themselves and families. He wrote: "Men in whose homes old, rusty revolvers had been found during the last few days cried aloud that they did not dare ever again to return to their places of residence or business. In fact, it was a mass of seething, panic-stricken humanity."[181]

Searches for weapons in Jewish homes and arrests generally continued. Jews who still had wealth, despite the recent campaigns to deprive them of their property, were pinpointed.[182]

The Decree on an Atonement Fine for Jews with German Citizenship (November 12, 1938) levied Jews with one billion reichsmarks as payment to the German Reich for the destruction caused by the Nazis.[183] Ordered by Field Marshal Göring in his capacity as Commissioner for the Four Year Plan, this was enforceable because a registry of all Jewish property had been compiled six months previously.[184] (Similarly, the order prohibiting Jews from possession of arms under penalty of imprisonment and "protective custody" was more enforceable because of the firearms registry laws.)[185] Jews were ordered to repair all damage that had been done to business-es and homes on November 8-10, and the Reich confiscated Jewish insurance claims. Jews were excluded from economic activity in the Reich by the year's end.[186]

A Swiss newspaper reported from Berlin on November 11 under the headline "Numerous Arrests?" the following:

> Last night the Gestapo started to arrest Jews in Berlin and in other German cities. Most of those arrested were respected Jewish personalities. At a reception for the press, the Reich Minister for Propaganda [Goebbels] denied that there had been any arrests; when asked again later, however, [his office] said that the arrests had been made in connection with Himmler's decree prohibiting Jews from owning arms. The explanation given was that the Jews had retained weapons even though the Chief of the German police in his latest decree had threatened to punish them with protective detention of 20 years.[187]

Reporting from Frankfurt, the British Counsel observed that for several days beginning on the evening of November 10, SS troopers and Gestapo agents intruded into Jewish homes to conduct search-es and seizures. If any arms or a large sum of money were found, the occupants were arrested for illegal possession of arms or for hoarding funds.[188]

French and Swiss newspapers saw *Reichskristallnacht* as the cul-mination of earlier anti-Semitic measures of the Reich and as "pre-meditated destruction":

> To illuminate the recent events one now better under-stands the special liabilities imposed on the Jews in recent times. Events since last June make clear the obvi-ous methods of their measures. They have simplified the destruction. One method was to confiscate their arms from them, rendering the operation without danger. The other demanded from them a formal declaration of assets (currency, jewelry, pieces of furniture, carpets), which facilitated the confiscation thereof. All was ready.[189]

A month after the pogrom, the Gestapo in Munich issued a

memorandum to the police, commissars, and mayors concerning the regulation requiring Jews to surrender all weapons. It also explained how the regulation was to be implemented:

> All weapons of all kinds in the possession of Jews are for-feited to the Reich without payment of compensation and must be surrendered.
>
> This includes all firearms including alarm (starter) pistols and all cutting and stabbing weapons including the fixed blade if like a dagger.
>
> Requests by emigrating Jews to have their weapons returned to them shall not be granted.
>
> A list shall be made of all weapons that belonged to Jews and the list shall be sent to this office by January 5, 1939. The weapons shall be well packaged and, if in small numbers, sent as parcel, and if in larger numbers, by freight.
>
> Because this will have to be reported to the Gestapo office in Berlin, this deadline will absolutely have to be observed.[190]

Thus, over a period of several weeks, Germany's Jews had been disarmed. The process was carried out both by following a combination of legal forms and by sheer lawless violence. The Nazi hierarchy could now more comfortably deal with the Jewish question without fear of resistance.

V. Afterword: Precluding Armed German Resistance to Nazism

The disarming of the Jews made individual or collective resistance in the future impossible. After *Reichskristallnacht*, the historical record does not reflect that German Jews unlawfully obtained or used arms as tools of resistance. In fact, the *Reichsvertretung der Juden in Deutschland* (National Representative Organization of Jews in Germany), the German-Jewish leadership, insisted that Jewish activities be legal. Militant resistance was rejected as futile and provocative of reprisals.[191] The *Reichsvertretung* did sanction the financing of escapes by opening illegal bank accounts,[192] but it also helped to register Jews selected for deportation and to ensure transportation arrangements for deportees.[193]

Yet it is a myth, observes Arnold Paucker, that Jews did not resist Nazism. Most Jews capable of bearing arms came forward, wherever possible, to fight either in regular armies or as partisans in every European country.[194] The exception was in Germany, where "there was virtually no armed resistance of any sort, and thus no armed Jewish resistance either."[195] German Jews could not be faulted for not instigating military adventurism.[196] Paucker does not speculate on how the course of history could have been altered had German opponents of Nazism, including both Jews and non-Jews, been better armed, more unified, and ideologically more inclined to resistance.

After Hitler launched World War II by attacking Poland in 1939, many Germans blamed him for failing to spare Germany an armed conflict. Anti-Nazi sentiment existed. Opined the London *Times*: "All this does not imply that Germany is ready for a revolution. Civilians are disarmed, and so powerless...."[197] Germans generally longed for, it was asserted, the return of legality, freedom, and human dignity.[198]

> When the Nazis conquered France (as in other countries), they proclaimed that failure of civilians to surrender all firearms within twenty-four hours would be punishable with the death penalty, and they executed many who failed to comply.[199]

> Nor would the Nazis trust ordinary German firearm owners. In addition to the law and regulations already in place, a secret Gestapo order in 1941 established a system of central registration of persons obtaining firearms other than military officers, police, and political leaders.[200]

The existence of firearms regulations providing for records on all individuals lawfully possessing firearms, coupled with searches and seizures of firearms from the houses of potential dissidents, guaranteed that firearms would be possessed only by supporters of Nazism. These firearms policies made it far easier to exterminate any opposition, Jews, and unpopular groups.

German resistors were different than their European counterparts in that there was no maquis or partisan force.[201] The German resistance to Hitler was not characterized by any armed popular movements or uprisings against the Nazi regime. Lone individuals or small military cliques with firearms or bombs sought to kill Hitler himself.[202] Heroic as these attempts were, how might the course of history been different had Germany (not to mention the countries Germany would occupy) been a country where large numbers of citizens owned firearms without intrusive legal restrictions and where the right to keep and bear arms was a constitutional guarantee?[203]

Three million Germans were imprisoned for political reasons in the years 1933 to 1945, and tens of thousands were executed. "These numbers reveal the potential for popular resistance in German society—and what happened to it."[204] The same could be said about the far larger numbers of victims of the Holocaust and the mass killings of unarmed peoples of the countries occupied by the Nazis. Once again, what might have been the course of history had firearm ownership been more prevalent and protected as a constitutional right?

Such questions have never been discussed in scholarly publications because the Nazi laws, policies, and practices have never been adequately documented. The record establishes that a well-meaning liberal republic would enact a gun control act that would later be highly useful to a dictatorship. That dictatorship could then consolidate its power by massive search and seizure operations against political opponents, under the hysterical ruse that such persons were "Communist" firearm owners. It could enact its own new firearms law, disarming anyone the police deemed "dangerous" and exempting members of the party that controlled the state. It could exploit a tragic shooting of a government official to launch a pogrom, under the guise that Jewish firearm owners were dangerous and must be disarmed. This dictatorship could, generally, disarm the people of the nation it governed and then disarm those of every nation it conquered.

The above experiences influenced perceptions of fundamental rights in both the United States and Germany. Before entering the war, America reacted to the events in Europe in a characteristic manner. Seeing the Nazi threat and its policies, Congress passed the Property Requisition Act of 1941 authorizing the President to requisition certain property for defense, but prohibiting any construction of the act to "require the registration of any firearms possessed by any individual for his personal protection or sport" or "to impair or infringe in any manner the right of any individual to keep and bear arms."[205]

Today, Germany's *Grundgesetz* (Basic Law) includes the following provision: "When other avenues are not open, all Germans have the right to resist attempts to impose unconstitutional authority."[206]

If the Nazi experience teaches anything, it teaches that totalitarian governments will attempt to disarm their subjects so as to extinguish any ability to resist crimes against humanity.

End Notes

©Copyright 2000 by Stephen P. Halbrook. All rights reserved. The full text of this article appeared in the Arizona Journal of International and Comparative Law, vol. 17, no. 3, pp. 483-535 (2000). End notes here are in the style of the original article. The author holds a Ph.D. from Florida State University and a J.D. from Georgetown University. Located in Fairfax, Virginia, he litigates constitutional law issues in the federal courts, including the Supreme Court. His recent books include *Freedmen, the Fourteenth Amendment, and the Right to Bear Arms, 1866-1876* (Westport, Conn.: Praeger, 1998); *Target Switzerland: Swiss Armed Neutrality in World War II* (New York: Sarpedon, 1998); *Die Schweiz im Visier* (Verlage Novalis Schaffhausen/Rothenhäusler Stäfa, CH, 1999); and *La Suisse encerclée* (Geneva: Editions Slatkine, 2000). He may be contacted via his website at www.stephenhalbrook.com. The author wishes to acknowledge Therese Klee Hathaway for her assistance in German translations and the following for their research assistance: Katya Andrusz, Jay Simkin, Lisa Halbrook-Stevenson, Heather Barry, and Dave Fischer.

[1]*Davis v. United States*, 328 U.S. 582, 597 (1946) (Frankfurter, J., dissenting).

[2]*Hitler's Secret Conversations*, trans. Norman Cameron and R. H. Stevens (New York: Signet Books, 1961) 403.

[3]"But if watering down is the mode of the day, I would prefer to water down the Second Amendment rather than the Fourth Amendment." *Adams v. Williams,* 407 U.S. 143, 152 (1972) (Douglas, J., dissenting). "There is no reason why all pistols should not be barred to everyone but the police." Id. at 150-51.

[4]Besides gun control, the Nazis were supposedly ahead of their time in such socially-responsible causes as the eradication of tobacco use. Robert N. Proctor, *The Nazi War on Cancer* (Princeton University Press, 1999).

[5]U.S. Const., amend. II.

[6]On the history of this right, see this author's *That Every Man Be Armed: The Evolution of a Constitutional Right* (University of New Mexico Press 1984; reprint Independent Institute 1994); *A Right to Bear Arms: State and Federal Bills of Rights and Constitutional Guarantees* (Greenwood Press 1989).

[7]Infra, passim.

[8]See David B. Kopel, "Lethal Laws," *N.Y. L. Sch. J. Int'l & Comp.* L. 15 (1995); Don B. Kates & Daniel D. Polsby, "Of Genocide and Disarmament," 86 *Crim. L. & Criminology* 297 (1995). Although the disarming of the Jews as a prelude to and in the course of the Holocaust does not appear to be the subject of any historical study, numerous excellent studies have

been published on armed Jewish resistance in the Nazi-occupied countries. E.g., Simha Rotem (Kazik), *Memoirs of a Warsaw Ghetto Fighter and the Past Within Me* (1994); Anny Latour, *The Jewish Resistance in France, 1940-1944* (1970).

[9]Robert G.L. Waite, *Vanguard of Nazism: The Free Corps Movement in Postwar Germany, 1918-1923* (Cambridge: Harvard Univ. Press, 1952), passim.

[10]See id. at 59-71.

[11]*Reichsgesetzblatt* 1919, Nr. 7, 31, § 1.

[12]See id. § 3.

[13]*Reichsgesetzblatt* 1928, I, 143, 147, § 34(1).

[14]Waite, supra note 9, at 72-3, citing *Vorwärts*, March 10, 1919 (morning edition).

[15]See id. at 14.

[16]See id. at 73 & n.42, citing *Freiheit*, March 18, 1919.

[17]See id. at 73.

[18]See id. at 84-87.

[19]Id. at 91-92, quoting Rudolf Mann, *Mit Ehrhardt durch Deutschland, Erinnerungen eines Mitkämpfers von der 2. Marinebrigade* (Berlin, 1921), 71-72.

[20]See id. at 172-81.

[21]Id. at 182, quoting Maximilian Scheer ed., *Blut und Ehre* (Paris 1937), 43.

[22]See id. at 182, 194-95, 200-01.

[23]See id. at 268, 281.

[24]*Reichsgesetzblatt* 1920, Nr. 169, I, at 1553-57, §§ 1, 7.

[25]See id. § 2.

[26]See id. § 6.

[27]See id. § 4.

[28]A. Neuberg, *Armed Insurrection* (New York: St. Martin's Press, 1970), 81-104. This work was originally published under a pen name as *Der bewaffnete Aufstand* (1928).

[29]See id. at 194-95.

[30]*Reichsgesetzblatt* 1928, I, 143. A reprint of the German text with English translation is available in Jay Simkin and Aaron Zelman, *"Gun Control": Gateway to Tyranny* (Milwaukee, WI: Jews for the Preservation of Firearms Ownership, 1992), 15-25.

[31]See id. § 2(1).

[32]See id. § 5.

[33]See id. § 7.

[34]See id. § 10(1).

[35]See id. § 10(3)1.

[36]See id. § 11.

[37]See id. § 15.

[38]Id. § 16(1).

[39]Id. § 16(2).

[40]See id. § 17.

[41]See id. § 23.

[42]Id.

[43]Id.

[44]Id. § 24.

[45]See id.

[46]See id. § 25.

[47]See id.

[48]See id. § 26.

[49]Id. § 27.

[50]See id. § 34(1), citing *Reichsgesetzblatt*, 1919, Nr. 7, 31.

[51]Id.

[52]See Reichskommissar Kuenzer, *"Das Gesetz über Schußwaffen und Munition,"* Deutsche Allgemeine Zeitung, Apr. 13, 1928, at 1.

[53]Id.

[54]Id. (referring to *Reichsgesetzblatt* 1919, Nr. 7, 31).

[55]See id.

[56]Id.

[57]Id.

[58]*Ausführungsverordnung zu dem Gesetz über Schusswaffen und Munition,* 13 Juli 1928, *Reichsgesetzblatt* 1928, I, at 198. Reprinted in Simkin & Zelman, *supra* note 30, at 27.

[59]See *Reichsgesetzblatt* 1928, at § 12.

[60]See id. at § 14(3).

[61]See id. at § 10.

[62]*"Razzia in Charlottenburg,"* Der Bund (Bern), Feb. 2, 1933 (evening edition).

[63]"Red Terror Plans Alleged By Reich," *N. Y. Times,* Mar. 1, 1933, at 11.

[64]Id.

[65]See Hans B. Gisevius, *To the Bitter End: An Insider's Account of the Plot to Kill Hitler 1933-1944* (New York: Da Capo Press, 1998), 3-36.

[66]*Reichsverordnung zum Schutz von Volk und Staat* [Ordinance of the Reich President for the Protection of the People and the State], Reichsgesetzblatt 1933, I, 83, § 1.

[67]Id. § 5.

[68]See *N. Y. Times, supra* note 63, at 11.

[69]Id.

[70]Id.

[71]Id.

[72]Id.

[73]Frederick T. Birchall, "Hindenburg Drops Flag of Republic," *N. Y. Times,* Mar. 13, 1933, at 6.

[74]"Nazis Seek Sweep of Local Offices," *N. Y. Times,* Mar. 12, 1933, at 19.

[75]"Nazis Raid Home of President Ebert's Widow: Hindenburg Orders Inquiry of Flag Search," *N. Y. Times,* Mar. 15, 1933, at 11.

[76]Id.

[77]Id.

[78]Id.

[79]See "All News is Censored and Opposition Press Suppressed," *N. Y. Times,* Mar. 20, 1933, at 1.

[80]See id.

[81]See id.

[82]"Nazis Hunt Arms in Einstein Home," *N. Y. Times,* Mar. 21, 1933, at 10.

[83]See id.

[84]See "Hitler Cabinet Gets Power to Rule As a Dictatorship: Reichstag Quits Sine Die," *N. Y. Times,* Mar. 24, 1933, at 1.

[85]See id.

[86]Id.

[87]Id.

[88]Id.

[89]*Zur Verordnung des kommisarischen bayer. Innenministers vom 24.3.33. über Wehrverbände.* Found in BHStA, LRA Bad Tölz 133992, No2501c51.

[90]See Raphaël Lemkin, *Axis Rule in Occupied Europe* (Washington D.C.: Carnegie Endowment for International Peace, 1944), 15-16.

[91]Gisevius, *supra* note 65, at 103, 148-49 (1998).

[92]See id. at 608.

[93]See William L. Shirer, *The Rise and Fall of the Third Reich* (New York: Simon & Schuster, 1990), 157, 226.

[94]Staatsministerium des Innern. An 1. die Regierungen, KdJ. [et al.], Betreff: Vollzug der Verordnung über die Ablieferung der Militärwaffen, (March 28, 1933). Found in BHStA, LRA Bad Tölz 133992, No. 2501c51.

[95]Id.

[96]Id.

[97]Id.

[98]See id.

[99]Id.

[100]*Betreff: Ablieferung der Militärwaffen,* (March 29, 1933). Found in BHStA,

LRA Bad Tölz 133992, No. 572.

[101]Id.

[102]See "Raid on Jewish Quarter," *N. Y. Times,* Apr. 5, 1933, at 10.

[103]Id.

[104]Since it was Berlin's Jewish quarter, the Scheunenviertel would become the site of the 1938 anti-Jewish pogrom which changed the "Communist weapon" scare to the "Jewish weapon" scare described below. *Time Out Berlin* (1998), 53-54 . This area of Berlin has been renovated and the Neue Synagogue on Oranienburger Street rebuilt since the reunification of Germany in 1989. Id.

[105]"Gross-Razzia im Scheunenviertel," *Völkische Beobachter,* Apr. 5, 1933.

[106]Id.

[107]See *Reichsgesetzblatt* 1928, I, 143, § 23.

[108]"Permission to Possess Arms Withdrawn From Breslau Jews," *N. Y. Times,* Apr. 23, 1933, at 1.

[109]Der Reichsminister des Innern, Betrifft: Einfuhr von Schusswaffen, I A 8310/24.4 (May 31, 1933). Bundesarchiv Berlin (hereinafter "BA Berlin"), R 43 II/399, Fiche 1, Row 1.

[110]See *Reichsgesetzblatt* 1933, I, 367.

[111]See William Sheridan Allen, *The Nazi Seizure of Power: The Experience of a Single German Town 1922-1945* (New York: Franklin Watts, Inc., 1984), 184-86.

[112]Id. at 186.

[113]Id.

[114]Id. at 191.

[115]Id. at 192.

[116]The Security Police comprised the criminal police and the Gestapo (Secret State Police). Lemkin, *supra* note 90, at 15-16.

[117]*Reichsgesetzblatt* 1938, I, 265.

[118]Bayerische Politische Polizei, Waffenscheinen an Juden, February 5, 1936. Found in BHStA, B.Nr.51722.

[119]*Reichsgesetzblatt* 1938, I, 265, § 3. This relies on the English translation in Federal Firearms Legislation, Hearings before the Subcommittee to Investigate Juvenile Delinquency, Senate Judiciary Committee, 90th Cong., 2d Sess., 489 (1968). Another translation is in Simkin & Zelman, *supra* note 30, at 53.

[120]See id. § 29(1).

[121]See id. § 7.

[122]See id. § 9.

[123]See id. § 11.

[124]Id. § 12.

[125]See id. § 14.

[126]Id. § 15.

[127]E.g., Victor Klemperer, *I Will Bear Witness* 1933-1941, trans. Martin Chalmers, (New York: The Modern Library, 1999), xi, xiv, 275. In 1933, the head of the Reich Association of Jewish War Veterans actually sent a copy of a memorial book with the names of 12,000 Jewish German soldiers killed in World War I to Hitler, who acknowledged receipt with "sincerest feelings." Saul Friedländer, *Nazi Germany and the Jews: Vol. 1 The Years of Persecution, 1933-1939* (New York: Harper Collins Publishers, Inc., 1997), 15. In fact, Jewish participation was in proportion to the rest of the German population. Id. at 75. Jewish service in the armed forces was not banned until 1935. Id. at 117.

[128]*Reichsgesetzblatt* 1938, I, 265, § 18.

[129]Id. § 19.

[130]See id. § 23.

[131]See id. § 25.

[132]See id.

[133]See id.

[134]Id. § 26.

[135]See id. § 27.

[136]Id. § 23.

[137]Id.

[138]See id. § 31.

[139]See Verordnung zur Durchführung des Waffengesetzes, Reichsgesetzblatt [1938], I, 270. For a side-by-side comparison of the Nazi law and regulations and the United States Gun Control Act of 1968 and regulations, see Simkin & Zelman, *supra* note 30, at 83-107.

[140]See id. § 1. An English translation is available in *Federal Firearms Legislation, supra* note 119, at 496-503, and the German text and English translation are in Simkin & Zelman, *supra* note 30, at 64-75.

[141]See id. §§ 15-19.

[142]See id. at Anlage (Appendix) I & II.

[143]See id. § 25.

[144]See id. § 20.

[145]See id. at § 36.

[146]See Anthony Read and David Fisher, *Reichskristallnacht: The Unleashing of the Holocaust* (New York: Peter Bedrick Books, 1989), 60; see also Shirer, *supra* note 93, at 430.

[147]"Razzia auf Judenwaffen," *Der Angriff,* Nov. 9, 1938, at 14.

[148]"Bewaffnete Juden," *Fränkische Tageszeitung*, Nov. 9, 1938, at 2.

[149]"Berlins Juden wurden entwaffnet," *Berliner Morgenpost*, Nov. 9, 1938.

[150]"Entwaffnung der Berliner Juden," *Der Völkische Beobachter*, Nov. 9, 1938.

[151]"Waffenabgabe der Juden in Berlin," *Berliner Börsen Zeitung*, Nov. 9, 1938, at 1.

[152]Id.

[153]See id.

[154]See Read & Fisher, *supra* note 146, at 68.

[155]"Nazis Ask Reprisal in Attack on Envoy," *N. Y. Times*, Nov. 9, 1938, at 24.

[156]Id.

[157]Id.

[158]Read & Fisher, *supra* note 146, at 64.

[159]See id. at 66.

[160]See id.

[161]Id. See also Gerald Schawb, *The Day the Holocaust Began: The Odyssey of Herschel Grynszpan* (New York: Praeger, 1990), 20.

[162]Read and Fisher, *supra* note 146, at 64.

[163]Schawb, *supra* note 161, at 22.

[164]Id. Also quoted in Lionel Kochan, *Pogrom: 10 November 1938* (London: Andre Deutsch, 1957), 63-64, (citing Urteil des obersten Parteigerichts in dem Verfahren gegen Frühling u.a).

[165]See Read & Fisher, *supra* note 146, at 69, 70.

[166]Id. at 68. See also Rita Thalmann and Emmanuel Feinermann, *Crystal Night: 9-10 November 1938*, Gilles Cremonesi, trans. (New York: Holocaust Library, 1974), 59. For the German version and source of this document, see An alle Stapo Stellen und Stapoleitstellen, Berlin Nr. 234 404 9.11.2355, in *Trial of the Major War Criminals Before the International Military Tribunal: Nuremberg, November, 14, 1945 - October 1, 1946*, Vol. 25 (Buffalo, NY: William S. Hein & Co., Inc., 1995), 377.

[167]*Völkische Beobachter*, Nov. 10, 1938; see also *Berliner Börsen Zeitung*, Nov. 10, 1938, at 1; *Der Angriff*, Nov. 10, 1938, at 7. See also Joseph Walk, *Das Sonderrecht für die Juden im NS-Staat* (1981).

[168]"Nazis Smash, Loot and Burn Jewish Shops and Temples Until Goebbels Calls Halt," *N. Y. Times*, Nov. 11, 1938, at 1.

[169]See id.

[170]Id. at 4.

[171]Id.

[172]See id.

[173]See id.

[174]See id.

[175]"Vienna's Temples Fired and Bombed," *N. Y. Times*, Nov. 11, 1938, at 2.

[176]*Reichsgesetzblatt* 1938, I, 1571, reprinted in Simkin & Zelman, supra note 30, at 80-81.

177Id. § 1.

178See id. § 3.

179The regulation was widely noticed in the English-speaking press. E.g., "Jews Pay for Nazi Damage," *The Times* (London), Nov. 14, 1938, at 12a; "Ban on Firearms for Jews," *Boston Globe,* Nov. 12, 1938.

180See Schwab, *supra* note 161, at 25.

181*The Holocaust, Vol. 3, The Crystal Night Pogrom,* John Mendelsohn ed. (New York: Garland, 1982), 183-84.

182"Revenge Laws Drive Semites Out of Business," *Chi. Trib.,* Nov. 13, 1938, at 1g.

183See *November 1938: From "ReichsReichskristallnacht" to Genocide,* Walter H. Pehle ed. & William Templer trans. (New York: St. Martin's Press, 1991), 127.

184See "More Arrests, Jews to Pay for Nazi Damage," *The Times* (London), Nov. 14, 1938, at 12a.

185See *supra* notes 30-49 and 119-145 and accompanying text for discussion concerning firearms laws of 1928 and 1938.

186See *Reichsgesetzblatt* 1938, I, 1579. See also *The Times* (London), Nov. 14, 1938, at 12a.

187*Neue Zürcher Zeitung,* Nov. 13, 1938, at 2:1.

188See Read & Fisher, *supra* note 146, at 95 (citing British Acting Counsel General A.E. Dowden's reports from Frankfurt-am-Main: F0371/21638).

189*Journal de Genève,* Nov. 16, 1938, at 8, quoting Jour-Echo de Paris. *The Swiss Neue Zürcher Zeitung,* Nov. 15, 1938, 1, under the headline "The Annihilation Campaign Against the German Jews," reported the following:

As with the action of last summer, the wave of persecution of Jews has spread to Gdansk [Danzig]. There were attacks on shops and raids for weapons. The Gauleiter [Nazi Party Provincial Chief] declared yesterday that Gdansk wanted to get rid of all Jews, even of those with Polish citizenship.

190Geheime Staatspolizei Staatspolizeileitstelle München, An Polizeipräsidium München et al., Betreff: Waffenablieferung durch Juden. 19 December 1938. Found in BHStA, B.Nr. 39859/38 II G Ma.

191Konrad Kwiet, "Resistance and Opposition: The Example of the German Jews," in *Contending With Hitler: Varieties of German Resistance in the Third Reich,* David Clay Large ed. (Washington, D.C.: German Historical Institute, 1991), 65-66.

192See id. at 67.

193See id. at 72-73.

194Arnold Paucker, *Jewish Resistance in Germany: The Facts and the Problems* (Berlin: Gedenkstätte Deutscher Widerstand, 1988), 3.

195Id.

[196]See id.

[197]"Liberation from Nazism," *The Times* (London), Feb. 10, 1940, at 5e.

[198] See id.

[199]E.g., *Le Matin* (Paris), June 27, 1940, at 1 (proclamation); *Le Matin,* Sept. 22, 1941, at 1 (execution of persons for "illegal possession of arms"). This is the subject of a forthcoming study by this author.

[200]Geheime Staatspolizei, Staatspolizeileitstelle München, An die Landräte in Oberbayern et al., Betreff: Überwachung und Kontrolle der Waffen- und Munitionsverkäufe, 21 January 1941. Found in BHStA, B.Nr. 28115/41, II Schd./Roh.

[201]See Claudia Koonz, "Choice and Courage," in *Contending With Hitler, supra* note 191, at 60.

[202]See Anton Gill, *An Honourable Defeat: A History of German Resistance to Hitler, 1933-1945* (New York: Henry Holt, 1994), *passim.*

[203]See David I. Caplan, "Weapons Control Laws: Gateways to Victim Oppression and Genocide," in *To Be a Victim: Encounters with Crime and Injustice,* Diane Sank and David I. Caplan eds., (New York: Plenum Press, 1991), 308-11.

[204]Peter Hoffman, "The Second World War, German Society, and Internal Resistance to Hitler," in *Contending With Hitler, supra* note 191, at 122.

[205]P.L. 274, 55 Stat. 742 (1941). This was passed "in view of the fact that certain totalitarian and dictatorial nations are now engaged in the willful and wholesale destruction of personal rights and liberties." Rept. No. 1120 [to accompany S. 1579], House Committee on Military Affairs, 77th Cong., 1st Sess., at 2 (Aug. 4, 1941). Rep. Paul Kilday, the sponsor, explained: "Remember that registration of firearms is only the first step. It will be followed by other infringements of the right to keep and bear arms until finally the right is gone." 87 Cong.Rec. 7101 (1941). *See also* S. Halbrook, "Congress Interprets the Second Amendment: Declarations by a Co-Equal Branch on the Individual Right to Keep and Bear Arms," 62 *Tenn. L. Rev.* 597, 618-31 (Spring 1995).

[206]Basic Law, Art. 20, § 4, quoted in Large, "Uses of the Past: The Anti-Nazi Resistance Legacy in the Federal Republic of Germany," in *Contending with Hitler, supra* note 191, at 180.

Chapter Ten:
Nazi Germany: To Disarm and To Kill

The Nazi German government aggressively disarmed German civilians, especially Jews, in the early years of the Third Reich. See Table 10A for key features of the German "gun control" laws. As the Nazis invaded other countries, they imposed "gun control" on the people of those lands as well. Once disarmed and rendered defenseless, the civilian victims met the full horror of the Nazi death machine.

Most Americans know that the Nazi German government carried out a calculated campaign to destroy all persons of the Jewish faith (i.e., Jews, or persons of the "Jewish race"). Most Americans know about the concentration camps and death camps built in Germany, Austria and Poland, and that Jews were imprisoned and killed by the thousands and millions in those camps.

Many Americans do not fully realize this fact: *it wasn't just the Jews.*

When thinking of Nazi Germany, its "gun control" program, and its persecution of the Jews, many non-Jewish people feel sorry, some even feel a sense of guilt — but they also see the whole issue as one of Nazis vs. Jews. People nowadays can place the Third Reich and its Holocaust in a special category of history — it was something that happened to Jews, it had something to do with Jewishness and Naziism. The persecution, the death camps, did not affect anybody else... they think.

It wasn't just the Jews.

Fact is, between 1933 and 1938, many concentration camps

were built to hold in "protective custody" the enemies of the state. They were built to isolate, punish, torture and kill Germans who opposed the Nazi regime.[1] For example, the infamous prison camp at Dachau was built for that purpose, and until 1938, the overwhelming majority of the 6,000 inmates were political prisoners.[2] Likewise the death camp at Auschwitz started as camp for political prisoners, mostly Polish people who were not necessarily Jews.[3]

As described in the preceding chapter, the "gun control" laws of Germany existed before the Nazi government came to absolute power. Those laws operated to disarm all Germans, not just the Jews.

Who were the victims of the Nazi murder machine? Jews, yes, but millions of non-Jews also. Drawn from the work of Professor R. J. Rummel, here are the civilian death counts, figures so huge that they stun the imagination:[4]

Total civilians killed:	20,946,000 men, women and children
Gypsies:	258,000 killed
Homosexuals:	220,000 killed
Slavs (Eastern Europe):	10,547,000 killed
Jews:	5,291,000 killed

In the death camps and other "institutions," the Nazis killed a total of 11,283,000 people (including Jews, Gypsies, political prisoners, campus rebels, dissidents, critics of the regime, pacifists and others).[5]

By forced labor: 1,861,000 people died.

By forced euthanasia: 172,500 people were killed.

Non-combatant civilians were murdered by the Nazis all over Europe: 256,000 French, 406,000 Hungarians, 64,000 Italians, 51,000 Belgians, and many more. About 12,250,000 Russian civilians were killed as well.

One million children under 18 years of age were victims of Nazi mass murder.

It wasn't just the Jews. The victims could be anybody.

The White Rose: A Lesson in Dissent[6]
by Jacob G. Hornberger[7]

The date was February 22, 1943. Hans Scholl and his sister Sophie, along with their best friend, Christoph Probst, were scheduled to be executed by Nazi officials that afternoon. Hans, a medical student at the University of Munich, was 24. Sophie, a student, was 21. Christoph, a medical student, was 22. What brought them to this fate?

Hans and Sophie Scholl were German teenagers in the 1930s. Like other young Germans, they enthusiastically joined the Hitler Youth. They believed that Adolf Hitler was leading Germany and the German people back to greatness.

Their parents were not so enthusiastic. Their father, Robert Scholl, told his children that Hitler and the Nazis were leading Germany down a road of destruction. Later, in 1942, he would serve time in a Nazi prison for telling his secretary: "The war! It is already lost. This Hitler is God's scourge on mankind, and if the war doesn't end soon the Russians will be sitting in Berlin."

Gradually, Hans and Sophie began realizing that their father was right. They concluded that, in the name of freedom and the greater good of the German nation, Hitler and the Nazis were enslaving and destroying the German people. They also knew that open dissent was impossible in Nazi Germany, especially after the start of World War II. Most Germans took the traditional position: once war breaks out, it is the duty of the citizen to support the troops by supporting the government.

But Hans and Sophie Scholl believed differently. They believed that it was the duty of a citizen, even in times of war, to stand up against an evil regime, especially when it is sending hundreds of thousands of its citizens to their deaths.

The Scholl siblings began sharing their feelings with a few of their friends Christoph Probst, Alexander Schmorell, Willi Graf as well as with Kurt Huber, their psychology and philosophy professor.

One day in 1942, copies of a leaflet entitled "The White Rose" suddenly appeared at the University of Munich. The leaflet contained an anonymous essay that said that the Nazi system had slowly imprisoned the German people and was now destroying them. The Nazi regime had turned evil. It was time, the essay said, for Germans to rise up and resist the tyranny of their own government. At the bottom of the essay, the following request appeared: "Please make as many copies of this leaflet as you can and distribute them."

The leaflet caused a tremendous stir among the student body. It was the first time that internal dissent against the Nazi regime had surfaced in Germany. The essay had been secretly written and distributed by Hans Scholl and his friends.

Another leaflet appeared soon afterward. And then another. And another. Ultimately, between 1942 and 1943, there were six leaflets published and distributed by Hans and Sophie Scholl and their friends: four under the title "The White Rose" and two under the title "Leaflets of the Resistance."

The members of The White Rose, of course, had to act cautiously. The Nazi regime maintained an iron grip over German society. Internal dissent was quickly and efficiently smashed by the Gestapo. Hans and Sophie Scholl and their friends knew what would happen to them if they were caught.

People began receiving copies of the leaflets in the mail. Students at the University of Hamburg began copying and distributing them. Copies began turning up in different parts of Germany and Austria. The members of The White Rose did not limit themselves to leaflets. Graffiti began appearing in large letters on streets and buildings all over Munich: "Down with Hitler! . . . Hitler the Mass Murderer!" and "Freihart! . . . Freihart! . . . Freedom! . . . Freedom!"

The Gestapo was driven into a frenzy. It knew that the authors were having to procure large quantities of paper, envelopes, and postage. It knew that they were using a duplicating machine. But despite the Gestapo's best efforts, it was unable to catch the perpetrators.

On February 18, 1943, Hans' and Sophie's luck ran out.

They were caught leaving pamphlets at the University of Munich and were arrested. A search disclosed evidence of

Christoph Probst's participation, and he too was soon arrested. The three of them were indicted for treason.

Four days after their arrest, their trial began. The presiding judge, Roland Freisler, chief justice of the People's Court of the Greater German Reich, had been sent from Berlin. Richard Hanser, historian of the student movement, described the trial of the students before Freisler:

> He conducted the trial as if the future of the Reich were indeed at stake. He roared denunciations of the accused as if he were not the judge but the prosecutor. He behaved alternately like an actor ranting through an overwritten role in an implausible melodrama and a Grand Inquisitor calling down eternal damnation on the heads of the three irredeemable heretics before him.... No witnesses were called, since the defendants had admitted everything. The proceedings consisted almost entirely of Roland Freisler's denunciation and abuse, punctuated from time to time by halfhearted offerings from the court-appointed defense attorneys, one of whom summed up his case with the observation, "I can only say fiat justitia. Let justice be done." By which he meant: Let the accused get what they deserve.

Freisler and the other accusers could not understand what had happened to these German youths. After all, they all came from nice German families. They all had attended German schools. They had been members of the Hitler Youth. How could they have turned out to be traitors? What had so twisted and warped their minds?

Sophie Scholl shocked everyone in the courtroom when she remarked to Freisler: "Somebody, after all, had to make a start. What we wrote and said is also believed by many others. They just don't dare to express themselves as we did." Later in the proceedings, she said to him: "You know the war is lost. Why don't you have the courage to face it?"

In the middle of the trial, Robert and Magdalene Scholl tried to enter the courtroom. Magdalene said to the guard: "But I'm the mother of two of the accused." The guard responded: "You should have brought them up better."

Robert Scholl forced his way into the courtroom and told

the court that he was there to defend his children. He was seized and forcibly escorted outside. The entire courtroom heard him shout: "One day there will be another kind of justice! One day they will go down in history!"

Robert Freisler pronounced his judgment on the three defendants: Guilty of treason. Their sentence: Death.

They were escorted back to Stadelheim prison, where the guards permitted Hans and Sophie to have one last visit with their parents. Hans met with them first, and then Sophie. Richard Hanser wrote:

His eyes were clear and steady and he showed no sign of dejection or despair. He thanked his parents again for the love and warmth they had given him and he asked them to convey his affection and regard to a number of friends, whom he named. Here, for a moment, tears threatened, and he turned away to spare his parents the pain of seeing them. Facing them again, his shoulders were back and he smiled....

Then a woman prison guard brought in Sophie... Her mother tentatively offered her some candy, which Hans had declined. "Gladly," said Sophie, taking it. "After all, I haven't had any lunch!" She, too, looked somehow smaller, as if drawn together, but her face was clear and her smile was fresh and unforced, with something in it that her parents read as triumph.

"Sophie, Sophie," her mother murmured, as if to herself. "To think you'll never be coming through the door again!" Sophie's smile was gentle. "Ah, Mother," she said. "Those few little years...." Sophie Scholl looked at her parents and was strong in her pride and certainty. "We took everything upon ourselves," she said. "What we did will cause waves." Her mother spoke again: "Sophie," she said softly, "Remember Jesus." "Yes," replied Sophie earnestly, almost commandingly, "but you, too." She left them, her parents, Robert and Magdalene Scholl, with her face still lit by the smile they loved so well and would never see again. She was perfectly composed as she was led away. Robert Mohr [a Gestapo official], who had come out to the prison on business of his own, saw her in her cell immediately afterwards, and she was crying. It was the first time

Robert Mohr had seen her in tears, and she apologized. "I have just said goodbye to my parents," she said. "You understand..." She had not cried before her parents. For them she had smiled.

No relatives visited Christoph Probst. His wife, who had just had their third child, was in the hospital. Neither she nor any members of his family even knew that he was on trial or that he had been sentenced to death. While his faith in God had always been deep and unwavering, he had never committed to a certain faith. On the eve of his death, a Catholic priest admitted him into the church *in articulo mortis* (at the point of death). "Now," he said, "my death will be easy and joyful."

That afternoon, the prison guards permitted Hans, Sophie, and Christoph to have one last visit together. Sophie was then led to the guillotine. One observer described her as she walked to her death: "Without turning a hair, without flinching." Christoph Probst was next. Hans Scholl was last; just before he was beheaded, Hans cried out: "Long live freedom!"

Unfortunately, they were not the last to die. The Gestapo's investigation was relentless. Later tried and executed were Alex Schmorell, 25, Willi Graf, 25, and Kurt Huber, 49. Students at the University of Hamburg were either executed or sent to concentration camps.

Today, every German knows the story of The White Rose. A square at the University of Munich is named after Hans and Sophie Scholl. And there are streets, squares, and schools all over Germany named for the members of The White Rose. The German movie "The White Rose" is now found in video stores in Germany and the United States. As Richard Hanser wrote, "Their actions made them enduring symbols of the struggle, universal and timeless, for the freedom of the human spirit wherever and whenever it is threatened."

Table 10A
Key Elements of German "Gun Control" Laws [8]

Date	Law / Regulation	Effect
January, 1919	Regulations of the Council of the People's Delegates on Weapons Possession	"All firearms, [and] all kinds of firearms ammunition, are to be surrendered immediately"; severe penalties for disobedience.
March, 1919	Executive orders (during uprisings)	Anyone caught possessing firearms is to be shot without trial.
Aug. 7, 1920	Law on the Disarmament of the People	Empowers a *Reichskommissar* to define weapons subject to confiscation.
Mar. 18, 1928	Law on Firearms and Ammunition (replacing earlier laws)	Government registration and licensing of everyone having anything to do with firearms or ammunition (manufacture, repair, possession, carrying, etc.); licenses available only to persons of "undoubted reliability."
Mar. 28, 1931	Law Against Unauthorized Use of Weapons	Prohibits carrying firearms, clubs or "stabbing weapons" outside of home or business (except permit holders and government authorized personnel).
Dec. 8, 1931	Fourth Regulations of the President...on the Defense of Civil Peace, Part 8, Ch. 1	Authorizes police to place all firearms and ammunition into custody for "public security" reasons; requires all license applicants to prove their "need" for firearms; requires licenses for manufacture and sale of clubs and "stabbing weapons."
Mar. 18, 1938	Weapons Law	Imposes special controls on handguns; excludes Jews from any firearms business; prohibits anyone who is "hostile to the government" or "may endanger public security" from possessing firearms, clubs or "stabbing weapons," exempts Nazi party organs and govenment officials.
Nov. 11, 1938	Regulations Against Jews' Possession of Weapons	Prohibits Jews from possessing any firearms, ammunition, clubs or "stabbing weapons."

End Notes

[1]Feig, Konnilyn G. 1979. *Hitler's Death Camps: The Sanity of Madness.* New York: Holmes & Meier Publishers, p. 23.

[2]Feig 1979, p. 51.

[3]Fischer, Klaus P. 1995. *Nazi Germany: A New History.* New York: The Continuum Publishing Company, p. 507.

[4]Rummel, R.J. 1996. *Death by Government.* New Brunswick, NJ: Transaction Publishers, pp. 111-112, 119.

[5]See *The World Book Encyclopedia.* 2001. Chicago: World Book, Inc. Vol. 9, p. 296 (in the death camps, 6 million Jews and up to 5 million non-Jews perished).

[6]Full text appeared first in *Freedom Daily,* January 1996, a publication of the Future of Freedom Foundation. Copyright, all rights reserved.

[7]Mr. Hornberger is founder and president of The Future of Freedom Foundation, which is headquartered in Fairfax, Virginia. (www.fff.org) The information in this story is drawn from Scholl, Inge. 1983. *The White Rose: Munich 1942-1943.* 2d edition. Middletown, Conn: Wesleyan Univ. Press; Hanser, Richard. 1979. A Noble Treason. New York: G. P. Putnam's Sons; Gill, Anton. 1994. *An Honourable Defeat: A History of German Resistance to Hitler,* 1933-1945. New York: Henry Holt & Co., pp. 188-195.

[8]Sources: Simkin, Jay and Aaron Zelman. 1992. *"Gun Control": Gateway to Tyranny.* Milwaukee, WI: Jews for the Preservation of Firearms Ownership; Halbrook, Stephen P. 2000. Nazi Firearms Law and the Disarming of the German Jews. *Arizona Journal of International and Comparative Law.* Vol. 17, pp. 483-535.

Chapter Eleven:
Rwanda

Between April 7 and July 19, 1994, genocide in the African nation of Rwanda resulted in 800,000 deaths.[1] That amounts to about 11% of the country's population killed in just over 100 days — about 80% of its Tutsi population exterminated.[2]

Hatred + Government + Disarmed Civilians = Genocide

All three factors that seed the Genocide Formula were present in Rwanda.

Hatred

Hatred in Rwanda came from two main sources. The first source was the long-standing tribal rivalry between the Hutus and the Tutsis. In Rwanda, the Hutus were 90% of population, the Tutsis were only 9%. Historically, the Tutsis had dominated political life in the land. Although the Tutsis and Hutus inter-mingled and often intermarried, there remained latent tribal resentments. When Belgium controlled Rwanda in the early 1900's, the Belgians tended to play one tribe against the other, favoring Tutsis over Hutus, and thus building tensions between them.[3] Political unrest turned violent when Hutus rebelled against Tutsis in 1959, resulting in 150,000 deaths and another 150,000 Tutsi refugees leaving the country.[4]

In neighboring Burundi, the minority Tutsis maintained control over the largely Hutu nation. Responding to a Hutu rebellion in 1972, Burundi's military moved to exterminate all educated Hutus — many uneducated Hutus were killed as well. This calculated genocide resulted in at least 100,000 killed and 200,000 Hutus fleeing to Rwanda.[5] Burundi's genocide inspired Hutu hatred and increased persecution of Tutsis in Rwanda.

The second source of hatred was deliberate racial baiting and a government-sponsored anti-Tutsi propaganda campaign.[6] Although anti-Tutsi prejudice, ostracism and violence had been occurring steadily for years in Rwanda, the central government jumped firmly on the bandwagon after the Rwandese Patriotic Front (RPF) started a revolt in October 1990.[7] The RPF consisted mostly of Tutsis and openly sought to overthrow the Hutu-controlled regime. The government responded by deeming all Tutsis to be supporters of the RPF. Hutus who disagreed with that view were considered traitors.

In June, 1994, during the genocide, the UN Commission on Human Rights reported the extremist Hutu organizations directly incited ethnic hatred and violence:

> False rumours and tracts designed to inflame ethnic hatred and encourage violence are constantly circulating in Rwanda. The Tutsi are portrayed, for example, as "bloodthirsty, power-hungry and determined to impose their rule on the people of Rwanda by means of the gun."[8]

Radio stations controlled by the government and by Hutu agitators did "not hesitate to call for the extermination of the Tutsi." One of the stations, called the "killer radio station," proclaimed that "by May 5, the cleansing of the Tutsi must be completed" and that "the grave is still only half full, who will help us to fill it?"[9]

The Hutu Ten Commandments had been circulating widely and generating ethnic hatred.[10] The first three "commandments" targeted Tutsi women as hostile "agents" and warned all Hutus against having anything to do with them. Other commandments declared that every Tutsi was dishonest and Hutus who dealt with Tutsis were traitors. Hutus were directed to unify against "their common Tutsi enemy." The eighth commandment chillingly said: "Hutus must stop having mercy on the Tutsis."[11]

After identifying Rwanda's internal enemies as the Tutsis and their fellow travelers, the government began to arrest them. Tutsis who were educated, prosperous, or who had traveled abroad were the first to be arrested. Prominent Hutus who might be out of step with the regime were also taken away.[12]

Government

Ethnic identity cards had been required for decades. When the genocide began, Hutu death squads and government troops stopped Rwandans, checked their identity cards, and carted off or immediately executed Tutsis.[13] One American writer dubbed these identity cards as "death tickets for Tutsis during the genocide."[14]

After Belgium gave Rwanda its political independence in 1962, political power increasingly became concentrated in the central government and a single ruler or party. By elections in 1960, the people had selected a Hutu-dominated government which persisted as a Hutu President was elected in 1962 and remained in office until overthrown by Hutu military officers in 1973.

Tutsi exiles in neighboring Burundi attacked the Rwanda government in late 1963 without success. The government not only repelled the exile invasion, it also murdered about 10,000 Tutsis in two months, including almost all of the Tutsi politicians in Rwanda.[15] Not surprisingly, the government enacted independent Rwanda's first "gun control" law on November 21, 1964.[16]

Disarmed Victims

Civilians in Rwanda, most especially the Tutsis, were mostly unarmed people.[17] As the UN observers reported, "most of the massacres were carried out...against unarmed and defenseless people."[18] The killers were organized armed units and gangs of Hutu civilians who were given weapons for the purpose.[19] The most frequently used murder weapons were: machetes, firearms, nail-studded clubs (called *masus*), axes, and blunt instruments.

Inadequate Defense Tools

Victims often attempted self-defense. When the defenders' weapons were even comparable to the attackers', then the defenders could buy time. The killers would call in military forces for support, however. The military always had firearms with plenty of ammunition, and sometimes grenades and mortars as well. Firearms turned the tide against defenders who then would be tortured, gutted, maimed and murdered.

Eyewitness testimony and observer reports show unquestionably how vital it is for innocent civilians (men, women and children) to be armed when faced with violent attack.

Kigali province: Threatened by Hutu death squads wielding clubs and machetes, civilians in Ntarama took refuge in a church and nearby school. One survivor said, "We used stones, bows and arrows" to hold off the attackers for a week. The defenders' hope ended when "well-armed soldiers and interahamwe [killer gang - auth.] came towards the church attacking from three fronts.... Our young men and women were overwhelmed.... They made holes in the back wall and threw grenades through the holes.... The interahamwe then came in with their machetes and began massacring."[20]

The resisters who survived had wounded one soldier and killed another, and had obtained a gun from the dead man. Eyewitnesses reported, "One of the refugees.... knew how to use the gun. The next morning, two busloads of soldiers arrived.... People tried to keep up the resistance. But with only one gun, bows, arrows, and stones we were no match for all these soldiers with their guns. There were just too many soldiers. Everyone who could flee fled. They came in and attacked the wounded, weak, old, young or just frightened." Those tried to escape were chased toward a nearby river where more killer gangs awaited them. Rather than die by machete, "very many people jumped and drowned, including many women with babies strapped to their backs."[21]

Butare province: At a town meeting in Cyahinda, the mayor asked the people to surrender their weapons and promised the police would protect them. When some of the people questioned the order, the mayor commanded the police to shoot the people and many were killed in the building. Other townsfolk mounted a resistance: "The war of stones against bullets lasted for about three days. There were between eight and eleven gendarmes [policemen - auth.] who came and went, leaving the interahamwe to keep up the killing. They were more easily repulsed because they did not have guns." The resisters managed to kill three policemen — the attackers massacred more than 20,000 people.[22]

In Karama, between 35,000 and 43,000 people were slaughtered.[23] A survivor recalled, "We tried to defend ourselves with stones. [The attackers] shot bullet after bullet." The attackers kept shooting for nearly seven hours — "there was an endless hail of bullets" — until they ran out of ammunition. "Of course we had run out of stones long before they had run out of bullets."[24]

In Songa, the Rwandan Army helped murder several thousand people, mostly Tutsis. One witness reported: "The men put up a defense against the continuous attacks of the interahamwe. Our defense continued [for three days]. Because they were fighting interahamwe, our men had no problem repulsing them. But [then] soldiers arrived. After that it was a calamity. As soon as the soldiers arrived, they started shooting.... Everywhere, there was a hail of bullets.... Some of the men bravely continued to fight back with bows and arrows. But once the soldiers arrived, we did not have a chance.... the defense collapsed. How could men and boys armed with stones fight their bullets and grenades?"[25]

Byumba province: Refugees from interahamwe death squads had gathered in city buildings in Gishari. The police started to kill the refugees. A high school teacher recalled: "I saw some of the refugees go into the [offices] and come out with four or five rifles and ammunition. They started fighting back. It was then that the soldiers started to use the rocket-propelled grenades which killed far more people than the old hunting rifles the refugees had found.... The interahamwe came in to finish people off with machetes and [nail-studded clubs].... The firing, wounding and dying continued for what seemed a lifetime. [After the interahamwe and soldiers left] the place was full of dead people. Hundreds of families had been wiped out. Over a thousand people had been killed. Hundreds more were seriously wounded." The teacher pointed out: **"Many more would have died if those refugees had not found those rifles."**[26]

Similar stories replayed all over Rwanda during the genocide:

- Kabarando, Byumba province: Local "law enforcement" refused to help refugees under attack in a church. The refugees resisted initial attacks by throwing stones and broken bricks, but then the army set up three machine guns. After eight hours of shooting into the church, the attackers threw in grenades and then invaded the church, killing the remaining women and children.[27]

- Kibuye town, Kibuye province: Young people in a church tried, by hurling rocks and stones, to fight back against interahamwe and police guns and grenades. The attackers prevailed, killing nearly all refugees inside.[28]

- Gitesi, Kibuye province: Soldiers opened fire on refugees collected in a stadium. Refugees responded by throwing rocks, and occasionally by returning unexploded grenades. In a single day, some 12,000 refugees were murdered.[29]

- Cyangugu province: Four police officers were assigned to protect 8,000 refugees in a church compound against murder squads. The officers fought back bravely, so the attackers waited until they ran out of bullets. The provincial governor arrived on the scene, had the policemen removed, and the murder squads retreated. Later, however, the squads returned fully armed with guns, grenades, spears, swords, and machetes. The refugee men who fought back with stones were shot first, then the squads entered the area to butcher the rest.[30]

No Defense Tools

The vicious attacks, mutilations and murders of entirely defenseless people during the genocide defy accurate count. Children, particularly Tutsi boys, were targeted especially for killing. Many children who survived machete attacks live massively disfigured.[31] Words can barely convey the horrors of the Rwanda genocide. Observers on-site reported:

> The massacres are systematic in nature. Whole families are exterminated — grandparents, parents and children. No one escapes, not even newborn babies.... the victims are pursued to their very last refuge and killed there....[32] This barbarism does not spare either children in orphanages or patients in hospital.... Hutu staff working for Doctors Without Borders were obliged to kill their Tutsi colleagues.[33]

The Hutu attackers, the interhamwe, and especially the government agents and troops, were armed. Why weren't the Tutsis also armed for defense?

The answer is simple: Firearms were not available to the Tutsis, because of cost and "gun control" laws. Firearms were available to Hutu attackers because extremist groups and the government supplied the weaponry.[34]

Victim disarmament laws had existed in independent Rwanda since 1964. The Rwandan Decree-Law No. 12/79, issued in May, 1979, revoked the 1964 law and established the "gun control" laws in effect during the 15 years just before the 1994 genocide. That decree aimed to "control firearms and their ammunition," and it did so by imposing high license costs, registering all owners, prohibiting many types of firearms including concealable and "military style" weapons, giving unlimited power to government officials to disarm civilians, and giving unlimited possession rights to police and military forces only.

The result was: the disfavored group (Tutsis) were mostly unarmed people when their government and fellow countrymen (Hutus) turned against them. The Genocide Formula is fact.

Unarmed minority groups die when the armed majority decides to kill them.

Table 11A:
Highlights of Rwanda's 1979 "Gun Control" Law

(Decree-Law No. 12/79, May 7, 1979, printed in *Journal Officiel De La Republique Rwandaise,* June 1, 1979)
Article 3: Possessing "arms constituting the weapons of the Armed forces" is forbidden, except for military or professional use, or as permitted by the Minister of National Defense.
Article 4: No one may possess or carry a firearm of any type without a permit, except those authorized to carry military weapons.
Article 5: The Minister of National Defense may at any time order "the taking of an inventory of all firearms and ammunition" that are possessed according to permits.
Article 6: Officials may demand any permit holder to "justify the possession of the arm or arms mentioned on these permits;" those who lack the justification face penalties under Article 13.
Article 8: "When circumstances or national security require it," the Minister of National Defense may prohibit importing, dealing in, possessing or carrying firearms and ammunition in any given territorial area.
Article 9: Permits can only be issued to named individuals who offer "a sufficient guarantee" that they will keep the firearm and ammunition themselves and not allow third parties to have it even temporarily.

Article 10: Annual fees of 1,000 francs charged for permit to carry "modern" firearms. (Other fees for display models and obsolete guns.)
Article 12: All permits "are revocable in case of abuse, or when public security is in danger." The Minister of National Defense has the right to revoke the permits.
Article 13: Penalties for unlawful possession, sale, importation, or carrying of regulated firearms: prison from 7 days to 1 year, and/or a fine from 5,000 to 50,000 francs. Prison is mandatory with a term up to 10 years if the violation occurs "in regions in which military operations have taken place."
Article 14: Possession for any reason of prohibited firearms is prohibited.
Article 15: Prohibited firearms include collapsible rifles and "all offensive and concealable arms."
Article 16: Penalties for possessing prohibited firearms: Up to one year in prison or up to 15,000 francs. The Armed Forces are exempt from prohibition of firearms.
Article 17: Except for Armed Forces and police training and use, "it is forbidden to shoot and to carry loaded arms in all built-up areas and near dwellings."
Article 18: Penalty for violating Article 17: 15 to 30 days in jail, or a fine up to 2,500 francs.

Lists of Victims

The Hutu-controlled regime prepared lists of people targeted for destruction first during the genocide.[35] The general organizer of the genocide of Tutsis was the director of services in the Ministry of Defense and the Defense Minister himself.[36] It seems likely that the list of priority targets would be developed, at least in part, from the list of firearms permit holders, because the Defense Minister is the licensing and fee collecting authority. Cross-referencing the list of permit holders to a list of identity cards bearing the designation of "Tutsi", and the genocide planners would have all they needed to find and kill primary targets.

End Notes

[1]Prunier, Gerard. 1995. *The Rwanda Crisis: History of a Genocide.* New York: Columbia University Press, p. 265; *The World Book Encyclopedia.* 2001. Chicago: World Book, Inc. Vol. 16. ("World Book"), p. 572 (Rwanda entry).

[2]Prunier 1995, pp. 263-265.

[3]Gourevitch, Philip. 1998. *We wish to inform you that tomorrow we will be killed with our families:* Stories from Rwanda. New York: Picador USA, pp. 55-58.

[4]World Book, 572.

[5]Gourevitch 1998, 67.

[6]Gourevitch 85-88, 96 ; Commission on Human Rights. June 28, 1994. *Report on the situation of human rights in Rwanda.* R. Degni-Segui, Special Rappaorteur of the Commission. Resolution E/CN.4/S-3/1 of May 25, 1994. ("UN Report"), ¶¶ 25, 26, 58.

[7]Gourevitch 1998, p. 82.

[8]UN Report, ¶ 58.

[9]Ibid.

[10]Gourevitch 1998, pp. 87-88.

[11]Ibid., p. 88.

[12]Ibid., p. 83.

[13]Gourevitch 1998, pp. 90, 223; UN Report, ¶¶ 22, 60-61.

[14]Gourevitch 1998, p. 223.

[15]Prunier 1995, pp. 55-56.

[16]Republique du Rwanda. *Journal Officiel.* December 1, 1964, pp. 404-407.

[17]Gourevitch 1998, p. 90.

[18]UN Report, ¶ 21.

[19]UN Report, ¶ 25.

[20]Omaar, Rakiya. 1995. *Rwanda: Death, Despair and Defiance.* Revised ed. London: African Rights, pp. 262-63. [All citations to this reference are drawn from Simkin, Jay, Aaron Zelman and Alan M. Rice. 1997. *Rwanda's Genocide 1994: Supplement to Lethal Laws.* Milwaukee, WI: Jews for the Preservation of Firearms Ownership, Inc.]

[21]Omaar 1995, pp. 264-65.

[22]Ibid., p. 340.

[23]Ibid., p. 345.

[24]Ibid., p. 346.

[25]Ibid., p. 356.

[26]Ibid., p. 380.

[27]Ibid., pp. 380, 383.

[28]Ibid., p. 423.

[29]Ibid., 429.
[30]Ibid., pp. 457-466.
[31]Ibid., pp. 798-799.
[32]UN Report, ¶ 27.
[33]Ibid., ¶ 28.
[34]Ibid., ¶¶ 25, 60; Prunier 1995, p. 243)
[35]Prunier 1995, pp. 242-43, 246.
[36]Ibid., p. 240.

Chapter Twelve:
Ottoman Turkey

Who Was Protecting These Women and Children?

"I saw through the windows of the [building] a caravan of several hundred Christian women and children resting in the marketplace. Their sunken cheeks and cavernous eyes bore the stamp of death. Among the women, almost all of whom were young, were some mothers with children, or, rather, childish skeletons, in their arms. One of them was mad. She knelt beside the half petrified cadaver of a new-born babe. Another woman had fallen to the ground, rigid and lifeless. Her two little girls, believing her asleep, sobbed convulsively as they tried in vain to awaken her. By her side, dying in a scarlet pool, was yet another, beautiful and very young, the victim of a soldier of the escort. The velvety eyes of the dying girl, who bore every evidence of refinement, mirrored an immense and indescribable agony....

When the hour struck for departure, one after another of those filthy, ragged skeletons struggled to its feet and, taking its place in that mass of misery that shrieked silently to heaven, tottered off, guarded by a group of bearded gendarmes."[1]

How could it be that so many women and children were marched to death and murdered — without being able to resist? Surely they were the families of someone. Why were there no men to defend them? What left these victims unprotected?

The Armenian Genocide of 1915

To Ottoman Turkey belongs the infamy of conducting the 20th Century's first genocide. Between 1915 and 1917, the Turkish government planned and carried out the killing of all Armenians in the land — men, women, children. The goal was to eradicate 2,000,000 souls.[2] In that short two years, the Ottoman Turks systematically butchered between 1,000,000 and 1,500,000 unarmed, defenseless Armenian citizens of Turkey.[3]

This Armenian Genocide was not the first time Ottoman Turks had attacked and killed Armenian citizens in large numbers. The Muslim Turks had long hated and resented the Christian Armenians scattered across the Ottoman Empire. When law and order broke down or a disaster occurred, Muslim Turks would predictably attack the Armenians.[4]

The worst previous massacre took place between 1894 and 1896 under Sultan Abdul Hamid II, when Turks killed between 100,000 and 300,000 Armenians.[5] Because the Armenian victims were Christians, the "Christian" governments of Europe condemned the massacre and finally forced the Sultan to halt that genocide and to confer greater political equality and self-government upon the Armenian minority.[6]

History Delivers The Victims

What made possible the Armenian Genocide of 1915-1917? Consider the factors in this time sequence:

(1) The Ottoman Empire was a declining multi-cultural patchwork of competing ethnicities and interests, originally dominated by Muslim Turks.

(2) A supposedly "liberal-oriented" entity, called the "Young Turks," overthrew the Sultan's government in 1908 and forced the Sultan to establish full religious and political liberties for all Turkish citizens and a fully representative governmental system (to include Armenians).[7]

(3) Armenians had long been "rigorously prohibited from possessing firearms" and were generally not permitted to serve in the army. Armenians were largely excluded from the highest administrative posts, and they played little part in provincial governments.[8] [Young Turks did at times arm Armenian factions to help them overthrow the Sultan and consolidate power.[9]]

(4) Blaming the threat of a coup against their regime, the Young Turks declared a national emergency and suspended constitutional rights. The government turned to repression and terror, destroying internal opposition parties and suppressing minorities who sought more political autonomy.[10]

(5) The Young Turk government expanded "gun control" laws to apply to all Turks.[11] The laws banned unauthorized manufacture or importation of weapons (firearms), and forbade carrying of weapons, cartridges and gunpowder.[12]

(6) Domestic chaos and popular discontent rose against the Young Turks.

(7) A military coup briefly ousted the Young Turks in 1912, but members of the Young Turks seized back power violently and ruled autocratically for the next six years.[13]

(8) Many Muslim Turks still hated Christian Armenians.[14]

(9) As World War I broke out, Russia attacked Turkey and occupied more territory — among the Russian military forces were many Russian Armenians.

(10) During World War I, the European governments that had previously intervened to protect the Armenians had become wartime enemies of Ottoman Turkey and thus had no influence over how Armenians would be treated.

These historical elements set the stage for the Turkish government to commit genocide. Next came the deliberate decision to destroy all Armenians.

Deliberate Decision to Destroy

The Young Turk rulers quite literally decided to commit genocide. In a secret meeting, the Turkish minister of education said:

> "Let us think well. Why did we bring out this revolution? What was our aim?...It was to revive Turkism that I became your comrade, brother and fellow-traveler. I only want that the Turk shall live. And I want him to live only on these lands, and be independent. With the exception of the Turks, let all the other elements be exterminated, no matter to what religion or faith they belong. This country must be purged of alien elements. The Turks must do the purging..."[15]

At the same meeting, a Muslim religious leader spoke:

"Your servant is prepared to present a holy edict in this respect...Since the collective society is endangered, the individual becomes sacrificed. This is Kaidahi Fiykiyeh (the principle of Islam philosophy). Therefore they must all be killed, men, women and children, without discrimination."[16]

The same Muslim leader outlined the genocide program:

[Saying that we are mobilizing for war], we [take] into the army all those who can carry arms. We send them (the Armenians) to the front line of the battle. Then we will take them in a cross-fire between the Russians in front, and our special forces from behind. Having thus removed the menfolk, we give the order to our [believers] to exterminate the remainder of women and children, the oldsters and the sick and the maimed in one full sweep. ..."[17]

Summary of the June 26, 1915
Official Proclamation to Deport Armenians

Official Proclamation Provision	Announcement, Law or Effect
Preamble	"For a few years our Armenian compatriots, who are a part of the Ottoman population, have been, with foreign instructions, harboring wrong and lawless ideas. They have been injuring, besides their own comfort and interest, the tranquility and peacefulness of the Ottoman Empire, and of their other compatriots; committing bloody acts and even daring to join the enemy with whom our government is now at war and who is also the enemy of the Armenian people as a community. For the purpose of both protecting the peace and tranquility of the land and also of preserving the existence and safety of the Armenian population, our government has been compelled to undertake extraordinary measures and sacrifices and is obliged to deport the Armenian population into the interior provinces where they will reside in places indicated by the government until the end of the war. For this reason we point out that all Ottomans must obey literally the following orders."

Summary of the June 26, 1915
Official Proclamation to Deport Armenians (cont'd)

Item 1	"Five days from [this date] all Armenians, except the sick, are required to start by sections and villages under the guard of gendarmes."
Item 2	Permits Armenians to take "any portable goods." Forbids selling any other property, or storing that property with others for safekeeping. Promises that, because the deportation is "temporary," the government will store all such goods "in large strong buildings," and such property will be "given back" on return of the owners. The army may buy goods from Armenians. Violators face court martial.
Item 3	Roadside accommodations ("proper buildings") are to be prepared "to secure their comfort" and safety until arrival at temporary destinations.
Item 4	"The guards will use arms against those who threaten the life or goods of one or more of the Armenian population or dishonor any of them. Any such person will be at once arrested, sent to Court Martial and condemned to death."
Item 5	Armenians "who dare to use arms" to resist the deportation orders shall be "arrested dead." Persons who hide or help Armenians to hide face court martial and the death penalty.
Item 6	Armenians must turn in any and all firearms, bombs and daggers to the government. Severe punishment awaits any person who hides any of these items from the government.
Item 7	"The soldiers and gendarmes acting as escort are permitted and required to use arms and to kill those who try to seize by force or plunder the Armenians on the roads or in villages."
Item 8	Armenians may leave goods with the Imperial Ottoman Bank and other creditors to secure debts. Government may buy such goods when "necessary" for "military purposes."
Item 9	No animals may be taken on deportation, and will be bought by the army.
Item 10	"The officials of villages, towns, districts and provinces on the way must assist the Armenians as much as possible."

Preparation for Genocide

Once the plan was formulated, the Young Turks selected police chiefs, governors and other officials who were loyal to them and their cause. After being given the more detailed secret instructions for liquidating the Armenians, these officials were sent out to the Armenian towns. They waited for the telegram that starkly read "Take care of the Armenians" to begin the slaughter.[18]

The steps of the genocide plan fell into place:

✔ The Turkish government drafted over 200,000 Armenian men into the army, thus taking most of the men capable of resisting away from the Armenian areas.

✔ In February, 1915, the Minister of War issued this order to all army commanders:

> "In view of the present situation the total extermination of the Armenian race has been decided by an Imperial order. The following operations are to be performed to that effect:
>
> 1. All Ottoman subjects over the age of five years bearing the name Armenian and residing in the country should be taken out of the city and killed.
>
> 2. All Armenians serving in the Imperial armies should be separated from their divisions, without creating incidents, taken into solitary places, away from the public eyes, and shot.
>
> 3. All Armenian officers in the army should be imprisoned in their respective military camps until further notice.
>
> 48 hours after the above instructions are transmitted to the commanders of the army specific orders will be issued for their execution."[19]

✔ Armenian soldiers were disarmed and transferred to labor battalions, where they were killed by various means.[20] Some were worked to death. Others died of exposure, hunger and disease in the freezing winter. Still others were bound into groups, marched to a secluded area and shot.[21]

✔ Exterminating Armenians in the army still left many males who could fight and might have the weapons to do so.[22] The Turkish government thus directly confiscated as many weapons as possible from the Armenian civilians:

"Under the guise of wartime necessity and to protect against possible sabotage and rebellion by Armenians, the first stage was to demand throughout all towns and villages that Armenians turn in their arms or face severe penalties. Turk soldiers and police ransacked Armenian homes, and many suspected of having weapons were shot or horribly tortured."[23]

Government terrorism against civilians can drive them to extreme acts of attempted self-preservation. The Turkish civilian disarmament campaign "created such terror that Armenians bought or begged from Turkish friends weapons that they could turn in to authorities."[24] The Armenians' reaction was not altogether unreasonable because in some areas Armenians were expected to fulfill quotas of guns to be relinquished to authorities.[25] Where authorities suspected hidden firearms, they proceeded with house to house searches, torturing Armenians and their families to discover the locations of weapons.[26]

The procedure was confirmed by British and American sources:

A decree went forth that all Armenians should be disarmed. The Armenians in the Army were drafted out of the fighting ranks, re-formed into special labour battalions... The disarming of the civil population was left to the local authorities, and in every administrative centre a reign of terror began. The authorities demanded the production of a definite number of arms. Those who could not produce them were tortured, often in fiendish ways; those who procured [firearms to turn in], by purchase from their Moslem neighbours or by other means, were imprisoned for conspiracy against the Government.[27]

The Turkish search for weapons not only disarmed the people, it served the purpose of further thinning out the ranks of able-bodied and influential men. The observers thus reported:

Few of these [tortured or imprisoned] were young men, for most of the young had been called up to serve; they were elderly men, men of substance and the leaders of the Armenian community, and it became apparent that the inquisition for arms was being used as a cloak to deprive the community of its natural heads. Similar measures had preceded the massacres of 1895-6, and a sense

139

of foreboding spread though the Armenian people.[28]

The ultimate "gun control" — forcible confiscation — left the Armenians servile and helpless.

✔ There were more ways to eliminate the able-bodied Armenian men. Late in April 1915, the Turkish government arrested 235 prominent Armenians in Constantinople and "deported" them to the interior. These first victims were educated people, politicians, physicians, lawyers, teachers, clergymen and writers. Hundreds of others like them were taken away by the Turks in raids all over the country. Another 5,000 "blue collar" Armenians shortly met the same fate.

✔ Mopping up the remaining Armenian men was a grimly clever process. Proceeding from town to town, "a town crier or bulletin would call for all Armenian males over age 15 to appear by a certain time in the town square or in front of the central government building. Once they had gathered, the authorities then imprisoned them all. After a day or so, soldiers and police roped the prisoners together in batches, marched them out to a secluded spot, and slaughtered them."[29]

✔ Once the men capable of resisting the genocide were eliminated, and the civilians disarmed, the genocide of the women and children progressed as planned:[30]

1. Turkish authorities would order all Armenians in a town to prepare for internal deportation in a week.

2. The Armenians (then mostly women) were forbidden to sell their real property or livestock. They were forced to sell most other family and personal property for next to nothing, often to government officials. (After the deportation, the Armenians' abandoned real property and livestock was given to Muslim Turks.)

3. The Turks collected Armenian families into convoys — groups numbering between 200 and 4,000 women, children and old people. Although hired oxcarts with drivers would start the trip carrying some Armenians' belongings, these hirelings would quit and turn back within a few days, leaving the Armenians to hand carry what they could.

4. Through hot and dry summer months, the convoys were force marched over rough terrain where water was scarce. The

Turkish guards assigned to "protect" the deportees sometimes forbade them to stop for water, and killed stragglers. Those marchers who took too long to die of hunger, thirst or exhaustion, the Turk guards massacred.

5. During the march, Muslim villagers would attack the Armenians, plundering, raping and killing at will. When passing through mountainous areas, Kurdish tribes were encouraged to loot, rape, kidnap women and kill. The Turks released convicted criminals and literally invited them to attack the convoys.

6. In some cases, Turkish army troops were ordered to murder a whole convoy. In one well-known case, the Turkish 86th Cavalry Brigade attacked a large convoy from Erzindjan, stripped all the people of their clothes and led them naked to Kemakh Gorge. There the Turkish troops tied up the Armenians and threw them down a rock crag into the flowing Euphrates River. Some 20,000 to 25,000 Armenians, roughly half the population of their town, was swiftly murdered there in this manner or by bayonet.

7. Some Armenians, chiefly those from cities, were confined in concentration camps or transported in overcrowded cattle cars. Many were also force marched during part of their transportation. All of these victims died by the thousands, from disease, exposure, hunger and murder by troops and attackers.

8. The 10% or so of the Armenians who survived their "trips" arrived as naked diseased skeletons at concentration camps. Disease, starvation and mass execution ended most of their lives.

Propaganda: gun ownership proves disloyalty

Repeating a pattern found in persecutions worldwide, the Turkish government used a *gun scare* as a propaganda tool against targeted victims. To build more public support for rounding up Armenians, the government publicly charged that some rural Armenians still possessed firearms even after the confiscation order:

> The pattern was repeated for each town and city. Politicians and leading citizens were ordered to report to the authorities and jailed. Armenians were required to

hand over any arms in their possession and police searched their homes. Those arrested were forced, sometimes under torture, to confess their part in the general uprising. Such confessions were rarely obtained, and, with the Ittihad [ruling party -ed] lacking sufficient evidence to support its allegations of an insurrection, the government simply published as proof photographs of stocks of weapons and munitions seized in Armenian homes throughout the country, as if it were surprising that peasants and mountain-dwellers had kept rifles and gunpowder in spite of the order to hand over all weapons. Shortly afterwards, the men themselves were ordered to report and arrested. All those imprisoned were taken out into the country and either cut down or shot.[31]

Didn't Anyone Resist the Genocide?

Innocent Armenian citizens largely did not resist the deportation and destruction in 1915-1917, for several reasons:[32]

- Communication technology, especially in remote parts of the Ottoman Empire, was slow. Armenians did not know what was happening elsewhere and could not see the master plan unfolding.
- Armenians were mostly loyal and obedient citizens of the Empire. They obeyed the orders given to them.
- The Armenian leadership and intelligentsia had been killed.
- The Armenian men capable of fighting had mostly been drafted, called away, and killed.
- Weapons had been confiscated from civilians.

Where Armenians knew about the Turkish threat and possessed arms, there was fierce resistance. In the region of Van, Armenians fought desperately against the vastly more powerful Turkish army. An Armenian woman offered this eyewitness account:

Gradually we got news that the Turks wanted to finish off all the Armenians by massacring them. ... Every night, taking turns in homes, we had secret meetings to figure out when this was going to happen and how we could prepare to resist and defend ourselves. [The

Armenians preparing to resist] came to our house many times. They would do drills to get used to the rifles. Suddenly word came to us that the Turks were going to attack in three days. Everyone got ready; the men, who were the only fighters, positioned themselves in the basements and were ready with their rifles by small windows. ... The Protestant churches opened up their meetinghouses for the people to take cover, and waited for the outcome.[33]

The Turkish army had been marching through, sacking and burning Armenian villages in the region. About 24,000 Armenians were butchered, mostly women, children and the aged, in about 80 villages.[34] The American Ambassador to Turkey, Henry Morgenthau learned from two reputable American eyewitnesses how the triggering events took place on the auspicious date of April 20 in the year 1915:

"On April 20th, a band of Turkish soldiers seized several Armenian women who were entering the city; a couple of Armenians ran to their assistance and were shot dead. The Turks now opened fire on the Armenian quarters with rifles and artillery; soon a large part of the town was in flames and a regular siege had started."[35]

Morgenthau reported the inequality of forces in battle:

The whole Armenian fighting force consisted of only 1,500 men; they had only 300 rifles and a most inadequate supply of ammunition, while [the Turks] had an army of 5,000 men, completely equipped and supplied.[36]

The Armenian defenders, all civilians, held off the Turkish army for five weeks. Another eyewitness detailed how the defenders managed to do it:

The whole population was involved, because even we children used to go from house to house to gather the brass candle bars to make shells for the bullets. They even learned to make powder. Everyone was involved. Sometimes the fighting was at a very close range, from one house to the other. The Turks had all the ammunition and ours was very limited, we had to be very, very careful not to waste any. Some of the Armenians had the ingenuity that, when a Turk was killed, they pulled him in with a long pole to get the ammunition he was carrying.[37]

After a month of prolonged fighting, and when Armenian volunteers and Russian troops approached the city, the Turks pulled back. When the Turks returned six weeks later with reinforcements, however, the Armenian defenders packed up and fled to Russia.

But the Armenians Were Protected By Law!

Americans tend to trust their leaders, judges and laws. If the government promises to protect a citizen's goods, then an American would likely trust that promise. Most Americans cannot imagine how the Turkish government murdered about 1,500,000 people whom that government had promised to protect by law.

Indeed, the Turkish law assuring the Armenians protection was about as strongly-worded as a law could be. Under the Official Proclamation of June 26, 1915, which ordered the Armenians to be deported internally, the Ottoman Turkish government promised:

- that the deportation of Armenians was temporary
- that the Armenians' property would be safeguarded
- that Turkish escort troops would shoot to kill anyone who attacked or looted Armenians during the deportation
- that roadside inns would be available to Armenians "secure their comfort" during the trip
- that a Turkish military court would condemn to death anyone who threatened the life or goods of an Armenian or who even showed "dishonor" to an Armenian

The Ottoman Turkish government lied. That government organized and executed the plunder and murder of the very people whom it promised to so fiercely protect.

Lesson of the Armenian genocide: never be so trusting of a government to protect you that you give up your own means of self-defense.

A good government will never try to render its citizens defenseless — an evil government always will.

Table 12A
Key Turkish "Gun Control" Laws that Disarmed Victims[38]

Turkish Law Citation	Operational Language
Article 166, Ottoman Penal Code, June 4, 1911	"Whoever, without obtaining permission from the department concerned, manufactures within the Ottoman territories gunpowder…or prohibited weapons or cartridges for them or imports into the Ottoman territories [the same], or becomes a medium for this sort of smuggling, or transports or imports [the same items smugged] within the Ottoman territories…is, in addition to the confiscation of such, put in prison for from two months to two years, and a fine [5 to 50 'gold pieces' or 'lira'] is taken."
Article 166, Ottoman Penal Code, June 4, 1911	"Those who, without permission, carry or sell such prohibited cartridges, weapons, gunpowder or explosive substances are also punished with imprisonment for from one month to six months and by taking a fine [1 to 10 'gold pieces' or 'lira']."
Article 166, Ottoman Penal Code, June 4, 1911	"For the purposes of the Penal Code 'prohibited weapons' mean generally State or military weapons and revolvers of which the barrels are more than 15 centimetres." [15 cm = 5.9 inches — auth.]
Official Proclamation, June 26, 1915	Item 5. [Referring to the deportation order], "Armenians are compelled to obey the government's decision. If there be any persons among them who dare to use arms against soldiers or gendarmes, arms will be used against such persons and they shall be 'arrested dead.'"
Official Proclamation, June 26, 1915	Item 6. "Armenians being prohibited to carry any fire arms, they must surrender to the government all kinds of arms, pistols, bombs and daggers that they have in their houses or out of doors. The government has been informed about a quantity of these arms, and those persons who try to secrete them instead of delivering them up to the government will be very severely punished when the arms are discovered by the government."

End Notes

[1]Rummel, R.J. 1996. *Death by Government*. New Brunswick, NJ: Transaction Publishers, p. 220, quoting eyewitness account in De Nogales, Rafael. 1926. *Four Years Beneath the Crescent*. Translated by Muna Lee. New York: Scribners, at pp. 130-131.

[2]Rummel 1996, p. 209.

[3]Simkin, Jay, Aaron Zelman, and Alan M. Rice. 1994. *Lethal Laws*. Milwaukee, WI: Jews for the Preservation of Firearms Ownership ("LL"), p. 83, citing Yves Ternon, "Report on the Genocide of the Armenians of the Ottoman Empire, 1915-16", in Libaridian, Gerard (ed), Permanent People's Tribunal. 1985. *A Crime of Silence: The Armenian Genocide*. London: Zed

Books, Ltd., pp. 114, 120; Melson, Robert F. 1992. *Revolution and Genocide*. Chicago: University of Chicago Press, pp. 146-147.

4Rummel 1996, p. 210.

5Ibid.

6Ibid.

7Ibid.

8LL, p. 80, quoting Lynch, H.F.B. 1901. *Armenia: Travels and Studies*. New York: Longmans, Green and Co., p. 429.

9LL, p. 81, citing Hoffman, Tessa. "German Eyewitness Reports of the Genocide of the Armenians, 1915-16," in Libardian 1985, p. 71.

10Rummel 1996, p. 211.

11LL, p. 81.

12LL, pp. 81, 86-87.

13Rummel 1996, p. 211.

14Not all Turkish people hated and tormented Armenians. Many individual Turks were friendly and many tried to help their Armenian neighbors and friends when the deportation and genocide began. Miller, Donald E. and Lorna Touryan Miller. 1993. *Survivors: An Oral History of the Armenian Genocide*. Berkeley, Calif: University of California Press, pp. 182-186.

15Rummel 1996, p. 214, citing Turkish language sources.

16Ibid.

17Ibid.

18Ibid., p. 216, citing Lang, David Marshall. 1981. *The Armenians: A People in Exile*. London: George Allen & Unwin, p. 26.

19Ibid., p. 216, quoting Boyajian, Dickran H. 1972. *Armenia: The Case for a Forgotten Genocide*. Westwood, NJ: Educational Book Crafters, p. 333-334.

20Miller and Miller 1993, p. 41.

21Rummel 1996, pp. 216-217, citing Libaridian, Gerard J. "The Ultimate Repression: The Genocide of the Armenians, 1915-1917." in Walliman, Isidor and Michael N. Dobrowski (eds.). 1987. *Genocide and the Modern Age: Etiology and Case Studies of Mass Death*. New York: Greenwood Press, p. 204.

22Rummel 1996, p. 217 (direct quote).

23Ibid.

24Ibid.

25Miller and Miller 1993, pp. 41, 67.

26Ibid., pp. 41, 67-68.

27Viscount Bryce. 1916. *The Treatment of the Armenians in the Ottoman Empire, 1915-16* London: G. P. Putnam's Sons, p. 638.

[28]Ibid.

[29]Rummel 1996, pp. 217-18.

[30]Ibid., pp. 218-222 & notes 24, 33-35.

[31]Ternon, "Report on the Genocide of the Armenians of the Ottoman Empire, 1915-16", in Libaridian 1985, p. 106.

[32]Miller and Miller, p. 72.

[33]Ibid., pp. 72-73.

[34]Ibid., p. 76, quoting American Ambassador Henry Morgenthau.

[35]Ibid.

[36]Ibid., p. 73.

[37]Ibid., p. 73.

[38]Full text of Turkish laws with translations are found in LL, pp. 85-91.

Chapter Thirteen:
Uganda

Can "gun control" laws avert social disasters that result from military and political policies? Can such laws prevent tribal warfare and government-sponsored mass murder?

In Uganda's case, the laws not only failed to work — they achieved the worst results. Under the dictatorship of Idi Amin and a fully developed "gun control" scheme, between 1971 and 1979, 300,000 people were murdered by government agents and troops.[1] Based on the estimated total population of just over 10 million people, the average government murder rate for that nine-year period was 300 murders per 100,000 persons. Uganda's murder rate under severe "gun control" was over 30 times higher than that of the United States in the same time period (9.4 per 100,000).[2]

What factors set the stage for government murder in Uganda under Amin? There were several.

Hostile Peoples Forced Together

First, Uganda was a nation created by the British government. In the late 1800's, Great Britain controlled Egypt, and wanted to ensure that the Nile River's water supply would not be disturbed.[3] The previous kingdom of Buganda lay at the source of the Nile. When religious civil war broke out in Buganda, Britain took control of the country in 1894 as a "protectorate," and later made it a colony.[4]

Through a series of political and military maneuvers, Britain managed to transfer control of a large part of the territory neighboring kingdom of Bunyoro into the Uganda colony.[5] Similarly, other nearby tribal kingdoms were pulled under British control.[6] To form Uganda, these rival and mutually hostile tribes and lands were cemented together.

Britain apparently little cared that its colony would be a land divided by hate. The people of Bunyoro had historically been hostile to the people of Buganda, and had fiercely resisted the forced union.[7] Meanwhile, to get the Buganda forces to surrender their weapons, the British gave a privileged status to the Buganda province over the rest of Uganda.[8] This program of inequality among the peoples and provinces could only make inter-tribal resentment worse.

Rule By Foreign Or Hostile Occupation Forces

Second, the British strategy of military control was designed to keep the peoples of Uganda divided. The British military forces were organized such that "a soldier should be of a different race, a different (and distant) geographical origin, and a different religious faith from the population in the area of posting. The underlying rationale was that the army would be more effective if the troops did not feel a sense of identity with the local populations, but owed allegiance only to the administration."[9]

Troops from Sudan, then from India and Kenya, were imported to keep order in Uganda. By 1913, however, most of the British forces were African.[10] From that point on, the men of Uganda's military came mostly from the northern regions, not from the southern Buganda province. As most leaders in Ugandan society were from Buganda, there remained a tension between the military and civilian elements.

Society Divided Against Itself

Third, Ugandan society was fractured in five key aspects:[11]

(1) Buganda (in the south) and its people received privileged treatment and dominated the administration.

(2) Tribes within the country remained hostile; the Bunyoro people particularly resented the loss of territories.

(3) The peoples were divided by religious differences so severe that a civil war had erupted owing to them (Catholic vs. Protestant vs. Muslim).

(4) The military was comprised chiefly of northern tribesmen (who were typically less educated than the southern people of the Buganda province in the south).

(5) In economic matters, the people of Buganda dominated the farm sector, while people of Indian descent largely controlled commerce.

Victim Disarmament Laws

Fourth, the British-imposed system of "gun control" had made it difficult or impossible for Ugandan citizens to possess and use firearms. From 1955 to 1970, the Firearms Ordinance comprehensively controlled the lawful access and use of firearms. Just before Idi Amin took power, Uganda in 1970 replaced the older law with an essentially similar Firearms Act. The key elements of the 1970 Firearms Act were:

- National registration of all firearms and licensing of all firearms owners.
- Licensing officials could deny or revoke firearms licenses at will.
- Police could demand to inspect firearms and licenses at any time.
- No firearms could be imported sold or transferred between private citizens except with government approval via licensing.
- Firearms dealers and gunsmiths must be nationally registered and could be searched and inspected for regulatory compliance at any time.
- Firearms owners would be criminally liable for failure to store firearms in approved manner.
- No person (except a dealer) could manufacture or assemble any ammunition or firearm.
- The Firearms Act restrictions did not apply to members of the military, nor to others whom the government authorities might select.
- Government authorities under statutory order could ban or confiscate firearms in any region at any time.

    See Table 13A below for more details.[12]

About six months before the enactment of the 1970 Firearms Act, Uganda's Prime Minister Milton Obote had banned the possession of all firearms and ammunition (except government officials and others selected by the Prime Minister).[13] Prime Minister Obote also banned nearly all political parties.[14] The government monopoly on lawful firearms possession, followed by the highly restrictive 1970 Firearms Act, made it quite difficult or impossible for disfavored citizens to legally have firearms. Those who sought to obey the law would remain disarmed, or would submit themselves to continuous government identification and monitoring. Political parties that could have opposed a power grab had to operate secretly if at all.

Ascent of the Ruthless Tyrant

Fifth, within two months of his seizing power in January, 1971, Idi Amin concentrated all political power in himself. His personal decrees became law.[15] He became commander in chief of the military, and abolished all lower levels of government.[16] He outlawed all political parties, abolished the legislature and transferred its powers to the "Council of Ministers."[17]

To forestall resistance to his rule, Amin made it a punishable crime for three or more persons to be found together if any one of them were armed.[18] He also authorized any member of the military or prison authorities to make arrests without a warrant.[19]

Genocide Begins

To consolidate further his personal power, Idi Amin purged the Ugandan Army of soldiers who were hostile to him or otherwise suspect. Soldiers from the ethnic and language regions that did not strongly support Amin were his first targets. Thousands of soldiers were initially transferred away from central units, and then later killed. Soldiers transferred away were replaced by others deemed loyal to Amin, including soldiers from other countries. An estimated 16,000 military men became "missing" (dead) in 1971 alone.[20] By September 1972, Amin had rebuilt the Army in his image. By 1973, at 90,000 people had been murdered: soldiers, ordinary citizens, and many people just because they were related to a person seen as a threat to the Amin regime.[21]

When the Army purge was nearly complete, Amin ordered on August 4, 1972, that all Asians who were not citizens to leave the country in 90 days.[22] Approximately 50,000 Asians left Uganda as ordered, abandoning property to be seized by the Army.[23] Many Asians were robbed of their personal belongings and had their luggage confiscated as they tried to leave via airports.[24]

In December 1972, Amin ordered the "nationalization" (confiscation by government) of all British companies' property in Uganda, and gave Britons two weeks to leave the country.[25] The effect of expelling the Asians and seizing the British holdings was to severely damage the economy of Uganda.[26]

A small army numbering about 1,000 Ugandan exiles tried to overthrow Amin by force in September, 1972, but failed.[27] The overthrow attempt gave Amin the excuse, however, to murder more of his "enemies," including the Chief Justice, the Vice Chancellor of Makerere University, and the former Interior Minister who "was dismembered alive" and had "his severed head displayed on the end of a pole."[28]

Government Death Agencies

The Amin regime empowered three government agencies to terrorize the civilian population into submission. Their means: torture and murder. Amin created a Military Police unit in 1971, and empowered another force, the Public Safety Unit. Most feared and powerful of the agencies was the State Research Bureau, which was established supposedly as a military intelligence agency.[29]

By 1977, these three units had killed an estimated 189,000 persons.[30]

What sort of person ran the government death agencies? One Ugandan described them:

> Who ran the State Research Bureau? Who operated and served in those organs of human destruction which sent innocent men and women to their deaths on mere suspicion and over trivial rivalries centered on such petty issues as girl- or boy-friends or cars? Highly educated men, with post-graduate degrees [and] those who headed the key ministries such as Justice, the Interior, Regional and Local Government, and Defence, and of course the state's security organs.[31]

How did the government death agencies operate? Eyewitnesses described what they saw at the side of the State Research Bureau building in Kampala, Uganda:

> [a] bloodstained drainage gutter....Prisoners had been forced to lie down in the drain and were shot there so that their blood would not stain the premises. The next person to be executed was then forced to carry the body to the pile at the side of the building and then climb

into the gutter himself. Sometimes prisoners were forced to club the person next to them to death and then await their turn.[32]

Confirming the reality of the wholesale murder factory were the thousands of identity cards of victims found at the State Research Bureau after the fall of the regime.[33]

When Tanzanian army troops occupied Uganda in 1979, they found prison cells "where prisoners had been forced to eat the bodies of those who died. ...Broken, starved, incoherent prisoners were released. Mass graves of thousands were found, victims of the State Research Bureau. Most exhumed bodies had beaten heads. Many had been killed by strangulation. Children's bodies were found impaled on stakes."[34]

Do Armed Citizens Die Easy?

What if the civilians of Uganda had possessed and known how to use firearms? Would that fact have made any difference? Could Idi Amin's death machine have been slowed or stopped by armed civilians? Consider this incident:

> In theft, as in war, Amin's soldiers displayed no inclination to stand up to opposition. One heavily armed group approached the locked gate at the front of the home of Ricarda and Charles Hetsch, the first secretary at the French embassy. At the time only Ricarda Hetsch was at home, but she was no stranger to weapons. Her previous marriage had been to a white hunter in the Sudan, and Ricarda Hetsch herself was a crack shot and a cool head. When Amin's soldiers leveled their weapons and demanded the Hetsches' car, she calmly pulled a pistol from her clothing and fired off three shots that sent the raiders into flight, their automatic weapons dangling at their sides as they ran for their lives down the street.[35]

Who ultimately ended the blood-soaked tyranny of Idi Amin? It was not an uprising of the citizens; they were mostly disarmed, and many of the potential fighting men were already dead. It was the 1979 counter-attack by the Tanzanian army responding to an invasion by Amin's forces, that finally drove Amin out.[36]

A good government will never try to render its citizens defenseless — an evil government always will.

Table 13A
"Gun Control" Under Uganda's Firearms Act of 1970

Firearm Act Provision	Citation	Penalty for Violation
National regulation of firearms ownership by appointed "chief licensing officer."	Part I, §1	n.a.
Chief licensing officer appoints local police commander in districts to act at his direction.	Part I, §1 (1)-(5)	n.a.
Citizens prohibited from possessing firearms or ammunition without having a "valid firearms certificate" for each item.	Part II, §2	Fine and/or prison up to 10 years
Licensing officer may refuse to issue a firearms certificate for any reason or no reason.	Part II, §3 (4)(b-g)	n.a.
Firearms certificate can be issued only to persons who prove to the licensing official that they have "reasonable cause," are "competent to use a firearm," are at least 25 years of age, are "of sound mind and of temperate habits," will "ensure the safe custody" of firearm, and are "fit and proper" to have a firearm.	Part II, §3 (4)(b-g)	n.a.
To obtain a firearms certificate for a firearm to be used "for sporting purposes," the citizen must also obtain a hunting license.	Part II, §3 (5)	n.a.
Firearms certificates may be restricted in scope as the licensing official sees fit.	Part II, §3 (7)	n.a.
Licensing official may "suspend or revoke" a firearm certificate for any reason or no reason.	Part II, §4 (1)	n.a.
Firearms certificates may not be renewed unless the firearm is produced to the licensing official for inspection.	Part II, §7 (1)	n.a.
Police may demand to see a valid firearms certificate at any time from a person in possession of a firearm.	Part II, §8	Seizure of firearm
Police may demand at any time that a citizen produce for inspection the firearms and ammunition held under any certificate.	Part II, §9	Fine and/or prison up to 6 months
Citizens prohibited from manufacturing or assembling firearms or ammunition (unless a registered dealer or gunsmith).	Part II, §10	Life imprison-ment
Citizens prohibited from selling, transferring, or possessing, without a certificate, a firearm for testing or repair (unless a registered dealer).	Part II, §11 (1)(a)	Fine and/or prison up to 5 years.

Table 13A (continued)
"Gun Control" Under Uganda's Firearms Act of 1970

Firearm Act Provision	Citation	Penalty for Violation
Citizens prohibited from repairing or testing a firearm without a certificate (unless a registered gunsmith).	Part II, §11 (1)(b)	Fine and/or prison up to 5 years.
Firearms dealers and gunsmiths must be registered by licensing official.	Part II, §12-13	Fine and/or prison up to 5 years.
Firearms dealers and gunsmiths may be refused registration for any reason or no reason.	Part II, §12(2)	n.a.
Firearms dealers and gunsmiths must maintain log of all transactions (including identity of customer) and report all transactions to licensing official.	Part II, §16	Fine and/or prison up to 6 months
Prohibition of transfers of firearms and ammunition between private citizens, unless both parties hold certificates and report transaction to licensing official.	Part II, §20	Fine and/or prison up to 5 years
Citizens lawfully possessing firearms and ammunition required to keep them in "safe custody" at all times, and must not allow them to be lost, stolen, or used by any other person not lawfully entitled to do so.	Part IV, §29	Fine and/or prison up to 1 year
Citizens must not use firearm or "imitation firearm" to resist lawful arrest, or to "threaten violence" to any person.	Part IV, §31(1)	Prison up to 14 years
Citizens must not "display any firearm or imitation firearm" publicly in a manner that causes "alarm" to any person.	Part IV, §31(2)	Fine and/or prison up to 6 months
Citizens must not discharge any firearm, negligently or deliberately, publicly in a manner that causes "alarm" to any person.	Part IV, §31(3)	Fine and/or prison up to 2 years
Police officer with "reasonable cause" to suspect a violation of any provision of this Act, may search any premises, container or vehicle, and may seize any person, firearm or ammunition found.	Part IV, §33	n.a.
To verify compliance with this act, chief licensing officer may order a search of a firearms dealer "at all reasonable times" without a warrant.	Part IV, §34	n.a.

Table 13A (continued)
"Gun Control" Under Uganda's Firearms Act of 1970

Firearm Act Provision	Citation	Penalty for Violation
National authority by statutory order can prohibit carrying, sales or transfer of firearms, and can order confiscation of all firearms, in any region of Uganda.	Part IV, §40	for citizen opposition to such order: fine and/or prison up to 5 years.
None of this Act applies to members of the military.	Part IV, §43(a)	n.a.

End Notes

¹Simkin, Jay, Aaron Zelman, and Alan M. Rice. 1994. *Lethal Laws.* Milwaukee, WI: Jews for the Preservation of Firearms Ownership ("LL"), p. 280; Rummel, R.J. 1996. *Death by Government.* New Brunswick, NJ: Transactions Publishers, p. 94; Chirot, Daniel. 1994. *Modern Tyrants.* New York: The Free Press, p. 392.

²United States Department of Justice, Bureau of Justice Statistics. 1989. *Sourcebook Of Criminal Justice Statistics - 1989.* P. 365, Table 3.118.

³LL, pp. 269-70, citing Omara-Otunnu, Amii. 1987. *Politics and the Military in Uganda, 1890-1985.* New York: St. Martin's Press, p. 13.

⁴LL, p. 270, citing Omara-Otunnu 1987, p. 19.

⁵LL, p. 270.

⁶LL, p. 270, citing Omara-Otunnu 1987, pp. 17-18; and Mutibwa, Phares. 1992. *Uganda Since Independence.* Trenton, NJ: Africa World Press, pp. 2-3.

⁷LL, p. 270, citing Omara-Otunnu 1987, 17-20; and Mutibwa 1992, pp. 2-3.

⁸LL, p. 270, citing Mutibwa 1992, p. 3.

⁹LL, p. 270, citing and quoting Omara-Otunnu 1987, p. 24.

¹⁰LL, p. 270, citing Omara-Otunnu 1987, pp. 22-24.

¹¹LL, p. 271.

¹²Text of Firearms Act of 1970 in English is reproduced in LL, pp. 285-299.

¹³LL, p. 274, citing Republic of Uganda. *Subsidiary Legislation, 1969.* Statutory Instruments, 1969 No. 234, The Firearms Order, p. 593.

¹⁴LL, p. 274, citing Omara-Otunnu 1987, p. 89.

¹⁵LL, p. 275, citing Republic of Uganda. *Decrees: 1971.* The Interpretation Act (Modifications) Decree. Decree 3 of 1971, 4 Feb., p. 3.

¹⁶LL, p. 275, citing *Decrees: 1971.* The Armed Forces Decree. Decree 1 of 1971,

2 Feb., p. 1; and *Decrees 1971*. The Local Administrations and Urban Authorities Decree. Decree 2 of 1971, 2 Feb., p. 2.

[17]LL, p. 275, citing *Decrees: 1971*. The Parliamentary Powers Vesting Decree. Decree 8 of 1971, 12 Mar., p. 12; and *Decrees 1971*. The Suspension of Political Activities Decree. Decree 14 of 1971, 15 Mar., p. 17.

[18]LL, p. 275, citing *Decrees: 1971*. The Penal Code (Amendment) Decree. Decree 11 of 1971, 15 Mar., p. 17.

[19]LL, p. 275, citing *Decrees: 1971*. The Armed Forces (Powers of Arrest) Decree. Decree 13 of 1971, 15 March, pp. 19-20.

[20]LL, p. 276, citing Omara-Otunnu 1987, pp. 105, 107.

[21]LL, p. 276, citing Omara-Otunnu 1987, p. 126.

[22]LL, p. 277, citing Omara-Otunnu 1987, p. 119.

[23]LL, p. 277, citing Omara-Otunnu 1987, p. 119.

[24]LL, p. 277, citing Mutibwa 1992, p. 95.

[25]LL, p. 277, citing Mutibwa 1992, p. 96.

[26]LL, p. 277, citing Mutibwa 1992, p. 117.

[27]LL, p. 277, citing Mutibwa 1992, pp. 99-100.

[28]LL, p. 277, quoting from Mutibwa 1992, p. 100.

[29]LL, p. 277, citing Kyemba, Henry. 1977. *A State of Blood*. New York: Grosset and Dunlap, p. 112-114.

[30]LL, p. 278, citing Kyemba 1977, p. 116.

[31]LL, p. 278, quoting from Mutibwa 1992, pp. 120-121.

[32]LL, p. 278, quoting from Avirgan, Tony and Martha Honey. 1982. *War in Uganda*. Westport, CT: Lawrence Hill & Company, p. 149.

[33]LL, p. 278, quoting from Avirgan and Honey 1982, p. 149.

[34]Chirot 1994, p. 392, citing *The Guardian,* April 21, 1979, p. 6.

[35]LL, p. 280, quoting from Avirgan and Honey 1982, pp. 148-149.

[36]LL, p. 279, citing Omara-Otunnu 1987, p. 141; LL 280, citing Avirgan and Honey 1982, p. 3.

Chapter Fourteen:

The Soviet Union:
The Bone Yard of "Gun Control"

The Union of Soviet Socialist Republics (USSR) styled itself a "workers' paradise." Economically, the Soviet Union could never succeed because the government attempted to run the entire country by central planning. Trying to operate a national economy via budgets, targets, and bureaucratic plans and directives, resulted in colossal inefficiency, waste and poverty.[1]

The Soviet government did more than engineer a doomed social experiment that wasted resources and frustrated people. The Soviet government murdered its own citizens by the millions. "Gun control" laws made that megamurder possible.

Same Oppression, Different Day

Before its end in 1917, Russia had a long history of political violence and oppression of the people. The emperors and empresses of the Russian Empire exercised nearly absolute power for centuries. Local rulers owned whole villages and had extensive powers over the people living and working there. There was no tradition of religious tolerance: Jews and dissident Christians suffered direct persecution.[2]

Tsar Nicholas II of Russia gave up his throne on March 15, 1917. After a provisional government failed to lead Russia into victory during the on-going World War, a small group of Bolsheviks seized power on November 7, 1917. The Russian Empire ceased to exist.[3]

When Vladimir I. Lenin took power as the Bolshevik leader of the Soviet Union, the (Bolshevik) Communist Party numbered only about 115,000 members from a nation of about 130,000,000. Lenin was not elected by the Russian people; his party amounted to less than 1/10 of 1% of the population.[4]

Shortly after the Bolshevik takeover, a civil war erupted in the spring of 1918. The Bolsheviks (renamed the Russian Communist Party) fought to hold power against an alliance of military forces from the tsarist regime and troops from Britain, the United States, France and Japan.[5] A number of domestic insurgents from various regions in and around Russia also fought against the Communist government.[6]

Civil War: Excuse for "Gun Control"

At the start of the civil war, the Communist government enacted its first "gun control" measures. The first measure was a resolution of the Presidium of the All-Russian Central Executive Committee, adopted on April 1, 1918, and modified by addendum on April 3, 1918. That April 3 Resolution required any person who would possess a firearm to have a "certificate" or license issued by the Central Executive Committee (the national government).[7] Each firearms certificate had to be "serially numbered" and bear the signatures of the Chairman and the secretary of the Central Executive Committee, and bear the official seal of that Committee.

As a word of warning, the April 3 Resolution stated: "Every forgery of said certificates will be severely punished."[8]

On its face, the April 3 Resolution contained no exceptions and appeared to apply to everyone. The next "gun control" step was to carve an exception for persons who had received firearms certificates issued by the secret police (known as the Extraordinary Commissions, nicknamed "Cheka"). Thus, the Central Executive Committee adopted a resolution on April 27, 1918, to extend legal permission to persons holding the secret police certificates.[9] The grounds for the exception: "the protection of railway lines." Based on the wording of the April 27 Resolution, the government would confiscate weapons from persons who did not have a proper certificate.

As the civil war continued in 1918, with various rebellions and Communist repression, the embattled national government installed more "gun control" regulations to disarm actual and potential enemies.[10] By a resolution dated August 17, 1918, the

Central Executive Committee standardized the firearms certificate format and imposed new requirements. The new certificate identified the holder as a "Comrade" and "Party member," implicitly suggesting that only Communist Party members would be issued such a certificate.

The new certificate also provided for specifically identifying the revolvers by type and serial number, and both rifles and "edged weapons" by description.[11] Each certificate would have an expiration date.

In addition to revising the firearm certificate format, the August 17 Resolution required holders of previously-issued certificates to exchange them for the new certificates, and to register them with their local governments. All "comrades" were required to "get their certificates registered with the local Councils before exchanging them." If the certificates were not registered, the certificate would become "invalid." Local Councils were "strictly responsible" for verifying the certificates noting the expiration dates.

Single Murder Gives Propaganda Excuse to Confiscate Firearms

Days later, on August 30, 1918, one Fanny Kaplan shot and wounded Lenin. Kaplan was executed without a trial, and the assassination attempt served as the excuse for a wave of government terror across the country.[12] Lenin recovered quickly. The Council of People's Commissars responded by preparing a draft Decree on October 29, 1918, which ordered all citizens to surrender all firearms and ammunition, as well as sabers, to the authorities:

The Council of People's Commissars has resolved that :

1) All citizens in possession of machineguns, rifles, revolvers of all kinds, cartridges, and all models of sabres, are obliged, within a period of a week, to surrender them....[13]

Who would get the surrendered weapons? "All weapons surrendered are to be used by the Red Army...."[14]

What if a person does not surrender a weapon? "Concealment of weapons, delay in — or opposition to — the surrender of weapons are to be punished by the deprivation of freedom for a term from one to ten years."[15] This language suggests that merely "opposing" the surrender of weapons was a crime.

The October 29 Decree had real teeth. High ranking officials were held "personally responsible for using all available means to show full cooperation to Military Commissariats to receive the above-mentioned arms from the citizenry."[16] "Officials guilty of negligence in collecting weapons, or who oppose this collection, [were] subject to immediate dismissal and [were] later to be tried by military and revolutionary courts."[17]

Holding a political official "personally responsible" means that the official faced punishment if the Decree were not successfully carried out. The official who fell short in some way would not just lose his job; he would be criminally prosecuted. The Decree thus strongly motivated officials to implement it.

By expressly requiring officials to use "all available means," the Decree gave the officials the legal authority to use any and all forcible methods. Ominously the Decree required the officials to "show full cooperation." That phrase indicates that officials will be rewarded for "showing" their efforts — meaning that the more aggressively they "show" their cooperation, the more likely it is that officials would avoid punishment.

The bottom line: the firearms confiscation Decree of October 29 *strongly motivated* officials to *strongly enforce* the law. At a time when the Communist government was already trying to rule by force and terror, this Decree was another green light to brute force and oppression.

Lenin signed a somewhat modified Decree with accompanying Instructions, dated December 10, 1918. The December 10 Decree achieved the same objectives:

The Council of People's Commissars has resolved that:

1) All citizens and all civil organizations should surrender machineguns, rifles, revolvers of all kinds - whether working or defective - as well as cartridges, and all models of sabres....[18]

The deadline for turning in weapons was adjusted in the December 10 Decree, giving 7 days for citizens in Moscow and Petrograd, 14 days in provincial capitals, and 21 or 30 days in regions lying farther away from the major cities.[19] The December 10 Decree softened somewhat the language holding officials "personally responsible for using all means available" to confiscate weapons and for showing their "cooperation," but left unchanged the language holding officials personally accountable and criminally punishable for negligence in collecting the weapons or for opposing the collection.[20] Likewise, citizens who concealed, delayed or opposed the collection of weapons faced prison terms of 1 to 10 years.[21] The other provisions of the October 29 draft Decree appeared in nearly identical form in the December 10 Decree.

New in the December 10 Decree was a cash reward payable to citizens who discovered weapons that had not been turned in.[22] Citizens who found even inoperable firearms would be rewarded. Double cash awards were payable for discovering illegal machine guns.

With the December 10 Decree was also issued an "Instruction." That Instruction carved an exception to the Decree for Party members:

> The Military Commissariats are ordered not to take rifles and revolvers in the possession of members of the Russian Communist Party, if a request has been made by — and responsibility has been taken by — the Chairmen of the Committees of the Russian Communist Party; but every Party member for whom this request has been made can have no more than one rifle and one revolver.[23]

The Instruction also provided for recording the make and serial number of each firearm possessed by Party members.[24]

The December 10 Decree and Instruction thus commanded officials to confiscate firearms from those persons who had earlier obtained certificates and had registered under the previous Decree of August 17. *Registration had paved the way for confiscation.*

War Means Even Tighter "Gun Control"

War erupted between the USSR and Poland in spring of 1920. The Polish Army captured and held Kiev, the capital of the Ukraine, from early May until late June, 1920. These events likely triggered enacting more Soviet "gun control" laws.[25]

The Council of People's Commissars delivered a Decree on the Issuing, Keeping & Handling of Firearms on July 12, 1920.[26] In the words of the July 12 Decree, the new law was necessary "to combat the illegal keeping of arms and the negligent and unskillful use of [arms].[27] The Decree thus declared:

§1. The keeping and use of firearms is only permitted to those whose service-related firearms [Army and other military] as well as to persons to whom this right is given under [the December 10, 1918 Decree, another decree on hunting, etc.]

In a note the Decree authorized the Secret Police to make exceptions to these restrictions for persons outside of the stated categories. Otherwise, only military personnel and other specified Party members could lawfully possess firearms. Section 2 of the July 12 Decree provided that minors could be issued firearms only if done under the name of a responsible "manager" or other official.

Section 3 of the July 12 Decree imposed a "zero tolerance" rule upon those persons allowed to possess firearms:

§3. It is absolutely forbidden to hand over weapons to anyone, whether for temporary use, or for storage.

Section 4 of the Decree spelled out more "gun control" regulations.[28] Immediate arrest and jail time awaited any person guilty of "illegal possession" or "negligent handling" of firearms. Under Section 4, a person "legally accountable" for any of the following acts would be "immediately arrested" and "punished with a sentence of deprivation of freedom for a period of not less than six months":

a. "the illegal possession of firearms, even if the possession is not with criminal intent;

b. "shooting into the air, without special need in crowded [areas] ...";

c. "shooting without reason" by military on guard;

d. "the illegal issuance of weapons to persons not having a legal right to them, or to persons who are not entitled to have them";

e. "negligent handling of firearms resulting in an accident."

Section 5 of the Decree imposed serious punishment upon a person for "taking aim" where there "may be danger to other people":

§5. A person guilty of taking aim in a street, or in general at any place, where there may be a danger to other people, even if he fires his weapon without consequences, should be tried by administrative order, and punished by confinement in a concentration camp for up to three months.

Notice how the words of Section 5 presume guilt. Taking the language as written, it says that "a person guilty" of the offense "should be tried" and then "punished." This kind of phrasing shows how very different the legal culture was in Soviet Russia.

Under the British and American common law system, a person is not deemed "guilty" and then given a trial.[29] A person in a common law country is first accused, then given a trial to determine whether that person is guilty. Punishment follows only from a conviction after a trial. Section 5 of the Decree set up a Soviet equivalent of a formal lynching: "let's hang him after we give him a trial."

Section 6 punished persons who were liable for "issuing arms to others who do not know how to use them, and who do not take steps to familiarize themselves with the handling of weapons, if this negligence gives rise to an accident."[30] In other words, the authorities would punish anyone who issued a firearm to a person who (1) was unfamiliar with the firearm, (2) failed to get firearms training, and then (3) caused a firearms-related accident.

Section 7 imposed a "duty" on the secret police (and the "militia") to ensure that "weapons are to be found only on a person having the legal right to them." The secret police was also empowered "to hold legally responsible" any person who violated the Decree.[31]

The July 12 Decree by itself achieved two key purposes. First, it stacked onto existing laws, reinforcing strictly the rule that only military and Party members could possess firearms. Second, it created even more incentives for firearms owners and the secret police to "enforce the law." The Decree held officials criminally liable for any failure to restrict firearms possession and any failure to control who possessed firearms — and it empowered the secret police to enforce the Decree itself.

The war with Poland ended in October, 1920, and by mid-1921 the Communist government had quelled nearly all armed resistance to their regime.[32] The "gun control" laws were collected in Article 220 of the Criminal Code of 1922.[33]

"Gun Control" In Stalin's Criminal Code

Lenin died in 1924, and was succeeded by Josef Stalin. A new criminal code was established in 1925.[34] Under the 1925 code, unauthorized possession of firearms was punishable by three months of forced labor or a large fine.[35]

The 1925 code was replaced the following year, but it still contained Article 182 with its forced labor and fines:

> Art. 182: The preparation, possession, purchase or sale of explosive substances or bombs without the necessary licence, or any infringement of the regulations regarding the acquisition, possess and use of rifled firearms, [is punishable by]
>
>> forced labor for a period not exceeding six months or a fine not exceeding one thousand roubles, with confiscation in every case [of the offending items].[36]

If there were "aggravating circumstances of a particularly serious character," then the punishment would be increased to up to one year forced labor or two years imprisonment.[37]

Stalin Builds The Killer State

In the power vacuum after Lenin's death, Josef Stalin ascended. Stalin had for years administered the Communist Party under Lenin, and had managed to place his supporters into key positions within the Party and the government.[38] According to Robert Conquest, pre-eminent historian of the Soviet Union, Stalin's supporters "were truly disgusting characters by any standards, a cadre which had abandoned all normal or even Communist standards and which may be regarded as in effect a personal group of hatchet men, ready for any violence or falsification at the orders of their leader."[39]

Stalin, backed by a government loaded with hand-picked loyalists, then set about to place all economic power into the central government while personally gaining all political power. To build the nation into a world class economic power, Stalin had to force the only large and reasonably successful industry to pay for the transition. That industry, grain agriculture, employed or supported about 80% of the population.[40]

To generate the revenue, the farmers would have to sell their grain to the government at prices so low that the government could resell the grain at a profit.[41] True to doctrine, Stalin forced social-ism onto the farmers. Between 1929 and 1933, the Soviet Army and secret police agencies collectivized all farming, placing livestock, land and tools into huge government farms.[42]

"Forced collectivization" sounds clean, neat, scientific. What actually happened was systematic wholesale slaughter of men, women and children. Megamurder by government.

The plan was to liquidate or send to concentration camps about 5,000,000 farmers and their families.[43] Brutalizing those initial 5,000,000 people would serve as the terror threat, and cause all oth-ers to give in to collectivization.[44] Many farmers resisted, and the Army was called to put down insurrections.[45] To finally complete the forced collectivization process, starting in about 1930, whole regions of farmers in the Ukraine were deliberately starved to death.[46] One conservative estimate places the numbers of dead at 4,000,000.[47] Other researchers have estimated the numbers killed during the collectivization to be between 6,000,000 to 11,400,000.[48]

What is a "kulak"?

The Russian Communists singled out a category of people for extermination. Those victims were called "kulaks." Farm owners who owned "a couple of cows or five or six acres more than their neighbors" were declared kulaks.[49] Calculated gov-ernment propaganda inflamed popular hatred of the kulaks. One woman Communist activist reportedly explained: "What I said to myself at the time was 'they are not human beings, they are kulaks' ... In order to massacre them it was necessary to proclaim that kulaks are not human beings."[50]

Vicious hatred works. The Communist anti-kulak activists "would threaten people with guns ... calling small children 'kulak bastards,' screaming 'bloodsuckers!' ... They had sold themselves on the idea that the so-called 'kulaks' were pariahs, untouchables, vermin. They would not sit down at a 'parasite's' table; the 'kulak' child was loathsome, the young 'kulak' girl was lower than a louse. They looked on the so-called 'kulaks' as cattle, swine, loathsome, repulsive; they had no souls; they stank; they all had venereal diseases; they were enemies of the people and exploited the labor of others. ... And there was no pity for them."[51]

Eyewitness to Genocide:
A Communist Remembers

One Communist government employee recalled: "[We all] believed that the ends justified the means. Our great goal was the universal triumph of Communism, and for the sake of that goal everything was permissible – to lie, to steal, to destroy hundreds of thousands and even millions of people, all those who were hindering our work or could hinder it, everyone one who stood in the way."

What did "total collectivization" mean? Systematically robbing the farming families of their produce. Said the Communist employee, it meant "scouring the countryside, searching for hidden grain, testing the earth with an iron rod for loose spots that might lead to buried grain." The government raiders would search entire homes, rifling through personal belongings, ignoring the protests and cries of the women and children. The raiders felt justified because they were "accomplishing the great and necessary transformation .... the people who lived there would be better off for it; that their distress and suffering were a result of their own ignorance or the machinations of the class enemy." The government, the planners, the leaders who directed the robbery, even the government employees themselves "knew better than the peasants how they should live, and what they should sow and when they should plough."

In spring 1931: "I saw people dying from hunger. I saw women and children with distended bellies, turning blue, still breathing but with vacant, lifeless eyes. And corpses – corpses in ragged sheepskin coats and cheap felt boots; corpses in peasant huts, in the melting snow ... under the bridges ..." For some raiders, the suffering and dying of fellow Soviet citizens all around them did not cause them even to question their motives or their superiors -- they would still "take away the peasants' grain in the winter," and in the spring "persuade the barely walking, skeleton-thin or sickly-swollen people to go into the fields in order to 'fulfil the bolshevik sowing plan ...'"[52]

How could megamurder take place without anybody knowing it was happening? In July 1932, the government deprived all workers of the right to transfer to other jobs.[53] Farmers could not move to get work anywhere else. In December, 1932, the government required all persons to carry an internal passport with them at all times.[54] Soviet troops forcibly prohibited people from leaving their villages even to look for food.[55] Foreign visitors could not readily visit the afflicted areas. Circulating rumors, even if true, was punishable by death.[56] Because the victims were cut off from the rest of the world and could not travel or safely communicate, the news of their fate did not travel far.

Eyewitness to Genocide: Malcolm Muggeridge, Reporter

On a recent visit [in 1933] ... I saw something of the battle that is going on between the government and the peasants. The battlefield is as desolate as in any war and stretches wider; stretches over a large part of Russia. On the one side, millions of starving peasants, their bodies often swollen from lack of food; on the other, soldier members of the [Party] carrying out the instructions of the dictatorship of the proletariat. They had gone over the country like a swarm of locusts and taken away everything edible; they had shot or exiled thousands of peasants, sometimes whole villages; they had reduced some of the most fertile land in the world to a melancholy desert.[57]

The forced collectivization of farmers hugely failed. Stalin's response was to blame his political opponents. His strategy was to accuse his enemies of trying to wreck his plan to industrialize the nation. The "saboteurs" had to be found, arrested and publicly tried.[58] The tactic was to force those accused to confess to crimes, name others who were also involved, public abase themselves for their acts, and then be punished severely.[59]

Not surprisingly, an incident of "gun violence" initiated the campaign. An assassin shot the head of the Leningrad branch of the Communist Party on December 1, 1934. Robert Conquest wrote of that fateful incident:

This killing has every right to be called the crime of the century. Over the next four years, hundreds of Soviet citizens, including the most prominent political leaders of the Revolution, were shot for direct responsibility for the assassination, and literally millions of others went to their deaths for complicity in one or another part of the vast conspiracy which allegedly lay behind it.[60]

In fact, this single crime "was the keystone of the entire edifice of terror and suffering by which Stalin secured his grip on the Soviet peoples."[61] The assassin was tried, condemned and executed within a month of the shooting. Only decades later did the outside world learn that the assassination was organized by Stalin himself.[62]

For the next five years, until 1939, the secret police invented conspiracy theories by which to charge people with crimes against the state. There were alleged plans to assassinate Stalin and other officials, acts of industrial sabotage (an accident might be considered sabotage), and espionage by Soviets working for foreign governments and other enemies.[63] Table USSR-1 lists some of the statutes that were applied broadly to as many defendants as needed to fill quotas.[64]

The now-infamous show trials took place between 1935 and

Table 14A
Counter-Revolutionary Crimes

Source: Penal Code of the Russian Socialist Federal Soviet Republic, 1926, as amended through 1932 (His Majesty's Stationery Office, London: 1934), Chapter 1, Crimes Against the State (selected articles; emphasis added).

Article	Crime	Penalty
58(1)	"Any action is considered counter-revolutionary which is directed [a] towards the overthrow, undermining or weakening of the authority [any government entity], or [b] towards the undermining or weakening of the external security of the U.S.S.R. or of the fundamental economic, political, and national conquests of the proletarian revolution."	[definition only]
58(2)	"Any armed rising" or other act of revolt against the U.S.S.R.	"The supreme measure of social defense: **death by shooting**," or confiscation of all property, deprivation of citizenship, and banishment from the territory of the U.S.S.R.

Table 14A (continued)
Counter-Revolutionary Crimes

Article	Crime	Penalty
58(3)	"Communication with counter-revolutionary intent with foreign governments [or their agents], or aiding any foreign goverment at war with or blockading the Soviet Union."	[same penalties as 58(2) above]
58(4)	"Rendering assistance of any kind" to the "international bourgeoisie" that is adverse or hostile to the Soviet Union.	"Deprivation of liberty" for at least 3 years and confiscation of property; or under "aggravating circumstances" **death by shooting;** or loss of citizenship, confiscation of all property, and permanent banishment from U.S.S.R.
58(6)	"Espionage", i.e. obtaining specially protected data with intent to transmit to foreign governments or "counter-revolutionary" organizations or persons.	[Same penalties as 58(4) above]
58(7)	"Undermining" any aspect of the economy "with counter-revolutionary intent," including "working against" or "opposing" state institutions.	[Same penalties as 58(2) above]
58(8)	"Terrorism" against Soviet authorities.	[Same penalties as 58(2) above]
58(9)	"Destruction or damaging, with counter-revolutionary intent" of any public utility, function, or building.	[Same penalties as 58(2) above]
58(10)	"Propaganda or agitation containing an appeal to overthrow, undermine or weaken the Soviet authority…or the dissemination, preparation or possession of literature containing such matters."	[Same penalties as 58(2) above]
58(11)	Any "organized activity" directed towards "preparation or commission" of any of the crimes set forth in this chapter.	[Same penalties as set forth for the specific crimes implicated]
58(12)	Any failure by a person with "certain knowledge" to report any "counter-revolutionary crime" or the preparation for such a crime.	Deprivation of liberty for 6 months or more.

Table 14A (continued)
Counter-Revolutionary Crimes

Article	Crime	Penalty
58(14)	"Counter-revolutionary sabotage," i.e. failing to discharge a duty properly, either knowingly or with deliberate carelessness, with intent to weaken the government or its operations.	Deprivation of liberty for 1 year or more, confiscation of property; if under "aggravating circumstances," confiscation of all property and **death by shooting.**
59(1)	A "crime against the administration" includes any act that disturbs or obstructs the regular activities of the government and involves opposition to the government, or if it otherwise weakens "the power and authority of the Government."	[definition only]
59(3)	Theft of firearms, parts of firearms or ammunition from any government building or from the military.	Deprivation of liberty for 1 year or more; if done by force, 3 years or more; if under "aggravating circumstances," confiscation of all property and **death by shooting.**

1938. Those accused of crimes against the state would be forced to sign (usually false) confessions, implicate supposed accomplices, and publicly declare their guilt. As the current slate of "criminals" was executed, the next wave of defendants would be rounded up to go through the same cycle.[65]

By summer, 1937, the police, courts and jails were jammed far beyond capacity. There weren't enough workers to process all the defendants and criminals, and there weren't enough hours in the day. There wasn't enough transportation to handle the load. The jail cells and prison camps were veritably bursting at the seams. The "courts" were operating 24 hours a day.[66] By the end of 1938, the secret police agencies had files that could "prove" that nearly every important government official was a spy. Nearly half the urban population was logged in a secret police file.

Stalin's 1934-1941 megamurder cost about 10,000,000 lives.[67] Who were these people? "Old and young, healthy and sick, men and women, even infants and the infirm, were killed in cold blood.

They were not combatants in civil war or rebellions; they were not criminals. Indeed, nearly all were guilty of...nothing."[68]

Nearly all the victims were also *unarmed*. Soviet "gun control" made firearms ownership so rare and unpopular that few citizens could have even tried to resist the death machine. Professor Conquest documented the pre-genocide civilian disarmament:

> In 1929-30, a great effort had been made to prevent the peasantry [from] possessing arms. Registration of hunting weapons had become compulsory in decrees of 1926, 1928 and 1929, and rules were also established to ensure that "criminal and socially dangerous elements" should not be sold guns...[69]

Despite the efforts to disarm them, the peasants had continued to resist forced collectivization, occasionally using violence. There were a few serious riots and insurrections in the first half of 1930, so in August of that year "a massive arms search was ordered. By this time, however, few arms were left" among the civilian population.[70]

Stalin's Post War Genocide

Soviet megamurder did not end with World War II. Stalin's regime racked up another 10,000,000 corpses in its slave labor camps during the war. After the war, Stalin and his successors sent another 18,000,000 people to the camps and early death by forced labor.[71] Not all of these later 18,000,000 victims were Soviet citizens, and many of them were not killed as part of a plan to destroy resistance or to improve the economy. For these reasons, perhaps their deaths are less well linked to the "gun control" policies implemented in the 1920's. To the extent their deaths were needless, arbitrary, political or otherwise unjust, they were still victims of the Communist government — a government that reigned for nearly 72 years — a government that the unarmed population was powerless to stop.

Table 14B
Elements of Citizen Disarmament Policies in the USSR

Type of Law	Reference & Date	Effect
Licensing of any person who possesses a firearm; license certificates serially numbered and signed by officials of the Central Executive Committee.	Resolution of April 3, 1918	Identified and located law abiding firearm owners and users.
Exceptions to licensing requirements for persons holding certificates issued by the secret police.	Resolution of April 27, 1918	Government officials and Communist Party members could possess arms with less risk of punishment.
Confiscation of weapons from persons not holding valid license certificates.	Resolution of April 27, 1918	Empowered local authorities to disarm unlicensed persons.
Revision of certificate format, requiring relicensing of all firearms owners and users.	Resolution of August 17, 1918	Old certificates must be exchanged for new; only Party members could obtain new certificates; certificates bear an expiration date.
License certificates required for handguns, rifles and "edged weapons" (knives and swords).	Resolution of August 17, 1918	Identified and located all law abiding persons who possessed weapons; records types of weapons.
Penalties imposed on local officials who fail to verify the new certificates and expiration dates.	Resolution of August 17, 1918	Encouraged local enforcement of law.
Nationwide confiscation of all privately-held firearms (working or not), all ammunition and all "sabres."	Decree of December 10, 1918, item 1.	Persons holding license certificates now lost their firearms, unless they fit into an exception.
Severe criminal penalties for "opposition" to the confiscation program, and for delay or failure to surrender weapons.	Decree of December 10, 1918, item 11.	Prison terms of 1 to 10 years were imposed on persons who resisted weapons confiscation.
Severe criminal penalties imposed on local officials for opposing the confiscation, or for any negligence in collecting the weapons.	Decree of December 10, 1918, item 13.	Fear of penalties strongly motivated local officials to enforce the law, even against popular sentiment.
Rewards payable to citizens who discover weapons not turned in; double rewards for machine guns found.	Decree of December 10, 1918, item 12.	Enlisted support of citizens to report others to authorities; increased incentives to turn in firearms.

Table 14B (continued)
Elements of Citizen Disarmament Policies in the USSR

Type of Law	Reference & Date	Effect
Communist Party members, who receive approval, may retain their firearms (one rifle and one handgun maximum).	Instruction issued with December 10 Decree,	Exception for approved members of the government and military.
All confiscated firearms turned over to the military.	December 10 Decree, (above) Item 8.	Helped stock army with small arms.
Possession of firearms limited to military and authorized Party members.	Decree on the Issuing, Keeping & Handling of Firearms, July 12, 1920, section 1.	Reaffirmed existing "gun control" policy.
Absolute prohibition on allowing an unauthorized person to hold, use or store firearms for any period of time.	<same as above, section 3.>	"Zero tolerance" for unauthorized firearms possession.
Criminal penalties for "illegal possession" or "negligent handling" of firearms.	<same as above, section 4.>	Punishment for violating "gun control" laws; punishment of gun users for accidents caused by others.
Criminal penalties for issuing a firearm to an untrained person, when that person causes an accident with the firearm.	<same as above, section 6.>	Officials held personally liable for gun accidents and failing to ascertain the training background of gun users.
Duty of secret police to enforce the "gun control" laws.	<same as above, section 7.>	National law enforcement officers responsible for "gun control."
Secret police empowered to arrest and punish violators of the Decree.	<same as above, section 7.>	National law enforcement officers were prosecutors, judges and executioners in "gun control" matters.
Stealing of firearms, parts, or ammunition punishable by imprisonment or death.	Article 59 (3-a) and Article 182 of the Soviet Penal Code (1926)	Empowered authorities to impose prison or death sentence to enforce "gun control."

Eyewitnesses to Genocide:
Watching the Children Die

• Soviet collectivization spared no victims. Children living in farming communities suffered long and died slowly. One observer said the children looked like prisoners in Nazi death camps: "their heads like heavy balls on thin little necks, like storks, and one could see each bone of their arms and legs protruding from beneath the skin ... the entire skeleton was stretched over with skin that was like yellow gauze. And the children's faces were aged, tormented, just as if they were seventy years old."[72]

• Observers collected and published stories from children caught in the government starvation plan. One seven-year old boy reported that after his father died, his mother became bloated and couldn't move; she sent him away to fend for himself. Two other boys, just eight years old, had witnessed their parents become physically helpless or die ... the boys became homeless wanderers in search of food.[73]

• Dead and dying mothers and babies were the fruit of Soviet social planning: "Sometimes the mother would wander off with her last baby. There are many stories of mother and infant lying dead in the road or in a city street; others of a dead woman with a still living infant at her breast."[74]

• Starvation drove some parents in farm areas to give up their children to state-run orphanages. Some orphanages became death camps. When the Soviet-planned famine deepened, the orphanages became overcrowded. At one such orphanage, excess children reportedly were "transferred to a 'children's town' where they could ostensibly live 'under the open sky.' They got nothing to eat and starved to death away from the public eye, their deaths being listed as caused by a weakness of the nervous system." People outside the camp could hear "frightening inhuman cries" emanating from behind the walls. At night, trucks reportedly hauled away the bodies of dead children. The death toll overtaxed even the cemetery facilities: "The burial pits would be filled so high and covered so poorly that dogs and wolves would partly dig the bodies up."[75]

End Notes

1Roberts, Paul Craig and Karen LaFollette. 1990. *Meltdown: Inside the Soviet Economy*. Washington, D.C.: Cato Institute, pp. 75-85.

2Simkin, Jay, Aaron Zelman, and Alan M. Rice. 1994. *Lethal Laws*. Milwaukee, WI: Jews for the Preservation of Firearms Ownership ("LL"), p. 96.

3LL, p. 97.

4LL, p. 95.

5LL, p. 97.

6LL, pp. 97-98.

7LL, pp. 106-107 (Russian original and English verbatim translation), recorded in the State Central Archives of the October Revolution, F. 1235, document no. 15; published in *Pravda* No. 68, April 10, 1918, and in *Izvestia*, No. 71, April 11, 1918.)

8LL, p. 107.

9LL, pp. 108-109 (Russian original and English verbatim translation); recorded in State Central Archives of the October Revolution, F. 1235, document no. 36; published in *Izvestia*, no. 88, May 3, 1918.

10LL, p. 98.

11LL, p. 112-113 (Russian and English verbatim translation); recorded in State Central Archives of the October Revolution, F. 1235, Document No. 27; published in *Izvestia*, no. 177, August 18, 1918.)

12LL, p. 98.

13LL, pp. 118-123 (Russian and English verbatim translation); published in Institute of History, Academy of Science. 1968. *Decrees of Soviet Power*, Vol. IV. Moscow: USSR Publishing House for Political Literature, Moscow.

14LL, pp. 118-119, Decree, item 7.

15Ibid., Decree, item 10.

16Ibid., Decree, item 2.

17Ibid., Decree, item 11.

18LL, pp. 120-121 (Russian and English verbatim translation); Central Party Archives, F. 2, Document no. 7714, Collection of Laws, 1918, No. 93, p. 933; published in *Izvestia*, No. 272, December 12, 1918.

19LL, p. 121, Dec. 10 Decree, item 4.

20Ibid., Dec. 10 Decree item 13.

21Ibid., Dec. 10 Decree, item 11.

22Ibid., Dec. 10 Decree, item 12.

23LL, pp. 124-25 (Russian and English verbatim translation); Instruction, item 1.

24Ibid.

25LL, p. 98.

[26]LL, pp. 128-131 (Russian and English verbatim translation); recorded in the Central Party Archives, F.2, Document No. 14660; published in Collection of Laws, No. 69, p. 314, and *Izvestia*, No. 160, July 22, 1920.

[27]LL, pp. 128-29 (grammatical error in source).

[28]LL, pp. 130-31.

[29]Blackstone, William. *Commentaries*, vol. 4, ch. 27, p. 358; *Estelle v. Williams*, 425 U.S. 501, 503 (1976) (the "presumption of innocence, although not articulated in the Constitution, is a basic component of a fair trial under our system of criminal justice"); Weinstein, Martin A. 1988. *Summary of American Law.* Rochester, NY: Lawyers Co-operative Publishing Co., p. 179..

[30]LL, pp. 130-31.

[31]Ibid., pp. 130-131.

[32]Ibid., p. 98.

[33]Ibid., p. 98.

[34]Ibid., p. 101.

[35]Ibid.

[36]Ibid., pp. 144-45.

[37]Ibid., pp. 144-45.

[38]Thid., p. 99.

[39]Conquest, Robert. 1990. *The Great Terror: A Reassessment.* New York: Oxford University Press, p. 14.

[40]LL, pp. 99, 101.

[41]LL, p. 99.

[42]LL, p. 100.

[43]This program is also known as "dekulakization." Conquest, Robert. 1986. *The Harvest of Sorrow: Soviet Collectivization and the Terror-Famine,* New York: Oxford University Press, pp. 3-4.

[44]LL, p. 102, citing Ulam, Adam. 1974. *Stalin.* London: Allen Lane, pp. 324-25.

[45]LL, p. 102.

[46]Conquest 1986, p. 4.

[47]LL, p. 102, citing Ulam 1974, p. 346.

[48]LL, p. 102, citing Conquest 1990, p. 20; see Rummel, R.J. 1996. *Death by Government.* New Brunswick, NJ: Transaction Publishers, p. 83, table 4.1.

[49]Conquest, Robert. 2000. *Reflections on a Ravaged Century.* New York: W.W. Norton & Company, p. 94.

[50]Ibid.

[51]Ibid.

[52]Conquest 1986, p. 233, quoting eyewitness source.

[53]LL, p. 102.

54Ibid.

55Ibid.

56Ibid.

57Conquest 1986, p. 260, quoting eyewitness source.

58LL, p.102.

59Ibid., p. 103.

60Conquest 1990, p. 67.

61Ibid., p. 67.

62LL, p. 103.

63Ibid.

64Rummel 1996, pp. 80-81.

65LL, p. 103.

66LL, p. 103, citing Conquest 1990, p. 289.

67LL, p. 102; Rummel 1996, p. 83, table 4.1.

68Rummel 1996, p. 79.

69Conquest 1986, p. 154.

70Ibid., pp. 154-55.

71Rummel 1996, p. 83, table 4.1.

72Conquest 1986, p. 286, quoting eyewitness source.

73Ibid., p. 287.

74Ibid.

75Ibid., p. 291.

Oppressors Must Disarm
Their Victims

°

Chapter Fifteen:
Zimbabwe: None So Blind

The history of the Twentieth Century repeatedly proved this formula:

Hatred + Government + Disarmed Civilians = Genocide

At the cost of at least 60,000,000 civilian deaths, humankind should have learned the lesson. Yet the standard textbooks on government and political science scarcely refer to any genocide (except the Nazi holocaust), and none seem to suggest the Genocide Formula. Professor Rummel observed in 1996 that "library stacks have been written on the possible nature and consequences of nuclear war" but perhaps one book had been written about the very real fact of government megamurder.[1] Rummel further noted "in virtually no index to any general book on politics and government will one find a reference to genocide, murder, killed, dead, executed, or massacre. Such is not even usually indexed in books on the Soviet Union or China."[2]

Educated people should be able to spot the warning signs of genocide a mile a way. The vast majority cannot. Many people cannot see a pattern of government persecution even if they are the victims.

Zimbabwe is mixing the formula for genocide as this book is written. The victims barely see how potentially dangerous their situation has become.

Government-Sponsored Land Invasions

After a civil war that ended in 1980, the African-ruled nation of Zimbabwe was established from the former British colony of

Rhodesia. Many of the nation's farmers were white descendants of British settlers. While most of the whites were native-born, they formed a small minority in the country. In the late 1990's, Zimbabwe's President Robert Mugabe proposed a "land redistribution" plan, by which Great Britain would pay white farmers to give up their farms to black citizens.

The British government did not fulfill Mugabe's expectations. In November, 1999, Mugabe announced: "We want to warn the British that the future might see the people of Zimbabwe lose their patience and therefore seize land on their own."[3]

Mugabe sought a new constitution for Zimbabwe that would have allowed the government to seize land without paying compensation. A referendum of Zimbabwean voters defeated the proposed new constitution in February 2000. Thousands of "squatters" started, on February 28, 2000, to invade mostly white-owned farms. As the farm invasions broke out in all regions of Zimbabwe, observers believed that central government authorities were orchestrating the attacks.[5]

Mobs of self-styled "war veterans," many too young to have fought in the battles for independence from Britain, would crowd onto properties, announce that they were taking the farm, and blockade the owners inside their homes or demand that they leave. Farm laborers were threatened with death unless they stopped working.[6] By March 3, 2000, 70 farms had been occupied.

The farm invaders have not been peaceful. Early reports told of crowds surrounding homes, chanting, cutting down trees, tearing up crops, and threatening violence. One farmer reported a mob of 300 people armed with sticks and axes. An elderly white couple was beaten. Squatters, armed with knives, clubs, spears and guns, in April, 2000, sealed off for several days the home of one farmer, J.J. Hammond, demanding that he give up ownership of his property and leave in seven days.[7]

By April 8, squatters had seized and occupied 975 farm properties. Just hours after a brutal attack on a husband and wife by squatters, President Mugabe publicly encouraged the farm invasions, saying: "Those who have invaded the farms, they are going to stay. I support them. We will not remove them."[8]

Things only got worse. By June, 2000, over 1,200 farms had been invaded. Human rights observers had documented over 5,078 incidents of political violence against opponents of Mugabe's ruling party. At least 19 farm owners, farm workers and other opposition party supporters had been murdered. At least 417 houses and properties had been destroyed.[9]

No Defense Of Victims

While the threats, killings and destruction were on-going, police officers frequently did nothing.[10] President Mugabe, in an April 7 speech, blamed the farmers for the violence: "We appeal for the farmers to be reasonable... Let there be no clashes between them and the war veterans. There have been some cases of violence, but many of these have been due to resistance by the farmers."[11] In short, the victims deserve the blame for failing to surrender their homes and lands to armed mobs.

By July 8, it became clear that the Zimbabwean police and army were part of the invasion campaign. Some 1,684 properties had been invaded, while the government in many cases had transported, fed and paid the squatters. In some cases, Zimbabwean police and army troops actually conducted the invasion and occupation of farm properties.[12]

Genocide Formula In Place

All of the factors needed to support a genocide were falling into place by mid-2000. The first factor, Hatred, is plainly evident. Stemming from long resentment of British colonial rule, many black Zimbabweans could simply hate white people enough to want to take their property and expel or kill them. Reacting to the white farmers' resistance to the government's land grab, President Mugabe echoed racial themes when he said he would "declare the fight to be on... The white man has not changed."

The Hatred element also crops up as fierce envy of land owners, white and black. Mugabe has publicly declared: "Farmers are enemies of the state!"[13]

The second factor, Government, has been a major source of the persecution of farmers. President Mugabe and his ruling party have long favored "land redistribution," which means taking land from existing owners and giving it to others. Mugabe offered a constitutional amendment by which the government could seize land without compensating owners. When the amendment failed to pass, the government covertly sponsored and supported mobs of "war veterans" to seize the land by force.[14] The Zimbabwe National Army actively supplied food, vehicles and some 21,000 fully automatic AK-47 rifles to soldiers and squatters engaging in attacking and occupying farms.[15]

When pro-Mugabe thugs attacked a peaceful march by opposition party supporters on March 1, the police did nothing. A police inspector was reportedly asked whether "it was the role of the police to protect all Zimbabweans?" The inspector answered, "No, we are here to protect the interests of the government."[16]

In practice, there has been no equal protection under the law. Zimbabwe's highest court ruled that the farm invasions were illegal. Zimbabwean judges have ordered police to remove squatters, but the police ignored those orders.[17] The police became an arm of the executive branch, not a servant of the law nor a protector of the people.

"Gun control" then rapidly became the pivotal third factor. Farm invaders often managed to overwhelm farmers by sheer force of numbers, but some farmers were armed and could resist. Whether the victim was armed made the difference in many cases.

Kidnap-Murder

April 15, 2000:   On the second day of their siege of Dave Stevens' farm, the gang of land invaders got inside his home and kidnaped him. Stevens, father of four (including two-year-old twins) was driven in his own car to a town and murdered in an alleyway by the kidnappers. Five other farmers tried to rescue Stevens, but came under fire and retreated to a police building. Several policeman passively watched when the invaders broke in, took the men away at gun point and beat them. The gang forced two of the farmers to lie blindfolded under Stevens' corpse on the floor of a pickup truck, and transferred them to other vehicles, and abandoned them on a country road. After finally managing to untie themselves, the two men walked barefoot about 10 miles to a farm, and eventually were taken to a hospital.

Government-run radio reported that Stevens had shot and wounded some of the land invaders, but other farmers denied that claim. When a television crew tried to visit Stevens' farm, where several buildings including farm workers' quarters had been burned down, squatters threw spears and stones to drive them away.

Forty other farming families in the vicinity fled their homes to stay with friends far from the scene of the kidnaping and violence. Many planned to stay away until they were assured of their safety. Meanwhile their properties lay deserted at the mercy of the mobs.[18]

Odds: 70 to 1 Against

April 18, 2000: An hour before dawn, 70 armed men in cars and trucks invaded the farm owned by Martin Olds. The invaders held Olds' staff personnel at gun point, and eventually shooting erupted. Olds' polio-stricken wife and his two teenage children were not there, so he fought alone. Barricaded in his home and returning fire, Olds was hit in the leg. He splinted the leg with planks and fought on. The invaders set his house on fire to burn him out, but Olds continued to defend himself and his home as bullets flew through the windows and peppered the walls with holes.

Unlike the vast majority of white farmers who had given up their lands and livelihoods to squatters without resisting, Olds had previously told police that he would shoot anyone who tried to take his land and property.

Martin Olds was tough. A former elite militiaman and nationally-recognized karate expert, he had received an award from President Mugabe for bravery when he dived into the Zambezi River to rescue a young girl from a crocodile.[19]

Despite being wounded, Olds used his shotgun and rifle to hold off the mob for over three hours. Olds had called police for help, but the police not only ignored his call — the police prevented the ambulance from reaching him. When he ran out of ammunition, the invaders overwhelmed his position and riddled him with bullets at point blank range.

Shortly after this incident, the police campaign to disarm farmers began in earnest. One observer noted: "it became clear that the official goal was to render the victims defenceless even as the criminals were being armed."[20]

Waiting For The Mobs

April 18, 2000: Peter Robart-Morgan bucked the trend of surrender to return to his farm property after the kidnap-murder of his close friend, David Stevens. Robart-Morgan and his wife drove past the squatters camp to re-enter their property, prepared to defend it by force if necessary. The farm house is protected by razor wire, and Robart-Morgan won't travel even the short distance to his barns without securing the gates around the house. Inside the home is a well-stocked gun cabinet, although neither of the them carries a sidearm. "It's not my style," remarked Robart-Morgan, "but the mobs should know I will defend my home with my life."

The couple carries walkie-talkies with them at all times, however. The radios provide their only emergency link to neighbors 40 miles away. Farm families formerly living nearby had fled the violence, and they could get no assurances that the police would safeguard their return to their homes.

The Robart-Morgans's 6,000 acres of land includes the homes of some 100 farm worker families. The couple returned to help protect the workers from intimidation and violence from squatters. Everyone on the farm lives in fear of an attack at any time.[21]

The Nationwide Gun Search

The violence between squatters and farm owners, and the claim that farmers were trying to sabotage the nation's economy and overthrow the government, provided the pretext for the Mugabe government to search every farm property in Zimbabwe for firearms. In April 2000, squads of up to 20 police entered farm properties to search for weapons. Zimbabwe's Information Minister confirmed that police had orders to search all 4,000 white-owned farms for unlicensed firearms, ammunition, stockpiles of diesel fuel, and evidence of para-military training facilities.[22]

The Information Minister, Mr. Chimutengwende, reportedly said: "There is so much military activity on farms. So many white farmers have applied for licenses to train security guards. But we now know that this is for military purposes and it includes firearms training. They have many unlicensed weapons."[23]

Farmers reported that the searches were so detailed that "every single inch of the farmhouse was searched."[24] The national firearms licensing system gave police a list of firearms owners, so the searches included a check of licensed firearms as well.

As one observed noted: "Instead of protecting lives and property, with farm invasions and widespread violence increasing throughout Zimbabwe, the police had added to the harassment — turning to systematic searches of targeted farms to confiscate any 'illegal weapons' from the besieged farmers, their only means of protection."[25]

Using the government's firearms search program as a justification, some squatters invaded farm properties especially to disarm farmers. The invaders would raid farms and homes, remove all the guns they could find, and then turn the guns over to the police.[26] Firearms confiscation assured the squatters that they would encounter little homeowner resistance if they chose to invade.

Zimbabwe's "Gun Control" Laws

Zimbabwe maintains a comprehensive "gun control" law, first enacted in 1956, and known as the Firearms Act.[27] The laws are summarized below in Table 15A. Briefly stated, the Firearms Act:

- Forbids a person from possessing for any reason a firearm or ammunition without a firearms certificate.
- Forbids a person from possessing more ammunition for a lawfully owned firearm than is allowed by the certificate.
- Authorizes government officials to deny an application for a firearms certificate if the applicant doesn't have a "good reason" to have a firearm (or ammunition).
- Authorizes government officials to revoke a firearm owner's certificate when the owner becomes "intemperate" or no longer has a "good reason" to have the firearm.
- Authorizes police to demand to inspect firearms, ammunition, and certificates at any time.
- Allows only government employees to possess fully automatic firearms.
- Holds firearms owner criminally responsible for the loss or

theft of firearms, unless owner can prove innocence.

- Punishes any infraction of the Firearms Act, however technical, as a crime.
- Allows police to conduct weapons searches, with or without warrants, and to confiscate all firearms and ammunition from any person or place where the officer believes a violation of the Firearms Act has occurred or will occur.
- Authorizes police officers to request, and magistrates to grant such requests, to destroy any firearms seized by the police during a search.

Question: Which provisions of the Firearms Act protect law-abiding Zimbabwean property owners and their families from land invaders who attack with the approval of the national government?

Table 15A
Summary of Key Provisions of Zimbabwe Firearms Act

Firearms Act	Language / Effect of Statute	Penalty
§ 3	All firearms and ammunition are regulated by this Act. All air-powered guns over .177 caliber are regulated as firearms by this Act (by order of Minister of Home Affairs, Declaration of Specially Dangerous firearms Notice, 1998)	
§ 4 (1-3)	Unlawful to buy, acquire or possess any firearm or ammunition without a valid firearm certificate.	Fine and/or imprisonment of 5 years (min) to 10 years (or more).
§ 4 (4)	Unlawful to buy, acquire or possess any ammunition for any firearm unless a certificate is held for that firearm. Also, unlawful to buy, acquire or possess more ammunition than is specified on the firearms certificate.	Fine and/or imprisonment up to 1 year.
§ 5 (2)	Government official grants a firearm certificate if the applicant has "good reason" for buying or possessing firearm or ammunition, so long as the applicant's possession of them poses no "danger to the public safety or to the peace."	

Table 15A (continued)
Summary of Key Provisions of Zimbabwe Firearms Act

Firearms Act	Language / Effect of Statute	Penalty
§ 5 (3-5)	One certificate per firearm, valid for three years, renewable unless revoked. Applicant must present firearm for inspection and testing if requested.	
§ 5 (8)	Government official may revoke firearm certificate if owner "is of intemperate habits or of unsound mind or is otherwise unfitted to be entrusted with the firearm" or "no longer has a good reason for possessing that firearm."	
§ 6	Certificate holder must notify government official of any change of address and any "material" change in occupation, within 21 days of change.	Fine and/or imprisonment up to 6 months.
§ 10	Prohibition of manufacturing ammunition without government license or outside of the limits of that license. (License may be revoked at any time by government official "if he thinks fit" to do so.)	Fine and/or imprisonment up to 5 years.
§ 11	Prohibition of manufacturing firearms without government license or outside of the limits of that license. (License may be revoked at any time by government official "if he thinks fit" to do so.)	Fine and/or imprisonment up to 5 years.
§ 12	"Any police officer may demand" to know the identity and to inspect the firearm certificate "from any person whom he believes to be in possession of a firearm or ammunition."	Failure to produce certificate in 7 days, officer may seize firearm or ammunition.
§ 13	Any police officer may demand that firearm certificate holder produce his firearms or ammunition for inspection, at any time set by the officer.	Failure to comply results in fine.
§ 18 (1)	May not sell or give a firearm or ammunition to any person lacking a firearm certificate or other legal authorization.	Fine and/or imprisonment up to 2 years.
§ 18 (2)	Every person who sells, gives or lends a firearm to any person other than a firearms dealer or proper certificate holder, must report the transaction to government officials by registered mail.	Fine and/or imprisonment up to 2 years.
§ 19	Firearms dealers must maintain register of all firearms and ammunition transactions. Dealers must allow any police officer to enter the premises and inspect all stock and the transaction register. Dealers who cease business must turn over register to government official.	Fine and/or imprisonment up to 5 years.

Table 15A (continued)
Summary of Key Provisions of Zimbabwe Firearms Act

Firearms Act	Language / Effect of Statute	Penalty
§ 24 (1)	Only those "in the service of the state" or expressly authorized by the government may possess or conduct any transaction involving a fully automatic firearm or ammunition for same. All others are forbidden.	Fine and/or imprisonment up to 5 years.
§ 28	Persons possessing firearms and ammunition must take "reasonable" precautions to ensure that these are not lost, stolen, or accessed by unauthorized persons. Burden lies with firearms owner to prove that precautions were reasonable.	Fine and/or imprisonment up to 1 year.
§ 29	Any person having a firearm or ammunition, with or without certificate or other legal authorization to possess firearms, must report to the nearest police station within 24 hours of when the firearm or ammunition is lost, stolen or destroyed.	Fine and/or imprisonment up to 2 years.
§ 31	Court that convicts a person of any offense under the Firearms Act may order forfeiture of any or all firearms or ammunition possessed by that person, and may cancel any or all firearms certificates of that person.	
§ 32(1-2)	On "reasonable grounds" supported by information given under oath, a magistrate or justice of the peace may grant a search warrant to police to search (by force if necessary) any place named in the warrant, and to search every place and every person in that place.	
§ 32(2-3)	Police may seize, detain and obtain permission to destroy any firearms found by an officer during a search, if the officer suspects that any violation of the Firearms Act has been or will be committed with that firearm or ammunition.	
§ 34	"Any police officer…or…any other person authorized by the [government]…may at any time enter and inspect any premises used for: (a) the storage of ammunition or firearms." (No warrant required.)	
§ 35	All persons must give to police all information they have about the manufacture, location and storage of firearms or ammunition, and must not in any way obstruct police in collecting this information.	Fine and/or imprisonment up to 6 months.

Table 15A (continued)
Summary of Key Provisions of Zimbabwe Firearms Act

Firearms Act	Language / Effect of Statute	Penalty
§ 37	All firearms certificates and permits will be maintained by the police in a centralized government file.	
§ 42	The Firearms Act does not apply to "the State." Government employees may possess firearms or ammunition only as authorized by the State.	

Victims Bewildered by Falling Dominoes of Persecution

Reports streaming out of Zimbabwe between 1999 and 2001 showed the government's attitude toward the farmers: that the farmers' land should be taken without compensation, that the farmers were economically draining the economy and the cause of the nation's ills. President Mugabe authorized and then openly encouraged squatters to do with private force what his government had wanted to do by confiscation laws: take the farm lands and drive off the farmers.

When the farm invasions began in February 2000, the government, army and police did next to nothing to prevent or stop the attacks and violence against farmers. Meanwhile, due to previously enacted "gun control" laws, the government knew where licensed guns were kept and who had them. A nationwide firearms license check and confiscation program started just after some farmers tried to defend their properties and lives by force of arms.

"It's like the beginnings of genocide"

The Genocide Formula was playing out against the farmers of Zimbabwe. Consider these statements (below) showing the fear and confusion of the victims, and then ask yourself: Were these people educated enough about the warning signs of genocide? Would these people have benefitted from understanding the Genocide Formula?

- A leader of the Commercial Farmers Union described the farm invasions in February, 2000: "It's breaking out in all regions.

It's clearly orchestrated by a central authority. We're having difficulty getting the authorities to react."[28]

- One farmer stated, in April 2000, that before the squatters murdered one of his neighbors, he had "never felt so close to black Zimbabweans since independence. Mugabe is trying to split us up ahead of the elections. But we have never felt so close. We feel left out as whites. No one, but no one, supports Mugabe down here. They remember the massacres of the 1980's, they are scared and they won't say anything, but they remember."[29]

- Commenting upon the reported attack and brutal beating of two elderly farm owners, one woman remarked: "Mugabe is so unstable that it really worries me. He could just wake up in the morning and decide to ethnically cleanse us. I'm not leaving — we just have to remain determined and see this through — but this man is just so frightening." Another farmer said: "We [farmers] care about this country, but look what he [Mugabe] says about us."[30]

- After learning that the local police did nothing to intervene in the kidnaping and murder of one farmer or to stop the beatings of several other farmers in April, 2000, the president of the Commercial Farmers Union said: "This has been our biggest fear all along. When you are outside the rule of law, the danger every minute is very great." Farmers in the area were reportedly "pinning their hopes on the army, which they regard as more credible than the police."[31]

- Hearing the reports of a farmer attacked and killed by squatters in April, 2000, one farmer said:"How many more of us are going to die before Zimbabwe pulls itself back from the brink?"[32]

- Referring to the police campaign to inspect all firearms licenses and confiscate "illegal" firearms, one farmer observed: "It is psychological action. It is harassment of the citizenry, giving us one hassle after another." Another stated: "I'm so sad that they have to use us all as scapegoats. It's almost like the beginnings of genocide."[33]

The Lesson of Zimbabwe: Minorities who fail to prepare for self-defense against their own government are easy targets of the Genocide Formula.

A good government will never try to render its citizens defenseless — an evil government always will.

South Africa Smoldering

Press coverage of the Zimbabwe land invasions and related violence has been scant in the United States. Moral outrage at the persecution has been virtually non-existent. Yet in South Africa, farmers have been suffering violence and murders for a decade.

According to Agri South Africa, the South African farmers' union, there have been over 4,241 attacks against farmers since 1991. The union counted at least 618 farmers who have been killed between 1994 and the year 2000. Other observers estimate more than 1,000 farmers killed, and that many violent attacks go uncounted.

In recent years, the South African government, like the Mugabe regime in Zimbabwe, has been planning "land redistribution" schemes. South African farmers see the parallels in Zimbabwe and fear their land will be forcibly taken. The long-term history of violence against farmers is viewed by many as politically motivated to intimidate the farmers. As one observer noted: "The South African feelings at the moment — every farmer you speak to — they're waiting for something to happen."[34]

As if planning for genocide, the government of South Africa in 1999 proposed "anti-gun" legislation that would outlaw 90% of legally-owned firearms. Under this victim disarmament proposal, all of the 2.5 million licensed gun owners would be required to reapply for their licenses. In addition,

• All applicants would be screened and have to undergo psychometric testing; any applicant having a domestic violence conviction or any "inclination" toward violence would be disqualified.

• License fees would be increased by a factor of 10.

• Licenses for handguns would be limited to one (1) per person.

• License holders would be limited to possessing only 100 rounds of ammunition.[35]

Imagining the victim disarming effects of this proposed "gun control" scheme brings to mind the story of Martin Olds. Mr. Olds was the Zimbabwean farmer who was killed by an armed mob when he ran out of ammunition to defend his home. Given the history of violence and murder of farmers in South Africa, this "gun control" proposal's limits on numbers of guns and ammunition diabolically work against the lonely defender who faces attacks by gangs. If the South African government turns hostile to the farmers, as did that of Zimbabwe, then the underpowered defenders will have no hope at all. The comprehensive licensing system will provide the road map for gun confiscation as well.

End Notes

[1]Rummel, R.J. 1996. *Death by Government*. New Brunswick, NJ: Transaction Publishers, p. 26.

[2]Ibid., p. 27.

[3]Blair, David. 1999. Mugabe warning over farms. *Electronic Telegraph*. Nov. 22. (www.telegraph.co.uk).

[4]Blair, David. 2000. Mugabe moves nearer to seizing whites' land. *Electronic Telegraph*. Jan. 21. (www.telegraph.co.uk)

[5]Blair, David. 2000. Farmers blame Mugabe for squatter invasion. *Electronic Telegraph*. Feb. 29. (www.telegraph.co.uk)

[6]Blair, David. 2000. White farms invaded as Mugabe ignores poll. *Electronic Telegraph*. March 3. (www.telegraph.co.uk)

[7]Zimbabwe ruling party approves seizure of white-owned land. *Seattletimes.com,* April 7, 2000. (www.seattletimes.com)

[8]Blair, David. 2000. Mugabe blames farmers for squatter violence. *Electronic Telegraph*. Apr. 8. (www.telegraph.co.uk)

[9]Hammond, Peter. 2000. Zimbabwe in ruins. *WorldNetDaily*. June 2. (www.worldnetdaily.com)

[10]Hammond, June 2, 2000; Blair, March 3, 2000.

[11]Mugabe Threatens to Takeover White Farmers' Land. UPI, April 8, 2000. Stored on www.newsmax.com.

[12]Blair, David. 2000. Police and army join in Zimbabwe farm occupation. *Electronic Telegraph*. July 8. (www.telegraph.co.uk)

[13]Hammond, June 2, 2000.

[14]Dougherty, Jon E. 2000. Mugabe's terror 'carefully orchestrated.' *WorldNetDaily*. May 16. (www.worldnetdaily.com)

[15]Muleya, Dumisani. 2000. Army steps up role in farm invasions. *Zimbabwe Independent Online.* May 5. (www.mweb.co.zw/zimin)

[16]Hammond, June 2, 2000.

[17]Ibid.

[18]Blair, April 17, 2000.

[19]Kiley. 2000. They wanted him out and wanted him dead. *London Times.* April 19. (www.sunday-times.co.uk)

[20]Hammond, June 2, 2000.

[21]McGrory, Daniel. 2000. Farmer defies mob at the gate to return home. *London Times.* April 19. (www.sunday-times.co.uk)

[22]Blair, David. 2000. Police search besieged farms for guns. *Electronic Telegraph.* April 18. (www.telegraph.co.uk)

[23]Ibid., quoting witness.

[24]Ibid., quoting witness.

[25]Hammond, June 2, 2000.

[26]Blair, Apr. 18, 2000.

[27]*Butterworths Statute Law of Zimbabwe.* Volume 1, Rev. ed. 1996, Chap. 10:09, pp. 769-779.

[28]Blair, Feb 29, 2000.

[29]Kiley, Apr. 19, 2000.

[30]Blair, Apr. 8, 2000.

[31]La Guardia, Anton & David Blair. 2000. Armed mob murders farmer. *Electronic Telegraph.* Apr. 17. (www.telegraph.co.uk)

[32]McGrory, Apr. 19, 2000.

[33]Blair, Apr. 18, 2000.

[34]Archer, Stephan. 2000. South Africa: Genocide Fears Raised. *Newsmax.com.* Jan. 25. (www.newsmax.com)

[35]Roberts, Bronwen. 1999. New law to outlaw 90% of legally owned guns. *Daily Mail & Guardian.* July 12. (www.mg.co.za))

Chapter Sixteen:
In America:
When a Race Is Disarmed

The experience of black people in America proves beyond a shadow of a doubt: *Armed oppressors have absolute power over unarmed victims.*

Some readers might dismiss this book's message by saying that the history of genocide and mass murder in other countries does not apply to America: "That's ancient history." "It can't happen here." "Our Constitution wouldn't allow it."

The facts say the opposite. Government-sponsored oppression did happen here on such an overwhelming scale that few modern Americans can even grasp it. Hundreds and thousands of books and articles and speeches have described every aspect of it. Perhaps Americans have heard about it too much, but understood the fundamental truths too little.

Certainly this book cannot possibly present all of the history and details of black slavery, racist terrorism, discriminatory laws and policies, and thousands of lynchings. One point, however, can and must be made: *because they were unarmed and undefended, black people in America suffered world-class oppression in America.*

Slavery in America

Millions of black people lived as slaves in America until 1865. In 1790, there were over 697,000 black slaves; by 1860 there were over 3.9 million.[1] In the South where slavery was legal and common, black slaves numbered about one-third of the total population. Three-quarters of the slave population lived on large farms and small plantations, where the number of slaves would be less than fifty, and where the owner and master was personally involved in directing their work.[2] In fact, by 1860, approximately 350,000 white families owned the roughly 4 million slaves — on average, the slaves outnumbered the white families by 10 to 1.[3]

Many slaves in America lived at a higher standard of living than did non-slaves in other parts of the world.[4] That fact does not change the basic immorality of owning human beings as property. Whatever their living conditions in economic terms, slaves were held captives, forced to work, and beaten, raped and brutalized in myriad ways.

Frederick Douglass, escaped slave and leader of the movement to abolish slavery, described the system of slavery:

> The law gives the master absolute power over the slave.
> He may work him, flog him, hire him out, sell him, and
> in certain instances, kill him, with perfect immunity.[5]

Slave Resistance

To control such a large number of slaves, either as a percentage of the population or in the groups on plantations, the slave masters had to be armed, and the slaves unarmed. Only because the masters had a virtual monopoly on physical force could slavery and brutality continue.

Force was needed especially because the slaves consistently worked against the system. Resistance to slavery appeared everywhere, and took these forms:[6]

- Playing ignorant, stupid, injured or lame
- Obtaining education in violation of rules
- Women (and their husbands) fighting masters' and overseers' attempts to force sexual favors
- Repeatedly disobeying orders, despite whippings
- Pilfering crops, food items and other property from owners
- Singing pro-freedom songs couched as religious hymns
- Slowing down or stopping work all at once
- Setting fire to woods and buildings
- Poisoning the masters' food
- Sabotaging farming and industrial equipment
- Planning, attempting, and succeeding in escapes
- Self-mutilation
- Suicide

Slavery in the American South was not a relaxed, carefree existence for any of the parties involved. Conspiracies and outright rebellion against slavery occurred often enough to impel state and local governments in slave states to deploy slave patrols, forbid meetings of black people, forbid free black people from entering the state, and forbid importation of slaves from places where revolts might be expected.[7]

William Loren Katz, author, examined the realities of slave rebellion:

> By the nineteenth century, slave holder power rested on thousands of well-trained troops and command of communication and transportation. Slaves began with few weapons, no military training, and perhaps a hope of seizing an enemy arsenal. They had no experience with guns, no way to practice being an army, and few places to hide once the militia appeared.[8]

Slaves with Guns

Which slave rebellions most terrified the slave owning society? The rebellions where the rebels had the magic ingredient: *firearms.*

In the Stono Rebellion of 1739, about 20 blacks seized a warehouse of guns and ammunition in South Carolina. Thus armed, they attacked and killed a number of whites and destroyed several houses, tried to rally other slaves to join them, and began a march that ended only after a pitched battle with government forces.[9]

Starting with six slave men, Nat Turner in 1831 started a rebellion aimed at conquering Southampton County, Virginia. Organized with a plan, the small band stealthily went from house to house, killing all whites and gathering slaves into their team. Over 50 white people were killed, most of them having had no chance to defend themselves. The rebels gathered weapons, ammunition and money from each house, until they numbered nearly 60 armed men. When a party of 18 armed white men surprised the rebels and commenced firing, the rebels returned fire, injuring several and chasing the whites away. Only when another white party arrived to join the fight did the slave rebels scatter.

Many of the slave rebels were caught, tried and executed, including the leader, Nat Turner.[10] Because of this rebellion, laws restricting slaves were further strengthened, e.g., prescribing the death penalty for inciting insurrection and criminal penalties for teaching slaves to read and write.[11]

Most dramatic was the 1791 armed revolution in the French Caribbean island of San Domingo (now called Hispaniola) where 80% of the population was enslaved under harsh conditions. Massive slave revolts in that year, with fearful atrocities committed by both sides, spelled the end of slavery by the following year.

A former slave, Toussaint L'Ouverture, commanded the army and formed a new government in San Domingo. His army of former slaves repulsed Spanish and British invasions. Napoleon rejected the new government's constitution in 1801, however, and sent large forces to restore direct French rule in the island. L'Ouverture was captured, but his successors continued the war and defeated the French in 1803.[12]

The San Domingo slave revolution worried U.S. slave owners because it could have inspired American blacks to likewise revolt. If armed former slaves could defeat Napoleon's armies, then what would happen if American blacks got the inspiration — and the firearms?

"Gun Control" – The Racists' Solution

Before slavery in the United States was permanently ended in 1865, white-run governments had enacted many "gun control" laws that heavily restricted or prohibited black people from owning firearms. The fear of slave uprisings was enough reason to motivate the governments to disarm black slaves, but there were many free blacks living in slaveholding states. Professors Robert Cottrol and Raymond T. Diamond have explained why free blacks were targeted:

> The threat that free blacks posed to southern slavery was twofold. First, free blacks were a bad example to slaves. For a slave to see free blacks enjoy the trappings of white persons — freedom of movement, expression, and association, relative freedom from fear for one's person and one's family, and freedom to own the fruits of one's labor — was to offer hope and raise desire for that which the system could not produce....[A] slave with visions of freedom threatened rebellion.[13]

The second "threat" was that free blacks would help slaves to rebel. Limiting the freedom of free blacks was a way to lessen the dangers. The various states passed laws to control free blacks, which:[14]

- limited how many could meet in a group
- restricted choices of employment
- limited trading and socializing with slaves
- allowed "patrols" to question, search and summarily punish free blacks
- restricted or prohibited possession of firearms.

To control the blacks in America, the governments tried many different approaches, but one method was always part of the plan: disarmament. After the Civil War and passage of the 13th, 14th and 15th Amendments, governments could no longer openly enslave black people — but they did try "gun control" to keep black people under control. Table 16A describes many of the "gun control" laws enacted in America, both before and after the Civil War, that worked to disarm blacks and other minorities.

Some state court judges have admitted the racial motivation for these "gun control" laws in the South. Discussing a Florida "gun control" statute, Judge Buford of the Florida Supreme Court in 1941 stated its purpose plainly:

> I know something of the history of this legislation. The original Act of 1893 was passed when there was a great influx of negro laborers in this State drawn here for the purpose of working in the turpentine and lumber camps. The same condition existed when the Act was amended in 1901 *and the Act was passed for the purpose of disarming the negro laborers* and to thereby reduce the unlawful homicides that were prevalent in turpentine and saw-mill camps and to give the white citizens in sparsely settled areas a better feeling of security. *The statute was never intended to be applied to the white population and in practice has never been so applied.*[15]

An Ohio Supreme Court judge also observed that "gun control" laws in Southern states had roots in the "race issue" and showed "a decisive purpose to entirely disarm the negro."[16] As the "gun control" laws in the South did not entirely prohibit firearms ownership, however, blacks sometimes were empowered to defend themselves against violence.

Table 16A: Racist Disarmament Laws[17]

Black persons excluded from militias
(United States, 1792)

Slaves cannot use any weapon, even in self-defense
(Louisiana, 1806, 1811)

Slaves cannot possess gun without master's permission
(So. Carolina, 1819)

White citizen patrols empowered to invade and search homes of any Black person — to look for and take any guns or other weapons
(Florida, 1825, 1831, 1847, 1861)

Black persons must have license to carry a firearm, or have a judge's approval
(Florida, 1825, 1828) (Delaware, 1831)

Guns banned — applies only to free Black persons
(Virginia, 1831) (Maryland 1831) (Georgia, 1833)
(No. Carolina, 1844) (Mississippi, 1852)

Guns banned — applies only to slaves
(Florida, 1840) (Texas, 1840) (No. Carolina, 1845)
(Mississippi, 1852)
(Georgia 1860)

Blacks must obtain gun licenses from local police
(Mississippi, 1865)
(Louisiana, 1865)

Total gun ban — applies to Black persons only
(Alabama, 1866)

Ban of all inexpensive handguns (the only kind that poor Black people could afford)
(Tennessee, 1870, 1879) (Arkansas, 1882) (Maryland, 1988)

Supreme Court rules that Federal gov't has no power to protect Black citizens against private (non-government) attacks on their rights
(United States, 1875)

High taxes on sale of handguns (to prevent poor Black persons from buying them)
(Alabama, 1893)
(Texas, 1907)

Ban of all handguns — except for police and their deputies
(So. Carolina, 1902)

Sellers of firearms required to keep records on buyers; the records included indication of the race of the buyer
(Mississippi, 1906)

Police control who can buy guns (permits frequently denied to minorities)
(New York, 1911)

Florida Supreme Court judge admits that gun control law aimed to disarm poor Black persons
(Florida, 1941)

Gun Control Act (passed "not to control guns but to control Blacks" after race riots in California, New Jersey, and Mississippi)
(United States, 1968)

Gun bans, warrantless searches of public housing, confiscation of firearms (effectively deprives poor people of right to possess firearms)
(Illinois, 1988) (Virginia, 1990)
(United States, 1994 [law not passed])
(Maine, 1995 [law struck down])

Bitter Fruit of "Gun Control:" Lynching:

The end of legal slavery did not end oppression of blacks in America. Immediately after the end of the Civil War, many of the formerly slave states enacted "black codes." These were laws that (1) required black farm workers to sign labor contracts requiring them to work for their employers for a year, (2) barred blacks from serving on juries, (3) prevented blacks from testifying against or suing whites in court, and (4) required blacks to have jobs and homes or face penalties ("vagrancy laws").[18] At the same time, these states imposed "gun control" laws on blacks only. (See Table 16A above) Roy Innis, National Chairman of the Congress of Racial Equality (CORE), noted: "The specter of a black man with the right of a freeman, bearing arms, was too much for the racist to bear."[19]

Although the earliest "black codes" were partially invalidated by the 14th Amendment and other federal laws, the Supreme Court restricted the federal government's power to enforce civil rights for black people.[20] The result Professors Cottrol and Diamond noted was "blacks would have to look to state government for protection against criminal conspiracies" and that "gave the green light to private forces, often with the assistance of state and local governments," to try to "subjugate the former slaves and their descendants."[21] Threats of violence intimidated blacks so that they would live and work as second class citizens without even the effective right to vote.[22]

State and local governments and officials, hostile to blacks, enforced laws that allowed public and private discrimination.[23] Worse still, the governments and their officials often did precious little to protect blacks from mobs, terrorism, and lynching.

Between 1882 and 1968, there were 3,446 black people lynched (i.e. killed unlawfully by mobs).[24] The typical case involved a group of armed white men seizing a black man (or sometimes a woman) on suspicion of committing an insult or a crime, and then killing the victim in a public and especially brutal way.

Victims would be beaten, sliced, dragged through the streets, shot, hanged or burned alive. In some lynchings, the victims would be mutilated also. Large crowds would sometimes form to watch and cheer.[25]

Sometimes the given "reasons" for lynchings included charges of real crimes such as arson, rape, theft, or murder. Far too often the victim was not guilty and had never had any benefit of due process. Other times victims were lynched for being too familiar with or talking to a white woman, hindering a lynch mob, failing to show "respect," or working to help get black people registered to vote. And sometimes there was no "reason" for the lynching at all — the mob apparently just felt like torturing and killing a black person.[26]

Why was it possible for lynchings to take place so frequently? Because generally black people were unarmed — due to their poverty, the laws that discouraged their having weapons, and their lack of community defense planning. Sometimes an individual target of a mob would be armed and able to hold off attackers for a time. In one case, before he was tortured and burned to death, an armed black man had held off the mob for hours until his ammunition ran out.[27]

Lynchings were common for another reason: the police frequently did not effectively protect many black people. Sometimes non-protection was deliberate policy: Senator Coleman L. Blease of South Carolina *bragged* in 1930 that, as governor of his state, he had not called out the state militia to protect blacks against mobs.[28] Other times the police or militia were too little or too late.[29]

What About the Second Amendment for Blacks?

The Second Amendment to the U.S. Constitution declares: "A well-regulated militia being necessary to the security of a free state, the right of the people to keep and bear arms shall not be infringed." Before the Civil War, black people were not considered citizens of the United States and thus the Second Amendment did not protect their rights.

After that War, slavery was abolished, the Fourteenth Amendment was adopted, and the Freedmen's Bureau laws were passed. The framers of the Amendment and laws had openly discussed their intention that freedmen (former black slaves) should have their Constitutional rights, including their right to keep and bear arms, protected against state government laws aimed at returning the blacks to a second-class, disarmed status.[30]

Rep. Thaddeus Stevens argued that the "rights, privileges and immunities" of citizens, as protected by the Fourteenth Amendment, should include all of the citizens' unalienable rights:

> What are those rights, privileges, and immunities? Without excluding others, three are specifically enumerated — life, liberty, and the pursuit of happiness... It follows that everything necessary for their establishment and defense is within those rights.... Disarm a community and you rob them of the means of defending life. Take away their weapons of defense and you take away the inalienable right of defending liberty.... The fourteenth amendment, now so happily adopted, settles the whole question.[31]

Enjoying their new freedom and exercising their rights, blacks in 1867 formed citizen militias in the District of Columbia for example. Public figures and newspaper editorials supported the right of blacks to do so, despite fears of an insurrection and legal moves to stop them.[32]

Not surprisingly, when several whites were charged with disarming and massacring blacks and thereby violating the blacks' Constitutional rights, the whites' lawyer argued to the U.S. Supreme Court that the Second Amendment protected the right to bear arms only "for the purpose of maintaining, in the states, a well-regulated militia."[33] Walking in the footsteps of racist killers, gun prohibition lobbyists still make the same argument about the "militia" clause of the Second Amendment today. Regrettably, several federal courts have agreed with that argument as well.[34]

Armed Defense Saves Lives

There have been scattered cases when a single armed person held off a lynching. In Columbia, South Carolina, in 1917, the jailer's 14-year-old daughter holding a revolver single-handedly held a mob at bay and protected a black prisoner for quite a while until her father returned to the jail.[35] More often, successfully stopping a lynch mob or terrorist attack required a group of armed citizens.[36]

For example, in 1891 a black militia unit guarded a jail in Memphis for several nights to protect 100 black prisoners who were at risk of lynching. When the threat seemed to have passed, the militia left — and a mob stormed the jail and lynched three of the prisoners. In many unpublicized cases, armed black men stood guard to ward off lynchers and deter other mob violence.[37]

During the period of the Civil Rights movement, the white supremacist Ku Klux Klan intimidated and terrorized black people and white civil rights workers all over the South. Klan-inspired and other racist violence flared, with attacks on civil rights demonstrators, riots, bombings and murders.[38] Armed volunteers were organized to defend civil rights workers, the most well-known being the Deacons for Defense and Justice.[39]

In 1965 the Deacons formed over 50 chapters in Louisiana, Mississippi and Alabama, to protect blacks and civil rights workers by force of arms. Because they promised to meet force with force, the Deacons successfully deterred terrorist attacks.[40] For this work many of the Deacons preferred to carry rifles.[41]

Defense work rarely required actual shooting. As one organizer of the Deacons put it, "The showing of a weapon stops many things. Everybody wants to live and nobody wants to die."[42] When this man became known as a Deacon, he was able to drive away harassers just by his *reputation for being armed:*

> "I didn't have to [brandish a firearm] — they know me. I showed my face. That was weapons enough. And they know whenever they see me, my gun and the Deacons are close."[43]

"Gun Control" is Race Control

The founder of the National Black Sportsman's Association, General Laney, gave his opinion of "gun control":

> Gun control is really race control. People who embrace gun control are really racists in nature. All gun laws have been enacted to control certain classes of people, mainly black people, but the same laws used to control blacks are being used to disarm white people as well.[44]

Robert Sherrill, a well-known journalist strongly opposed to widespread firearms ownership, angrily charged in 1973 that the federal Gun Control Act of 1968, being worthless to "control guns", was instead a reaction rooted in thinly-veiled racial fears:

> The Gun Control Act of 1968 was passed not to control guns but to control blacks, and inasmuch as a majority of Congress did not want to do the former but were ashamed to show that their goal was the latter, the result was that they did neither.[45]

Sherrill noted that after "the horrendous rioting of 1967 and 1968, Congress again was panicked toward passing some law that would shut off weapons access to blacks..."[46] The Gun Control Act of 1968 ("GCA 68") was supposed to be that law.

To fashion a law designed to "shut off" minority groups' access to weapons, what better example to use than the Nazi Weapons Law of 1938? Comparing the 1938 Nazi law (extending the reach of its predecessor, the 1928 "Law on Firearms and Ammunition") to GCA 68, the parallels between the laws stand out:

- similarities in firearms transaction record keeping and reporting,
- the delegation of authority to a bureaucrat to permit or restrict certain types of weapons and ammunition,
- the requirement that the buyer establish his qualifications to obtain a firearm,
- the concept of "sporting purpose" as a class of firearms.[47]

Who was instrumental in preparing and getting GCA 68 enacted? The late Senator Thomas Dodd, then Chairman of the Special Subcommittee to Investigate Juvenile Delinquency, and member of the Senate Judiciary Committee. According to a Senate document now publicly available, Senator Dodd asked the Library of Congress to deliver to him an English translation of the Nazi "Law on Weapons of March 18, 1938" at about the time the GCA 68 was being fashioned in Congress.[48] Senator Dodd had worked with prosecuting attorneys at the Nuremburg trials of Nazi leaders after World War II, and the evidence suggests that he possessed a German-language copy of the Nazi Weapons Law before he contacted the Library of Congress for the translation.

So it seems that American legislators in 1968 enacted a Nazi-like "gun control" law designed to disarm a feared minority group. Historical experience with the Genocide Formula proves that combining racial fears, powerful government, and civilian disarmament moves a nation closer to genocide.

Whether it was Divine Providence or the sturdy traditions of liberty and a democratically-elected government answerable to the people,[49] America was spared a massive persecution or race war in the late 1960's. If the federal government grows much stronger and the three elements of the Genocide Formula interplay once more, will America escape genocide again?

End Notes

[1]Foner, Eric and John A. Garraty, eds. 1991. *The Reader's Companion to American History*. Boston: Houghton Mifflin Co., p. 991.

[2]Ibid.

[3]Katz, William Loren. 1990. *Breaking the Chains: African-American Slave Resistance*. New York: Ethrac Publications, p. 20.)

[4]Reader's Companion, p. 991.

[5]Katz 1990, p. 19.

[6]See Katz 1990; and Bauer, Raymond A. and Alice H. Bauer. 1942. Day to Day Resistance to Slavery. *Journal of Negro History*. Vol 27, Oct. 1942, 388-419. Reprinted in Grant, Joanne, ed. 1968. *Black Protest: 350 Years of History, Documents and Analysis*. Second Edition. New York: Random House, p. 38.

[7]Wish, Harvey. 1937. American Slave Insurrections Before 1861. *Journal of Negro History*. Vol 22, July, pp. 229-320, reprinted in part in Grant 1968, p. 29)

[8]Katz 1990, p. 113.

[9]Katz 1990, p. 101; Grant 1968, pp. 30-31.

[10]Higginson, Thomas Wentworth. 1861. Nat Turner's Insurrection. *Atlantic Monthly*. Vol. 8., Aug., pp. 173-87, excerpted in Grant 1968, pp. 46-52.

[11]Grant 1968, pp.15-16.

[12]Katz 1990, pp. 104-107. (Today, the nations of Haiti and Santo Domingo divide the island.)

[13]Cottrol, Robert J. and Raymond T. Diamond. *The Second Amendment: Toward an Afro-Americanist Reconsideration*, 80 Georgetown L. J. 309, 335 (1991).

[14]Ibid., pp. 336-338 (citing sources).

[15]*Watson v. Stone*, 4 So. 2d 700, 703 (Fla. 1941)(concurring opinion of Judge Buford)(emphasis added).

[16]State v. Nieto, 130 N.E. 663, 669 (Ohio 1920)(dissenting opinion of Judge Wanamaker).

[17]Sources for chart: Cottrol, Robert J. and Raymond T. Diamond. 1991. The Second Amendment: Toward an Afro-Americanist Reconsideration. 80

Georgetown Law Journal. Vol 80, pp. 309, 331, 336-38, 344-46, 348, 354-55 (citing historical sources); Tahmassebi, Stefan. 1991. *Gun Control and Racism.* George Mason Univ. Civil Rights Journal. Vol. 2, pp. 67, 70, 74, 80, 97, 98; Funk, T. Markus. 1995. Gun Control and Economic Discrimination: The Melting-Point Case-in-Point. *Journal of Criminal Law & Criminology.* Vol 85, pp. 764, 797; Cramer, Clayton E. 1995. The Racist Roots of Gun Control. *Kansas Journal of Law & Public Policy.* Vol. 4 (Winter), p. 17; Tonso, William R. 1985. Gun Control: White Man's Law. *Reason.* (December), p. 23; Kates, Don B., Jr. (ed.). 1984. *Firearms and Violence: Issues of Public Policy.* Pacific Institute for Public Policy Research, pp. 459-60, 476-78, 482-85; *United States v. Harris,* 106 U.S. 629 (1882); *United States v. Cruikshank,* 92 U.S. 542, 548-49 (1875); *Watson v. Stone,* 4 So.2d 700, 703 (Fla. 1941)(concurring opinion of Justice Buford); *http://www.nra.org/crimestrike/csrace.html* (February 1998).

[18]Cottrol and Diamond 1991, p. 344.

[19]Innis, Roy. 1991. Bearing Arms for Self-Defense: A Human and Civil Right. *The Alliance Voice.* Sept., p. 18.

[20]Cottrol and Diamond 1991, p. 348.

[21]Ibid.

[22]Ibid.

[23]Ibid., pp. 349-350.

[24]Cottrol & Diamond 1991, p. 352. Another source estimates about 5,000 black people lynched from 1859 to 1962. Ginzburg, Ralph. 1962. *100 Years of Lynchings.* Baltimore, MD: Black Classic Press, p. 253.

[25]See Ginzburg 1962, collecting dozens of newspaper stories.

[26]Cottrol & Diamond 1991, pp. 352-53, citing Ginzburg 1962 and other sources.

[27]Cottrol & Diamond 1991, p. 353; Ginzburg 1962, pp. 114-116.

[28]Ginzburg 1962, p. 187.

[29]E.g., Ginzburg 1962, pp. 126-128,132-135, 136-37, 141-142.

[30]Halbrook, Stephen P. 1998. *Freedmen, The Fourteenth Amendment, and the Right to Bear Arms,* 1866-1876. Westport, CT: Praeger Publishers, pp. 1-44.

[31]Ibid., p. 109 (citing Cong. Globe, 40th Congress, 2d Sess. 1967 (March 18, 1868).)

[32]Ibid., pp. 76-78.

[33]Ibid., p. 169 (quoting the brief filed in the Supreme Court in the case of *United States v. Cruikshank,* 92 U.S. 542 (1876)).

[34]See *United States v. Emerson,* 46 F. Supp. 25 598, 608-609 (N.D. Tex. 1999) (invalidating statute that violates Second and Fifth Amendment, noting other federal decisions that restrict the scope of the Second Amendment); Denning, Brannon P. 1996. Can the Simple Cite Be

Trusted?: Lower Court Interpretations of *United States v. Miller* and The Second Amendment. *Cumberland Law Review.* Vol. 26, p. 961-1004 (discussing cases, e.g. *Cases v. United States,* 131 F.2d 916 (1st Cir. 1942); *United States v. Tot,* 131 F.2d 261 (3d Cir. 1942); and *United States v. Hale,* 978 F.2d 1016 (8th Cir. 1992)).

[35]Ginzburg 1962, pp. 111-112.

[36]Cottrol & Diamond 1991, p. 354. See Polsby, Daniel D. and Don B. Kates, Jr. 1997. Of Holocausts and Gun Control. *Washington Univ. Law Qtly.* Vol. 75, p. 1237 (discussing effectiveness of armed resistance to the Ku Klux Klan, especially in the 1910's and 1920's).

[37]Ibid.

[38]Ibid., pp. 355-56.

[39]Interview with Charles R. Sims, conducted by William A. Price, reporter for the *National Guardian* newsweekly, on Aug. 20, 1965, in Bogalusa, Louisiana, reprinted under the title of "Armed Defense," in Grant 1968, at pp. 336-37.

[40]Cottrol & Diamond 1991, p. 357.

[41]Armed Defense in Grant 1968, p. 339.

[42]Ibid., p. 340.

[43]Ibid.

[44]Tonso, William R. 1985. Gun Control: White Man's Law. *Reason Magazine.* December, pp. 23-25.

[45]Sherrill, Robert. 1973. *The Saturday Night Special.* New York: Charterhouse, p. 280 (italics added).

[46]Ibid., p. 283.

[47]Simkin, Jay and Aaron Zelman. 1993. *"Gun Control": Gateway to Tyranny.* Revised edition. Milwaukee, WI: Jews for the Preservation of Firearms Ownership, Inc., pp. 1, 14, 106.

[48]Ibid., p. 130 (letter from Lewis C. Coffin, law librarian at the Library of Congress, to Senator Thomas J. Dodd, July 12, 1968). Article detailing Senator Dodd's connection to the Nazi law and GCA 1968, with photocopy of this letter, was also published in *Guns & Ammo* magazine, May 1993, pp. 30-33.

[49]Rummel 1996, p. 27, concludes that the way to prevent "democide" (genocide) is to restrain the power of government, e.g. by maintaining a vibrant democratic political culture. When government obtains absolute power, hell breaks loose.

Righteous Defense:
A Judeo-Christian Duty

Chapter Seventeen:
How "Gun Control" Threatens Jews and Righteous Gentiles[1]

Some Jews and Jewish organizations support "gun control" or take no position on the issue. Yet it flies in the face of centuries of Jewish history and tradition to favor policies that disarm victims. Jewish law mandates armed self-defense if that is necessary to preserve an innocent life. The Jewish experience shows, beyond any shadow of a doubt, that when Jews have been disarmed they have been victimized.

For a Jew to urge "gun control" is a self-destructive and evil act. Some Jews who back "gun control" don't know the facts. On the other hand, Jewish "gun control" militants are cut from the same cloth as the Jews who urged non resistance to the Nazis and even helped to arrange deportations to death camps. Jews who urge "gun control" similarly betray their fellow Jews.

When a vocal and visible Jewish minority supports "gun control," it hurts all Jews because it:

1. Creates ill will against all Jews on the part of millions of decent, law-abiding American gun owners. These Americans become righteously angry as they see their civil right to own firearms being taken away for no fault of their own.

2. Makes Jews appear to be "criminal lovers" in the eyes of millions of Americans who are increasingly upset by our government's failure to curb criminals of all types.

3. Will recreate in America the vulnerability with which Jews have lived in many lands over the centuries, and which too often resulted in bloody persecutions at the hands of govern-

ment officials or violent mobs.

4. Promotes public policies based on irrationality rather than analysis. It is irrational and dangerous for people to blame things (like guns) for the evil actions of people. The trend to blame "guns" instead of criminals is dangerous, because Jews often have been made scapegoats when irrationality replaces analysis.

Each of these four results works against the interests of America's Jews. We (Jews) are a small part of the vast, peace-loving and law-abiding majority in America that makes this such a wonderful country in which to live, work, and worship. We have a great interest in defending these values of the American majority. One of those values is the fundamental right to self-defense, which includes the right to keep and bear arms.

Long-held Jewish beliefs support those rights. Well-known teachings from a range of Jewish sources show that Jews are commanded:

1. To ensure their own defense against evildoers.
2. To be skilled in the use of weapons for self-defense where the situation requires it.
3. Not to show compassion to those who deserve none.
4. To clearly distinguish between evildoers and upright persons.

Our long and rich history shows that when Jews failed to follow these rules, for whatever reasons, they brought great disasters upon themselves.

A Basic Duty of Jews

Our position is really not controversial within Judaism, because it is based on long established principles. The relationship between G-d and the Jewish people is such that a Jew must fulfill specified obligations if he is to receive Divine blessing and help. Neither worldly nor spiritual benefits are generally gained without effort.[2]

A Jew must live in order to carry out these Divine commandments, so his life must be preserved. Therefore a Jew is required to exercise caution in all activities, so as to protect himself or herself against undue risks of harm.[3] A person cannot rely on prayer alone in defending himself; he must take appropriate steps before Divine help will be available.

Using lethal force for self-defense

Jewish law and thought greatly respect the sanctity of life, so that means Jews have a duty to oppose attackers. Lethal force should be used to save innocent lives, such as to defend oneself or to prevent an attack on another person.

In cases where a person is attacked, the mandate of Jewish law is crystal clear: "he who comes to kill you, arise and kill him."[4] Thus, if a Jew is reasonably certain that someone is coming to kill him or her, he or she must kill the would-be murderer.

When an attacker is pursuing another person to kill him, then using force is mandated. A Jew who sees such an incident is obliged to kill the attacker, if that is necessary to save the life of the person in peril.[5]

A Jew who is obligated to kill an attacker, but who does not do so, violates the law set forth in Leviticus 19:16, "thou shall not stand idly by the blood of your brother," and other commandments.[6] This injunction is very severe: it is related to the prohibition against murder. Some Jewish authorities would consider the failure to protect an endangered person to be the passive form of the act of murder.[7]

People responsible for protecting others carry an awesome obligation. In Ezekiel 33:6, the A-mighty imposes a high duty on guardians of the people, saying:

> But if the watchman sees the sword coming and does not blow the trumpet to warn the people and the sword comes and takes the life of one of them,... I will hold the watchman accountable for his blood.

The Sixth Commandment expresses a powerful bias in favor of life, and against the taking of innocent life: "Thou shall not murder."[8] Sometimes this command has been translated as "thou shall not kill," but this cannot be correct, because elsewhere the Hebrews (including the Jews) were ordered to kill the Midianites,[9] the Amalekites, and many of the Canaanites.[10] As the A-mighty is consistent, we would not expect him to command us to violate his own commandment.

Distinguishing between the righteous and the evil doers

Jewish law and thought require that the law-abiding person not be treated the same as the evildoer. The concept first appears in Genesis. The A-mighty warned Noah of the impending, all-destroying flood. Noah was told to build an ark in which to preserve himself and all other non human life. Noah was spared from the flood because he was "perfect in his generation," i.e., Noah did not do the evil things that moved the A-mighty to unleash the deluge.[11]

The story of Noah clearly proves that the upright person must be treated differently from the evildoer. The same concept recurs with dazzling clarity later in Genesis.[12]

The A-mighty told Abraham that everyone in the cities of Sodom and Gomorrah would be destroyed because of their evil deeds. Nonetheless, Abraham implored the A-mighty to spare all of the people in the cities, because he felt that some upright persons might be living there. Abraham actually challenged G-d, saying: "Will you also stamp out the righteous along with the wicked?... it would be sacrilege to You to do such a thing, to bring death upon the righteous along with the wicked; letting the righteous and the wicked fare alike. It would be sacrilege to You! Shall the Judge of all the earth not do justice?"

The A-mighty agreed to spare the cities if 10 righteous persons could be found. Not even that few decent persons were to be found, so the cities were destroyed. Yet the A-mighty sent an angel just to lead out of the city the only righteous persons — Lot and his family. So important was it to separate the righteous from the evildoers that the angel told Lot that the destruction could not commence until Lot was in a safe place.[13]

The Ninth Commandment also requires separating the law-abiding from the evildoer in legal matters. The Commandment forbids a person from "testifying falsely," because false testimony could cause an innocent person to be punished.[14]

"Gun control" laws discourage private ownership of defense tools, thus making it harder for people to carry out their duty of defense. Sometimes these laws are employed to punish upright, peace-loving people who have committed no aggression. (Innocent citizens sometimes are punished severely for "gun law" violations to "set an example.") Violent criminals who are caught might also be punished under these same laws — which shows only that the righteous and the criminals are being treated alike. That result violates G-d's laws and Jewish tradition.

Those who advocate "gun control" measures that target the law-abiding in effect are testifying falsely against innocent persons. These advocates seek to create a new class of law-breaker — firearms owners — when the firearms owners have threatened or injured no one. These advocates thus are claiming that the firearms owners have done wrong, when in the overwhelming majority of case, they have not.

Not surprisingly, many persons who advocate "gun control" have also urged lenient treatment for violent criminals. These advocates show compassion to those who do not deserve it (criminals) and show cruelty to those to whom they should show compassion (law-abiding firearms owners).

The folly of showing mercy to evildoers

Some of these rules may seem to be rather harsh, but to show compassion to those who did not deserve it, such as an attacker, produces a double standard that always is harmful. Rabbi Shimon ben Levi has said, "all who act compassionately in instances requiring cruelty ultimately become cruel in instances requiring actions of compassion." Other sages state that a person who acts this way, "ultimately... is punished harshly."[15]

For example, King Saul was noteworthy for his inconsistent moral standards. He spared King Agag of Amalek from death, directly disobeying G-d's command delivered by the prophet Samuel to destroy every Amalekite. Samuel himself later executed Agag.[16] King Saul later wrongfully destroyed the priestly city of Nob.[17] Saul ultimately was deprived of the kingship of Israel which passed to David instead.

American legislators and judges behave the same way as Saul, with equally harmful results. They persistently show compassion to violent criminals, and then show cruelty to the law-abiding by imposing "gun control" and other restrictive laws on them. Showing leniency to those who repeatedly commit crimes, especially violent crimes, is very costly, and not just to the victims, and not just in money. All law-abiding Americans suffer as their freedoms are eroding. "Gun control" is only one of many examples of how criminals are being allowed to define the limits within which the law-abiding live. "Gun control" advocates help criminals by creating conditions favorable to criminals.

America is supposed to be the land of the free, but law-abiding Americans increasingly are not free. Instead, they huddle behind locked doors, window bars, alarms, and security guards. Criminals seem more free to do what they please, to whom they please, where they please, when they please, and as much as they please. This sad state of affairs results from mistakenly showing compassion to violent criminals.

Those who back "gun control" and similar policies that target or mainly affect law-abiding people are helping to make America into a zoo, one in which dangerous animals run free and the visitors are behind bars. With "gun control," people who claim to be compassionate deliberately victimize a group of law-abiding people. So, Patrick Purdy, who shot schoolchildren in Stockton, Calif., had several previous convictions for violent crimes but was still at liberty. Willie Horton, a convicted murderer on weekend release, killed again. Neither deserved compassion and should not have been shown any. As mercy was wrongly extended to them, law-abiding people paid with their lives. All law-abiding persons suffer from the "gun control" measures enacted by the same legislators and enforced by the same judges who wrongly showed mercy to these men.

Jews in exile: demoralized, disarmed, defenseless, disenfranchised, despoiled, destroyed

After the destruction of the Second Temple, in 70 CE (Common Era), Jews spent the next 1,878 years living in countries where they were at best a tolerated minority. In almost all of these places they were persecuted to some degree. They were usually forbidden to own arms. Faced with active persecution (e.g., mob violence, forced conversions, etc.) or passive persecution (e.g., punitive taxes, confiscations of property, confinement to ghettos, special dress codes), disarmed Jews found that flight proved to be a reliable means of salvation in the long run. That conclusion, though, ultimately produces catastrophic consequences.

All sorts of regimes have persecuted Jews in recent centuries. This list shows only a few of the more infamous examples:

Germany: 1096-99. Thousands of Jews slaughtered by crusaders on the way to the Holy land.

Spain: 1130-1269. Expulsion or conversion to Islam (Almohad regime)

England: 1144. Jews accused of ritual use of human blood.

England: 1290. Expulsion of Jews.

France: 1306. Expulsion of Jews.

Europe: 1347-51. Jews wrongly blamed for the Black Death, the Bubonic Plague epidemic that killed one-third of Europe's population, some 25 million people, spread by rat-borne fleas.

Spain: 1492. Expulsion of Jews.

Portugal: 1497. Expulsion of Jews.

Ukraine: 1648-49. Pogroms and riots against Jews.

Russia: 1783. Jews confined to certain regions of the country.

Russia: 1881. Pogrom after the murder of Czar Alexander II. While only one Jew was involved, Jews in over 200 cities and towns were brutalized.

France: 1894-1906. Army captain Alfred Dreyfus, a Jew, underwent court-martial on an espionage charge, in which the authorities used fabricated evidence to protect the well-connected actual culprit.

Russia: 1903. Kishniev Pogrom. Mobs, led by Russian government provocateur, massacre Jews in Moldavia.

Germany: 1933-45. Nazi regime murdered six million Jews (two-thirds of all European Jews, and three-quarters of all the Jews in German-controlled areas).

Syria, Iraq, Yemen: 1948. Jews forced to flee after Israel established and won its war of independence.

Russia: 1949-53. Stalin prepared a show trial of Jewish doctors accused of plotting to kill top Communists. Stalin's death intervened.

Algeria: 1964. Jews forced to leave after Algeria won independence from France.

Russia: 1967-85. Jews suffer intense official discrimination after Israeli victory in Six-Day War against Egypt, Jordan, and Syria (Russian allies).

Iran: 1979. Jews persecuted by fundamentalist Muslim regime after ouster of Shah.

Ethiopia: 1980-91. Jews held for ransom by Marxist regime and allowed to leave when ransom paid.

Most of the expulsions in the above list were accompanied by confiscations of property and had long lasting impacts. For example, Jews could not legally live in England for more than 350 years, until the end of the 17th century. Jews had no civil rights in France until Napoleon's era (1791-1815).

The impacts of 1,900 years of victimization: Jews don't matter

The history of the victimization of Jews had an even more harmful impact: it affected their treatment even in countries where they were not persecuted. For example, Jews have never been systematically persecuted in America by the government. There have been isolated incidents of violence against Jews, and non-life threatening discrimination (e.g., exclusion for certain schools, jobs and clubs).

In the 1930's, as Nazi oppression of Jews in Germany grew and then spread to other countries such as Austria (occupied by the Nazis in 1938), few countries — including America — wanted to give refuge to Jews fleeing for their lives. Some would-be refugees were even sent back to Germany!

During World War II, even after it was clear that the Nazis were exterminating Jews (and others), the U.S. government did not directly try to intervene. American bombers were never sent to destroy Nazi murder factories (e.g., Dachau, Buchenwald, Auschwitz in Poland) or even the nearby rail lines that supplied them. Although the object of the war was to destroy the Nazi regime, saving some of its intended victims was not a priority. Simply put, Jews just did not matter.[18]

Jews are not the only disarmed people to suffer horribly. This book catalogs the genocides and massacres of disarmed peoples of different races and religions that occurred in Europe, Africa, and Asia in the 20th century.

Many of these genocides and massacres occurred after the Holocaust and took place over several years. Yet, as in the case of the Jews, no one much cared. In many cases these mass killings were stopped only when a neighboring power intervened for reasons of its own.

Consider this question: Amnesty International is an organization that fights against the taking of political prisoners and seeks to liberate these victims. Would Amnesty International be needed if everyone in the world owned a military-type rifle and plenty of cartridges for it?

The impacts of 1,900 years of victimization: Jews forget how to defend themselves

Nearly 1,900 years of victimization has reshaped many Jews' attitudes toward ownership and use of arms. Increasingly, Jews disregarded their teachings and came to see arms only as a means by which they were oppressed. Each incident of victimization moved some to rely more completely on Divine protection. Prayer alone is not usually enough to stop aggression, however, if the people fail to use readily available means of self-defense.

Being treated as aliens (and being ineligible to own arms) for nearly 1,900 years has caused some Jews to forget the very notion that owning weapons is essential to fulfillment of the Torah's commands to defend life.

Neither the Torah nor the Talmud contains any direct equivalent of the Second Amendment to the United States Constitution that declares an individual right and duty to keep and bear arms. There was no need for such language in the Torah and Talmud, because the ownership of weapons by both the righteous and the evildoers is assumed. In that age-old view, what decided the outcome of battles between armed Jews and their armed enemies was not the supply and kind of weapons, but the will of the A-mighty.

When the Jews have upheld their Covenant to G-d, none could beat them. And when the Jews did not uphold their Covenant, their enemies prevailed against them. For example, the First and Second Temples in Jerusalem were destroyed by the Babylonians and the Romans, respectively, because the Jews no longer merited Divine help.

After their dispersal from Israel following the destruction of the Second Temple, the practice of armed defense often was not feasible because of government restrictions or simple poverty. As a result, Jews sought to be liked, or if that were impossible, invisible.

Jews tended to support a benevolent, prevailing power. But when the prevailing power was actively hostile as it became with the rise of the Church of Rome and, later, the spread of Islam, Jews found it more difficult to be liked, no matter how hard they tried. As a result, they were mainly defenseless and without protectors.

Jews slowly learned that invisibility was healthy. Jews tended to avoid actions that attracted official attention. Ultimately, in some countries (mainly in Western Europe) Jews were segregated by government decree. They had to live in special areas, called ghettos. It became ingrained in the Jewish psyche that invisibility was the key to survival. Failing that, flight was the last resort.

For most of the past 1,900 years, Jews almost always were oppressed by some government, whether national or local, which instilled hatred of Jews and encouraged viewing the Jews as scapegoats. To ensure that the Jews were submissive, often they were forbidden to own arms, whether edged weapons (e.g., swords) or firearms.

Alert Jews who had the means would flee from such evil regimes. Almost always, there was a haven somewhere. Jews who did not or could not flee often were massacred. Jews, who passed up chances to flee, forgot that the sanctity of life requires that one flee an overwhelming foe, if that would save one's life. Many ultimately paid with their lives.

Ironically, nearly 1,900 years of being victimized taught Jews that something so precious as life could be best defended by flight — but ultimately that proved to be a fatal teaching. It was in the 1930's and 1940's, when escaping from the Nazis proved nearly impossible, that the futility of relying on flight as a means of salvation was finally proved.

The Nazis' zeal to root out Jews made it particularly hard for Jews to hide. Only a few survived by hiding or by using false identities. Therefore we thank G-d for his kindnesses to them, and we applaud their courage and that of the righteous Gentiles in many countries who helped them, often at the risk of their own lives.

What needs to be done: learn from experience

We should learn from these experiences. But many Jews outside Israel still do not realize that in many cases the best defense of life is not flight — or concealment — but fight. This lesson from our Scriptures, forgotten by many for nearly 1,900 years, has been taught again but some Jews and self-appointed Jewish "leaders" have not grasped it.

These Jews respond to an upsurge in activity by America's tiny criminal minority by attributing inherent evil to the class of inanimate objects: firearms. These Jews have failed to grasp that weapons in the hands of the righteous protect lives from evildoers. Not understanding this key fact has cause inestimable damage to Jews throughout history. Unfortunately, more than a few of today's American Jewish leaders are cut from the same cloth as those who urged non-resistance to the Nazis, some of whom even helped the Nazis to organize deportations to the death camps. The "leaders" during the Nazi era betrayed their fellow Jews then, and some Jewish leaders now are doing exactly the same thing by backing "gun control."

The lessons of Jewish law and experience: Some Jews who back "gun control" are morally corrupt

Judaism exalts the sanctity of life.[19] Jewish law prescribes practices which enhance the length and quality of life, both physical and spiritual. Jewish law forbids practices which degrade or shorten life. Consequently, Jewish law mandates the use of lethal force against evildoers, when necessary to protect an innocent life. Jewish law also specifies clear penalties to be imposed upon evildoers, if carefully validated evidence of wrongdoing is found and presented to a competent court. Once again the emphasis of Jewish law on treating evildoers and upright persons very differently shines through.

When rightly understood, Jewish law and tradition view "gun control" as the essence of moral perversion. "Gun control" requires that all persons be treated as evildoers, and that the law-abiding and the evildoer be treated alike. In so doing, it deprives the righteous, law-abiding person of his advantage over the evildoer. The evildoers flourish.

Jews, more than other people, have suffered from arms control, and from lack of criminal control. Would the Holocaust have occurred had world powers crushed the Nazis in the early 1930's, before they went on their murderous rampage?

Could the Nazis and their allies have killed so many Jews in

Poland if Jewish "leaders," such as Adam Czerniakow, head of the Warsaw ghetto Jewish Council, had responded to the first Nazi brutalities in 1939 by leading open armed resistance? Mordechai Anielewicz and others urged armed resistance with stirring if not totally successful results — while Czerniakow had tried "working with" the Nazis ... selling out his people to death camps.

Only in mid-April 1943 did Warsaw's Jews begin to fight openly. They took action when the Nazis moved to deport the few Jews remaining there after hundreds of thousands had been sent to and gassed at the Treblinka death camp. Although the Nazis had superior forces and weapons, the Jewish fighters inflicted heavy casualties in the following weeks. Stung by these gutsy Jews' ferocity, the Nazis burned down the ghetto and took few prisoners. Mordechai Anielewicz, a commander of the Jewish fighting forces, and some 56,000 others, sanctified G-ds' name there.

Even Jews in concentration camps took up arms: in October 1943, inmates at the Sobibor death camp seized guns from guards, smashed some of the gas chambers, and escaped. A few survived; the Nazis promptly closed the camp. The lesson seems clear: had more Jews been skilled in the use of arms, more would have been ready and able to fight back, and many might have been saved.

The example of these Jewish heroes should inspire all Jews in America to reject immoral and dangerous "gun control," and instead to endorse criminal control. Jews should reject as irrational any policy that allows criminals and criminal conduct to define the civil rights of the innocent and law-abiding citizens.

Jews have been persecuted most harshly when supporters of such irrational policies have prevailed. Thus, the Nazis made all sorts of pseudo-scientific arguments to justify their persecution of the Jews, in order to make this evil easier for the German public to accept. Those who back "gun control" in America now do the same thing to law-abiding firearms owners. These decent citizens are now made scapegoats for years of hopelessly flawed public safety policies based on showing compassion to violent criminals. Jews who support "gun control" thus endorse a moral perversion so profound as to be frightening. If this perversion prevails, it will arouse righteous anger against those who support it. To the extent that Jews are seen supporting this perversion, the resulting backlash will endanger all of us. G-d, let this not be your will!

Conclusions:

1. Jewish law clearly demands we defend innocent life and have the means to do so.

2. Jewish history clearly shows that disarmed Jews were always horribly victimized.

3. Jewish "gun control" advocates create ill will against Jews.

4. Jewish "gun control" advocates are self-destructive.

5. "Gun control" makes Jews and vulnerable to those who hate us.

6. "Gun control" is moral perversion because it treats the law-abiding persons the same as the criminal.

End Notes

[1]Adapted from a 1991 article originally published by Jews for the Preservation of Firearms Ownership, Inc. (www.jpfo.org). End notes here are in the style of the original article.

[2]See, e.g. Deuteronomy 4:1-7, 4:13-14, 6, 7:12-16, 10:12-13.

[3]Deut. 22:8; Babylonian Talmud Tractate Berachos, 32b, discussing Deut. 4:9, 15; Shulchan Aruch, Choshen Mishpat 427 (specifically STF 10 which discusses cases when one is liable to judicial corporal punishment for recklessly endangering one's own life).

[4]Sanhedrin 72a, Berachos 58a & 62b; Makkos 85b; Midrash Tanchumah, Pinchas: 3 (4 in some editions). Rabbi Shlomo Yitzchaki (RaShi) cites these four Talmudic sources and Exodus 22:1. Rabbi Nissin Gaon states also that Berachos 58a derives from Exodus 22:1. According to the Midrash Tanchuma, Bamidbar Rabbah 21:5, and the M'eiri (Bais Ha B'chira on Sanhedrin 72a), the same concept derives from Numbers 25:17. In any event, the example in Sanhedrin 72 is based on Exodus 22:1-2 and applies this principle. Exodus 22:1 states: "If a thief is found breaking into a building's basement, and is struck so that he dies, there shall be no liability for the shedding of innocent blood." The Talmudic discussion stays that a thief who enters a building via the basement (i.e., covertly because people are likely to be present in the house) is deemed to be ready for a confrontation. The owner who seeks to protect his property should presume that the intruder has deadly intent. Although the intruder might actually only intend enter to steal, he is considered to be a "pursuer" — a would-be murderer. Therefore the intruder may be killed.

[5]Sanhedrin 73a, Maimonides, *Mishneh Torah* Nezikin, Hilchos Rotzeach V'Shmiras Nefesh 1:6-8, 10, 11; Tur Shulchan Aruch, Choshen Mishpat 425; reference the censored sections, specifically Shulchan Aruch Choshen Mishpat 425:1 [with Gaon Rabbenu Eliyahu of Vilna and B'er

Haitaiv] and 425:3. See also Maimonides, *Sefer Hamitzvos,* Positive Commandment 247 and Prohibition 293 and 297.

[6]See Mishneh Torah, ibid., 1:14-16; Shulchan Aruch, Choshen Mishpat 425:1 with M'iras Anayim; Lev. 19:16, Sifra (ad loc), specifically "... l'hatzilo b'nafsho" in some versions. Cf. Notes of the Gaon Rabbenu Eliyahu and the "Biur" of the Chofetz Chaim; Torah T'mimah, 109-110; Michas Chinuch, 237:1 and 4; Rabbi Shmuel ben Rabbi Meir, RaShBaM (ad loc); Deut. 22:26-27, Sifri, notes of the Gaon Rabbenu Eliyahu; Deut. 25:12, Sifri; Sanhedrin 73a and commentaries. Also see the various Sifrei HaMitzvos, *e.g.* HaChinuch 237, 600-601; Rabbi Saddiah Gaon's compilation, Negative Injunction 61, etc. Sefer Hamitzvos Hakatan, Prohibition 77. See also Shulchan Aruch 436:1 for related imperatives derived from this verse.

[7]Midrash Rabbah, Lev. 24:5. Rabbi Don I. Abarbanel. Deut. 25:11.

[8]Exodus 20:13.

[9]Numbers 31:2-18.

[10]Deuteronomy 21:17.

[11]Genesis 6, especially verses 9-19.

[12]Genesis 19:17-33.

[13]Genesis 19:15-22.

[14]Exodus 20:16.

[15]"Midas Ha'din poga'as bo", Midrash Rabbah, Ecclesiastes 7:16, Rabbi Shimon ben Levi. See Matnos Kehunah and Aitz Yoseif, Yoma 22b. See Further Midrash Tanchuma, Pinchas 3; Orchos Tsaddikim, Ch. 8; M'eiri, Sefer Hamidos, Section on Midos, Chapter on Compassion; Torah T'mimah, Ecclesiastes 7, Notes 70 and 72.

[16]I Samuel 15:10-33.

[17]I Samuel 22:19.

[18]See Perl, William R., *The Holocaust Conspiracy,* Shapolsky Books, New York, 1989.

[19]See Maimonides' *Mishnah Torah,* ibid, Ch. 1; Ch. 4:8-9.

Chapter Eighteen:

What Does the Bible Say about "Gun Control"?

A Christian View
by Larry Pratt[1]

The underlying argument for gun control seems to be that the availability of guns causes crime. By extension, the availability of any weapon would have to be viewed as a cause of crime. What does the Bible say about such a view?

Perhaps we should start at the beginning, or at least very close to the beginning — in Genesis 4. In this chapter we read about the first murder. Cain had offered an unacceptable sacrifice, and Cain was upset that God insisted that he do the right thing. In other words, Cain was peeved that he could not do his own thing.

Cain decided to kill his brother rather than get right with God. There were no guns available, although there may well have been a knife. Whether it was a knife or a rock, the Bible does not say. The point is, the evil in Cain's heart was the cause of the murder, not the availability of the murder weapon.

God's response was not to ban rocks or knives, or whatever, but to banish the murderer. Later (see Genesis 9:5-6) God instituted capital punishment, but said not a word about banning weapons.

Did Christ Teach Pacifism?

Many people, Christians included, assume that Christ taught pacifism. They cite Matthew 5:38-39 for their proof. In this verse Christ said: "You have heard that it was said, 'An eye for an eye and a tooth for a tooth.' But I tell you not to resist an evil person.

But whoever slaps you on your right cheek, turn the other to him also."

The Sermon on the Mount from which this passage is taken deals with righteous personal conduct. In our passage, Christ is clearing up a confusion that had led people to think that conduct proper for the civil government — that is, taking vengeance — was also proper for an individual.

Even the choice of words used by Christ indicates that He was addressing a confusion, or a distortion, that was commonplace. Several times in the rest of the Sermon on the Mount Christ used this same "you have heard it said" figure of speech to straighten out misunderstandings or falsehoods being taught by the religious leaders of the times.

Contrast this to Christ's use of the phrase "it is written" when He was appealing to the Scriptures for authority. For example, see Matthew 4 where on three occasions during His temptation by the devil, Christ answered each one of the devil's lies or misquotes from Scripture with the words: "it is written".

To further underscore the point that Christ was correcting the religious leaders on their teaching that "an eye for an eye" applies to private revenge, consider that in the same Sermon, Christ strongly condemned false teaching: "Whoever therefore breaks one of the commandments, and teaches men so, shall be called least in the kingdom of heaven..." (Matthew 5:19). Clearly, then, Christ was not teaching something different about self-defense than is taught elsewhere in the Bible. Otherwise, He would be contradicting Himself for He would now be teaching men to break one of the commandments.

The reference to "an eye for an eye" was taken from Exodus 21:24-25 which deals with how the magistrate must deal with a crime. Namely, the punishment must fit the crime. The religious leaders of Christ's day had twisted a passage that applied to the government and misused it as a principle of personal revenge.

The Bible distinguishes clearly between the duties of the civil magistrate (the government) and the duties of an individual. Namely, God has delegated to the civil magistrate the administration of justice. Individuals have the responsibility of protecting their lives from attackers. Christ was referring to this distinction in the Matthew 5 passage. Let us now examine in some detail what the

230

Scriptures say about the roles of government and of individuals.

Both the Old and New Testaments teach individual self-defense, even if it means taking the assailant's life in certain circumstances.

Self-Defense in the Old Testament

Exodus 22:2-3 tells us "If the thief is found breaking in, and he is struck so that he dies, there shall be no guilt for his bloodshed. If the sun has risen on him, there shall be guilt for his bloodshed. He should make full restitution; if he has nothing, then he shall be sold for his theft."

One conclusion which can be drawn from this is that a threat to our life is to be met with lethal force. After the sun has risen seems to refer to a different judgment than the one permitted at night. At night it is more difficult to discern whether the intruder is a thief or a murderer. Furthermore, the nighttime makes it more difficult to defend oneself and to avoid killing the thief at the same time. During the daytime, it had better be clear that one's life is in danger, otherwise, defense becomes vengeance, and that belongs in the hand of the magistrate.

In Proverbs 25:26 we read that "A righteous man who falters before the wicked is like a murky spring and a polluted well." Certainly, we would be faltering before the wicked if we chose to be unarmed and unable to resist an assailant who might be threatening our life. In other words, we have no right to hand over our life which is a gift from God to the unrighteous. It is a serious mistake to equate a civilized society with one in which the decent people are doormats for the evil to trample on.

Trusting God

Another question asked by Christians is "Doesn't having a gun imply a lack of trust that God will take care of us?"

Indeed, God will take care of us. He has also told us that if we love Him, we will keep His commandments. (John 14:15)

Those who trust God work for a living, knowing that 1 Timothy 5:8 tells us: "But if anyone does not provide for his own, and especially for those of his household, he has denied the faith and is worse than an unbeliever." For a man not to work, yet expect to eat because he was "trusting God" would actually be to defy God.

King David wrote in Psalm 46:1 that God is our refuge and strength, a very present help in trouble. This did not conflict with praising the God "Who trains my hands for war and my fingers for battle" (Psalm 144:1).

The doctrine of Scripture is that we prepare and work, but we trust the outcome to God.

Those who trust God should also make adequate provision for their own defense even as we are instructed in the passages cited above. For a man to refuse to provide adequately for his and his family's defense would be to defy God.

There is an additional concern to taking the position that "I don't need to arm myself. God will protect me."

At one point, when Satan was tempting Jesus in the wilderness, he challenged Jesus to throw himself off the top of the temple. Satan reasoned that God's angels would protect him. Jesus responded: "It is written again, 'You shall not tempt the Lord your God'" (Matthew 4:7).

It may seem pious to say that one is trusting in God for protection, and we all must, but it is tempting God if we do not take the measures that He has laid out for us in the Bible.

Role of Government

The Bible records the first murder in Genesis 4 when Cain killed his brother Abel. God's response was not to register rocks or impose a background check on those getting a plough, or whatever it was that Cain used to kill his brother. Instead, God dealt with the criminal. Ever since Noah the penalty for murder has been death (Genesis 9:5-6).

We see the refusal to accept this principle that God has given us from the very beginning. Today we see a growing acceptance of the idea that checking the criminal backgrounds of gun buyers will lessen crime but we should seldom execute those who are guilty of murder.

In Matthew 15 (and in Mark 7) Christ accused the religious leaders of the day of also opposing the execution of those deserving of death — rebellious teenagers. They had replaced the commandments of God with their own traditions. God has never been interested in controlling the means of violence. He has always made it a point to punish, and where possible, restore (as with restitution and excommunication) the wrongdoer. Control of individuals is to be left to self-government. Punishment of individuals by the civil government is to be carried out when self-government breaks down.

Man's wisdom today has been to declare gun free school zones which are invaded by gun-toting teenage terrorists whom we refuse to execute. We seem to have learned little from Christ's rebuke of the Pharisees.

Nowhere in the Bible does God make any provision for dealing with the instruments of crime. He always focuses on the consequences for an individual of his actions. Heaven and hell only applies to people, not to things. Responsibility only pertains to people, not to things. If this principle, which was deeply embedded in the common law, still pertained today lawsuits against gun manufacturers would be thrown out unless the product malfunctioned.

Responsibility rightly includes being liable for monetary damages if a firearm is left in a grossly negligent fashion so that an ignorant child gets the gun and misuses it. The solution is not to require that trigger locks be used on a gun to avoid being subject to such a law suit. Some might argue that this is nothing more than an application of the Biblical requirement that a railing be placed around the flat rooftop of a house where people might congregate (Deuteronomy 22:8). But trigger locks are to be used with unloaded guns — which would be as pointless as requiring a railing around a pitched roof where people do not congregate.

Surely in protecting against accidents we must not end up making ourselves more vulnerable to criminal attack, which is what a trigger lock does if it is in use on the firearm intended for self protection.

The firearm that is kept for self-defense should be available in an emergency. Rooftop railings have no correspondence to the need for instant access to a gun. On the other hand, guns that are not intended for immediate use should be kept secured as a reasonable precaution. But to make the owner criminally or monetarily liable for another's misuse violates a basic commandment of Scripture: "the righteousness of the righteous shall be upon himself, and the wickedness of the wicked shall be upon himself" (Ezekiel 18:20b).

Self-defense Versus Vengeance

Resisting an attack is not to be confused with taking vengeance which is the exclusive domain of God (Romans 12:19). This has been delegated to the civil magistrate, who, as we read in Romans 13:4, "is God's minister to you for good. But if you do evil, be afraid; for he does not bear the sword in vain; for he is God's minister, an avenger to execute wrath on him who practices evil."

Private vengeance means one would stalk down a criminal after one's life is no longer in danger as opposed to defending oneself during an attack. It is this very point that has been confused by Christian pacifists who would take the passage in the Sermon on the Mount about turning the other cheek (which prohibits private vengeance) into a command to falter before the wicked.

Let us consider also that the Sixth Commandment tells us "Thou shall not murder." In the chapters following, God gave to Moses many of the situations which require a death penalty. God clearly has not told us never to kill. He has told us not to murder, which means we are not to take an innocent life. Consider also that the civil magistrate is to be a terror to those who practice evil. This passage does not in any way imply that the role of law enforcement is to prevent crimes or to protect individuals from criminals. The magistrate is a minister to serve as "an avenger to execute wrath on him who practices evil" (Romans 13:4).

This point is reflected in the legal doctrine of the United States. Repeatedly, courts have held that the government has no responsibility to provide individual security. One case (Bowers v. DeVito) put it this way: "there is no constitutional right to be protected by the state against being murdered."

Self-defense in the New Testament

The Christian pacifist may try to argue that God has changed His mind from the time that He gave Moses the Ten Commandments on Mount Sinai. Perhaps they would want us to think that Christ canceled out the Ten Commandments in Exodus 20 or the provision for justifiably killing a thief in Exodus 22. But the writer of Hebrews makes it clear that this cannot be, because "Jesus Christ is the same yesterday, today and forever" (Hebrews 13:8). In the Old Testament, the prophet Malachi records God's words this way: "For I am the Lord, I do not change" (Malachi 3:6).

Paul was referring to the unchangeability of God's Word when he wrote to Timothy that "All Scripture is given by inspiration of God, and is profitable for doctrine, for reproof, for correction, for instruction in righteousness, that the man of God may be complete, thoroughly equipped for every good work" (2 Timothy 3:16-17). Clearly, Paul viewed all Scripture, including the Old Testament, as useful for training Christians in every area of life.

We must also consider what Christ told his disciples in his last hours with them: "...But now, he who has a money bag, let him take it, and likewise a sack; and he who has no sword, let him sell his garment and buy one" (Luke 22:36). Keep in mind that the sword was the finest offensive weapon available to an individual soldier — the equivalent then of a military rifle today.

The Christian pacifist will likely object at this point that only a few hours later, Christ rebuked Peter who used a sword to cut off the ear of Malchus, a servant of the high priest in the company of a detachment of troops. Let us read what Christ said to Peter in Matthew 26:52-54:

> Put your sword in its place, for all who take the sword will perish by the sword. Or do you think that I cannot now pray to My Father, and He will provide Me with more than twelve legions of angels? How then could the Scriptures be fulfilled, that it must happen thus?

In the companion passage in John 18, Jesus tells Peter to put his sword away and told him that He had to drink the cup that His Father had given Him. It was not the first time that Christ had to explain to the disciples why He had come to earth. To fulfill the Scriptures, the Son of God had to die for the sin of man since man was incapable of paying for his own sin apart from going to hell. Christ could have saved His life, but then believers would have lost their lives forever in hell. These things only became clear to the disciples after Christ had died and been raised from the dead and the Spirit had come into the world at Pentecost (see John 14:26).

While Christ told Peter to "put your sword in its place" He clearly did not say get rid of it forever. That would have contradicted what he had told the disciples only hours before. Peter's sword was to protect his own mortal life from danger. His sword was not needed to protect the Creator of the universe and the King of kings.

Years after Pentecost, Paul wrote in a letter to Timothy: "But if anyone does not provide for his own, and especially for those of his household, he has denied the faith and is worse than an unbeliever" (1 Tim. 5:8). This passage applies to our subject because it would be absurd to buy a house, furnish it with food and facilities for one's family, and then refuse to install locks and provide the means to protect the family and the property. Likewise it would be absurd not to take, if necessary, the life of a night-time thief to protect the members of the family (Exodus 22:2-3).

A related, and even broader concept, is found in the parable of the Good Samaritan. Christ had referred to the Old Testament summary of all the laws of the Bible into two great commandments: "'You shall love the Lord your God with all your heart, with all your soul, with all your strength, and with all your mind,' and your neighbor as yourself" (Luke 10:27). When asked who was a neighbor, Christ related the parable of the Good Samaritan (Luke 10:30-37). The Good Samaritan who took care of the mugging victim was acting as a neighbor to the victim. The others who walked by and ignored the victim's plight were not acting as neighbors to him.

In the light of all we have seen the Scriptures teach to this point, can we argue that if we were able to save another's life from an attacker by shooting the attacker with our gun that we should "turn the other cheek instead?" The Bible speaks of no such idea. It only speaks of our responsibilities in the face of an attack — as individual creatures made by God, as householders or as neighbors.

National Blessings and Cursings

The Old Testament also tells us a great deal about the positive relationship between righteousness, which exalts a nation, and self-defense. It makes clear that in times of national rebellion against the Lord God, the rulers of the nation will reflect the spiritual degradation of the people and the result is a denial of God's commandments, an arrogance of officialdom, disarmament and oppression.

For example, the people of Israel were oppressed during the time of the rule of the Judges. This occurred every time the people apostatized. Judges 5:8 tells us that, "They chose new gods; then there was war in the gates; not a shield or spear was seen among forty thousand in Israel."

Consider Israel under Saul: The first book of Samuel tells of the turning away of Israel from God. The people did not want to be governed by God; they wanted to be ruled by a king like the pagan, God-hating nations around them. Samuel warned the people what they were getting into — the curses that would be upon them — if they persisted in raising up a king over themselves and their families. Included in those curses was the raising up of a standing, professional army which would take their sons and their daughters for aggressive wars (I Samuel 8:11).

This curse is not unknown in the United States. Saul carried out all the judgments that Samuel had warned the people about. His build up of a standing army has been repeated in the U.S., and not just in terms of the military, but also the 650,000 full-time police officers from all levels of government.

Saul was the king whom the Israelites wanted and got. He was beautiful in the eyes of the world but a disaster in the eyes of the Lord. Saul did not trust God. He rebelled against His form of sacrifice unto the Lord. Saul put himself above God. He was impatient. He refused to wait for Samuel because God's way was taking too long. Saul went ahead and performed the sacrifice himself, thus violating God's commandment (and, incidentally, also violating the God-ordained separation of duties of church and state!)

Thus was the kingdom lost to Saul. And, it was under him that the Philistines were able to defeat the Jews and put them into bondage. So great was the bondage exerted by the Philistines that "Now there was no blacksmith to be found throughout all the land of Israel: for the Philistines said, 'Lest the Hebrews make them swords or spears.' But all the Israelites went down to the Philistines to sharpen each man's plowshare, his mattock, his ax, and his sickle;...So it came about, on the day of battle, that there was neither sword nor spear found in the hand of any of the people who were with Saul and Jonathan..." (1 Samuel 13:19-20; 22-23).

Today, the same goals of the Philistines would be carried out by an oppressor who would ban gunsmiths from the land. The sword of today is the handgun, rifle or shotgun. The sword control of the Philistines is today's gun control of those governments that do not trust their people with guns.

It is important to understand that what happened to the Jews at the time of Saul was not unexpected according to the sanctions spelled out by God in Leviticus 26 and Deuteronomy 28. In the first verses of those chapters, blessings are promised to a nation that keeps God's laws. In the latter parts of those chapters, the curses are spelled out for a nation that comes under judgment for its rebellion against God. Deuteronomy 28:47-48 helps us understand the reason for Israel's oppression by the Philistines during Saul's reign:

> Because you did not serve the Lord your God with joy and gladness of heart, for the abundance of all things, therefore you shall serve your enemies, whom the Lord will send against you, in hunger, in thirst, in nakedness, and in need of all things; and He will put a yoke of iron on your neck until He has destroyed you.

The Bible provides examples of God's blessing upon Israel for its faithfulness. These blessings included a strong national defense coupled with peace. A clear example occurred during the reign of Jehoshaphat. 2 Chronicles 17 tells of how Jehoshaphat led Israel back to faithfulness to God which included a strong national defense. The result: "And the fear of the Lord fell on all the kingdoms of the lands that were around Judah, so that they did not make war against Jehoshaphat" (2 Chronicles 17:10).

The Israelite army was a militia army (Numbers 1:3, ff.) which came to battle with each man bearing his own weapons — from the time of Moses, through the Judges, and beyond. When threatened by the Midianites, for example, "Moses spoke to the people, saying, 'Arm some of yourselves for the war, and let them go against the Midianites to take vengeance for the Lord on Midian'" (Numbers 31:3). Again, to demonstrate the Biblical heritage of individuals bearing and keeping arms, during David's time in the wilderness avoiding capture by Saul, "David said to his men, 'Every man gird on his sword.' So every man girded on his sword, and David also girded on his sword" (1 Samuel 25:13).

Finally, consider Nehemiah and those who rebuilt the gates and walls of Jerusalem. They were both builders and defenders, each man — each servant — armed with his own weapon. Those who built on the wall, and those who carried burdens loaded themselves so that with one hand they worked at construction, and with the other held a weapon. Every one of the builders had his sword girded at his side as he built (Nehemiah 4:17-18).

Conclusion

The wisdom of the framers of the Constitution is consistent with the lessons of the Bible. Instruments of defense should be dispersed throughout the nation, not concentrated in the hands of the central government. In a godly country, righteousness governs each man through the Holy Spirit working within. The government has no cause to want a monopoly of force; the government that desires such a monopoly is a threat to the lives, liberty and property of its citizens.

The assumption that only danger can result from people carrying guns is used to justify the government's having a monopoly of force. The notion that the people cannot be trusted to keep and bear their own arms informs us that ours, like the time of Solomon, may be a time of great riches, but it is also a time of peril to free people. If Christ is not our King, we shall have a dictator to rule over us, just as Samuel warned.

For those who think that God treated Israel differently from the way He will treat us today, please consider what God told the prophet Malachi: "For I am the Lord, I do not change..." (Malachi 3:6).

End Notes:

[1]Executive Director, Gun Owners of America, 8001 Forbes Place, Suite 102, Springfield, VA 22151. All Rights Reserved. This article has been previously published on the GOA Internet site at *www.gunowners.org*.

Chapter Nineteen:
Roman Catholicism and Self-Defense

How does the Roman Catholic Church view the right to self-defense and the duty to resist tyranny? In a nutshell, the Church's official statement of its views, the *Catechism*,[1] outlines a consistent Christian view.

Section 2263 of the *Catechism* states that using deadly force in the "legitimate defense of persons and societies" is not murder. Section 2264 explains the concept of defense further:

> Love toward oneself remains a fundamental principle of morality. Therefore it is legitimate to insist on respect for one's own right to life. Someone who defends his life is not guilty of murder even if he is forced to deal his aggressor a lethal blow.

The Church views armed defense as mandatory in some cases. Section 2265 of the *Catechism* states:

> Legitimate defense can be not only a right but a grave duty for someone responsible for another's life. Preserving the common good requires rendering the unjust aggressor unable to inflict harm. To this end, those holding legitimate authority have the right to repel by armed force aggressors against the civil community entrusted to their charge.

When government turns evil, what does the Catholic Church declare? Section 2242 states the moral duties plainly. First, citizens must not obey laws that violate fundamental rights:

> The citizen is obliged in conscience not to follow the directives of civil authorities when they are contrary to

the demands of the moral order, to the fundamental rights of persons or the teachings of the Gospel. Refusing obedience to civil authorities, when their demands are contrary to those of an upright conscience, finds its justification in the distinction between serving God and serving the political community.

Second, citizens may defend themselves and their fellows against abusive government:

When citizens are under the oppression of a public authority which oversteps its competence, they should still not refuse to give or to do what is objectively demanded of them by the common good; but it is legitimate for them to defend their own rights and those of their fellow citizens against the abuse of this authority within the limits of the natural law and the Law of the Gospel.

The Church cautions in Section 2243 that "armed resistance to oppression by political authority is not legitimate," however, unless the violation of fundamental rights is "certain, grave, and prolonged," all other means have been exhausted, there is no other alternative, resistance will not provoke worse violations, and there is a reasonable chance of success.

Based on these *Catechism* sections, it appears that the Church's doctrine fundamentally supports the concept of widespread civilian ownership of firearms for defense of individuals and the community, as well as a last resort against tyranny.

Following are three stories about Catholics and defensive firearms; two with happy endings, one giving a warning to future generations.

The "Patron Saint" of Handgunners

As a youth, Gabriel Possenti had been fairly well-to-do, a little wild, and an excellent marksman. He received a calling, however, and entered seminary in the mountain village of Isola, Italy. One day in 1860, soldiers in the army of Garibaldi stormed into the town, terrorizing the villagers, plundering and burning.

With the permission of his superior, Gabriel Possenti walked in the center of town, and, unarmed, faced down the attackers. One of the soldiers, pulling a young woman for likely rape, laughed at the young monk standing alone. Gabriel Possenti seized the snig-gering soldier's handgun from his belt, pointed it at the man, and demanded he release the woman.

As the one soldier freed the woman, another soldier came upon the scene. Gabriel Possenti grabbed the second man's gun as well. The rest of the soldiers came running toward Gabriel Possenti, now holding two guns.

At that charged moment, a small lizard ran across the road between Gabriel Possenti and the men. The lizard paused — the young monk took aim — and with a single shot hit the lizard. Then Gabriel Possenti pointed his two handguns at the gang of soldiers and told them to drop their weapons. They did.

Gabriel Possenti proceeded to march them around the village to put out the fires they started and then drove them out of town. The villagers were amazed and grateful, and celebrated Gabriel Possenti as "the Savior of Isola." Gabriel Possenti was canonized later for other reasons, but the St. Gabriel Possenti Society has been promoting him as the "the Patron Saint of Handgunners," and has asked the Vatican to make it official.[2]

Nuns With Guns

Roman Catholic nuns at the Sanctuary of the Virgin of Miracles in Bogota, Columbia, had personal knowledge of crime. Seven times burglars had broken into their facilities to steal chickens and religious relics. The nuns finally had to post a night patrol to guard the church and grounds.

One night in July 1999, two nuns heard strange noises in the halls of the Sanctuary of the Virgin of Miracles. Armed with a revolver, they confronted the intruder and ended up shooting him dead.[3] Initially the nuns were charged with the killing, but they eventually were exonerated.

Had the nuns failed to protect themselves and their home, their laxity might have invited more serious and violent criminal invasions. Their brave defense doubtless telegraphed the news to would-be criminals not to bother that church in the future.

When "Peacemaking" Gets People Killed

It was 1798 in Wexford County, Ireland. The United Irish organization struggled to start what became known as the

Rebellion of 1798, to throw off British rule as the American colonies had done. Father John Murphy, a Catholic priest, convinced most of his parishioners to pledge their allegiance to the British crown by signing an oath. It was a way he thought would avoid persecution.[4]

The British ordered a search of homes in Wexford to look for illegal weapons — firearms. Local men (mostly Catholics) in the North Cork militia carried out the searches with fearsome brutality. By May of 1798, people literally retreated from their homes and slept in the fields because the gun confiscators were burning houses at night. Uprisings and massacres all over Ireland had been reported, so people were worried.

The authorities had issued an Arms Proclamation requiring residents of Wexford to hand over their guns within 14 days. Father Murphy encouraged his parishioners to surrender their firearms. Many of the parishioners took his advice, relying on promises of British government protection.

Unfortunately, the local authorities and militia troops did not wait 14 days — torture and flogging began almost immediately to compel surrender of guns. Many Wexford people were shot before they could even comply with surrender demands.

Most of the Irish men of Wexford had rendered themselves defenseless by turning over their arms. One fateful day an English contingent fired into a crowd of men working the fields and set fire to the farm. In a fight between the Irish men and the soldiers, the senior lieutenant was killed. The next day, the English regiment took revenge by ravaging the whole region, burning over 170 homes — and Father Murphy's chapel.

On that turn of events, Father Murphy had a change of heart. He and about 1,000 men gathered to fight back, having perhaps 50 guns total. The North Cork militia attacked with 110 men, but the Wexford men drove them back. After a few other victorious encounters, however, the ill-equipped Wexford community defense force was driven out and slaughtered by cannon fire and massive attacks.

By cajoling the Wexford Catholics to surrender their weapons to their oppressors, Father Murphy opened wide the door to destruction of his people, their lands, and even his church. When he saw the government betray his people and the law, Father

Murphy tried to lead a defense force of men whom he earlier had helped disarm. Ultimately, he was executed for rebellion.

Sad as it is, the tale of Father Murphy describes perfectly the "gun control" idea: the government promises protection in exchange for the monopoly on power; the civilian leaders exhort the people to turn in their defense tools in the name of peace and safety. If the people comply and disarm themselves, then they become easy victims of persecution and murder by the next armed aggressor, whoever it might be.

David Dieteman, lawyer and scholar, wrote in a 2001 article: "The story of Father Murphy has rather obvious implications for America today. Rather than blindly surrender our freedoms and firearms in exchange for paper promises of 'protection,' Americans are better served to rely upon themselves."[5]

End Notes

[1]*Catechism of the Catholic Church.* 1994. St. Paul's Press.

[2]Story adapted from a publication by St. Gabriel Possenti Society. Arlington, VA. (www.possentisociety.com)

[3]Columbian nuns kill thief. 1999. *The Washington Times.* July 25.

[4]Story adapted from Dieteman, David. 2001. "Father Murphy and the Million Mom March." *LewRockwell.com.* Feb. 14. (www.lewrockwell.com) (citing Kee, Robert. 1972. *The Green Flag, Vol. 1: The Most Distressful Country.* New York: Penguin). The story is retold in an Irish folk song entitled "Boulavogue."

[5]Ibid.

Crime: Another Cost
of Victim Disarmament

Chapter Twenty:
Ban Guns, Crime Soars in Britain

In September, 1991, Roy Innis, National Chairman of the Congress of Racial Equality (CORE), noted a connection between anti-gun laws and high crime. He saw that places in American having the most restrictive anti-gun laws also have seven characteristics in common:[1]

1. They have the most crime.
2. They have the highest murder rate.
3. They have the largest number of illegal guns in criminal hands.
4. Illegal guns are available in the underground market in the widest variety.
5. The cost of a firearm is higher there than in less restrictive areas.
6. Criminals "are able to afford better guns than ordinary people, even better than the police."
7. Criminals are "more bold;" the environment is "safer for criminals but unsafe for the unarmed citizens."

Just a few years later, the British government unintentionally put Roy Innis' observation to the test. In June, 1997, the British Parliament enacted a ban on private possession of all handguns, including the relatively small .22 caliber pistols.[2] Ownership of pistols and long guns had already been tightly restricted.[3] At least 200,000 firearms of all types had been turned over to the government since 1996 in a general "amnesty" program. What was the result?

Most of the seven characteristics predicted by Roy Innis now apply in Britain after the "total gun ban":

On the first point, Britain's crime rate has soared. According to the British Home Secretary, Jack Straw, "levels of victimisation are higher [in England and Wales] than in most comparable countries for most categories of crime." Figures assembled for 1999 in the International Crime Victims Survey showed that "England and Wales were second only to Australia in "victimisation rates."[5] About 3.6% of people in England and Wales suffered violent crime in 1999, compared to 1.9% in the United States.

Overall, England placed second among the studied countries with 26% of its people suffering a serious crime. The United States with a 21% rate did not even place in the top ten.[6] In June, 2000, CBS News proclaimed Great Britain "one of the most violent urban societies in the Western world."[7]

On the second point, Britain's total murder rate has not greatly increased, but there has been "a rise in drive-by shootings and gangland-style executions.[8]

On the third, fourth and sixth points, criminals have access to greater numbers of a wide variety of high power firearms. According to reports in 2000, "Criminals have maintained a steady flow of smuggled guns, exhibition weapons reactivated in illegal 'factories' run by underworld leaders, and guns stolen from private collections."[9] Research data suggested that a third of "young criminals" (15-25 years of age) possess guns ranging from submachineguns to Luger pistols. What's more, according to national police detectives, "there is a move from the pistol and the shotgun to automatic weapons."[10]

While anti-gun lobbyists in Britain had claimed the handgun ban would reduce crimes committed with firearms, the opposite has occurred. The British Home Office revealed that armed crime rose 10% in 1998.[11]

The Home Office has also admitted that the handgun ban was never intended to combat firearms-related crime.[12] The figures thus far confirm that the gun ban did not reduce crime. Disarmed Britons now face a greater risk of crime. Indeed, the *Daily Telegraph* pointed out that "the main reason for a much lower burglary rate in America is householders' propensity to shoot intruders. They do so without fear of being dragged before courts and jailed for life."[13]

On the fifth point, whether the costs of firearms has risen or dropped on the underground market is uncertain. One report indicated that sub-machineguns and Luger pistols were selling to street criminals for a little as 200 British Pounds (a little over $300 US).[14]

On the seventh point, it is difficult to prove that criminals are less or more "bold" in Britain at this date. Crime data has shown, however, that half of the burglaries committed in Britain and Canada are "hot burglaries," i.e., the burglar enters when the resident is home. Only 13% of burglaries in the U.S. are "hot burglaries." The difference? Handgun ownership is tightly restricted in Britain and Canada, but much less so in the U.S.[15] In survey responses criminals in the U.S. admit that they "are much more worried about armed victims" than being intercepted by police.[16]

There seems little doubt that Britons are not feeling any safer being unarmed. Yet the Chief Constable of Norfolk advised rural gun-owning homeowners who might face burglars to "scream for help, shout and make a lot of noise" but "not shoot" at intruders.[17] The chief gave this advice, despite rising crime in Norfolk and the frank admission that "police help could take 20 minutes to arrive."[18]

Roy Innis has been just one of many Americans pointing out that "gun control" disarms innocent citizens who obey laws, while it has little or no deterrent effect on violent criminals. The British experience not only supports this conclusion — it also shows that criminal activity can increase when the victims are more likely to be unable to resist.

End Notes

[1]Innis, Roy. 1991. Bearing Arms for Self-Defense: A Human and Civil Right. *The Alliance Voice.* Sept., pp. 18-19.

[2]Copley, Joy. 1997. MPs vote to ban all handguns. *Electronic Telegraph.* June 12. (www.telegraph.co.uk)

[3]Kopel, David B. 1992. *The Samurai, The Mountie, and The Cowboy.* Buffalo, NY: Prometheus Books, pp. 76-78 (detailing British gun laws). (Book includes chapters on gun laws and effects in Japan, Canada, Australia, New Zealand, Jamaica, and Switzerland as well.)

[4]O'Neill, Sean. 2001. A quarter of English are victims of crime. *Electronic Telegraph.* February 23. (www.telegraph.co.uk)

[5]Ibid.

[6]Ibid.

[7]Kopel, David, Paul Gallant, and Joanne Eisen. 2001. Britain: From Bad to Worse. *Newsmax.com*. March 22. (www.newsmax.com)

[8]Ungoed-Thomas, Jan. 2000. Killings rise as 3M illegal guns flood Britain. *The Sunday Times*. January 16. (www.sunday-times.co.uk)

[9]Ibid.

[10]Ibid.

[11]Ibid.

[12]Ibid.

[13]Kopel, et al., 2001, Britain: From Bad to Worse, citing *Daily Telegraph*, June 29, 2000.

[14]Ungoed-Thomas, 2000.

[15]Lott, John R. Jr. 2000. *More Guns, Less Crime: Understanding Crime and Gun Control Laws*. Second ed. Chicago: University of Chicago Press, p. 5, citing Wright, James D. And Peter Rossi. 1986. *Armed and Considered Dangerous: A Survey of Felons and Their Firearms*. Hawthorne, NY: Aldine de Gruyter Publishers.

[16]Ibid.

[17]Ford, Richard. 2000. Don't shoot - scream, police tell farmers. *The (London) Times*. April 21. (www.times-archive.co.uk)

[18]Ibid.

Chaper Twenty-one:
Japan: Exception to the Rule?

For centuries, Japan has banned or rigidly limited most private ownership of firearms. During that time and until today, Japan has enjoyed a very low violent crime rate. Do these two facts prove that disarming civilians can drastically reduce violent crime? More importantly, does the example of Japan disprove the Genocide Formula?

The short answer is: no. Because of Japan's unique history, tradition, demographics, and its culture and social system, the Japanese crime rate is low and would be low — with or without the private ownership of firearms. Unfortunately, the Japanese culture and social system yields no guarantee against oppressive government. Rather, the Japanese system in the past unleashed militarism and brutality that caused death and destruction on a huge scale all over Asia. Even today many elements of a police state prevail in Japan.

Low Crime Rate -- With A Cost

David Kopel, scholar at the Independence Institute, examined the potential connection between firearms prohibition and low crime rates in several countries, including Japan, in his book *The Samurai, The Mountie, and the Cowboy.*[1] Kopel's research pinpointed several factors peculiar to Japan that account for the low crime rate there:

1. The police have broad powers to stop and search citizens on a hunch; police search citizens at will, usually with the citizens' permission.[2]

2. The Japanese population is 97% of one race: Japanese. Immigrants and their descendants can never become full

citizens.[3]

3. The differences in incomes and wealth between citizens is narrower than in some Western countries such as the United States.[4]

4. Policemen, even riot police, have rarely carried firearms; police officers rely mostly on martial arts and batons when necessary.[5]

5. Japanese people for centuries have lived in a culture of strict obedience to family and authorities, where an individual who deviated from society's expectations would bring shame and humiliation not only upon himself but upon his family and community.[6]

6. Accused criminals confess to their crimes about 95% of the time; the conviction rate in criminal trials is 99.91%.[7]

Summing it up, Kopel observed:

> Powerful social authorities, beginning with the father and reaching up to the state, create a strict climate for obeying both the criminal laws and the gun-control laws. The voluntary disarmament of the Japanese government reinforces this climate. Ethnic homogeneity and economic equality remove some of the causes of criminality. Simply put, the Japanese are among the most law-abiding people on earth... .[8]

Those same factors come with heavy costs to the Japanese people:

1. Police surveillance and intervention are part of citizens' daily lives. Once or twice a year, police prepare "residence information cards" for every home and person: logging who lives where, how many live in each house and their relationships, how much money each person has, where they work and whether they work late, what kind of car they own, even dating and sexual activity. The police maintain a file on every person in the country.[9]

2. Persons who are arrested may be detained for up to 23 days before being brought before a judge.[10] Because the police can release and then rearrest a suspect on a different charge or to prevent him from possibly destroying evidence, some defendants have been held in jail for months

without a hearing or bail.[11]

3. Suspects in custody usually cannot be visited except by their lawyers. Lawyer visits are strictly limited and very short, and sometimes denied entirely. Suspects can be questioned up to 12 hours per day, denied a bath for a week, or forced to stand up or lie down continuously in their cells. Seemingly endless questioning can induce suspects to falsely confess just to end the pressure.[12] Amnesty International reportedly called the Japanese police custody system a "flagrant violation of United Nations human rights principles."[13]

4. Defendants have no right to a jury trial.[14] Illegally obtained evidence is admissible in court, even when the evidence is a confession obtained by torture.[15]

5. The culture of shame has resulted in a very high suicide rate among Japanese people, including teenagers. Kopel reported that the suicide rate in Japan was twice as high as that in the United States.[16] More recent figures pegged the Japanese suicide rate at 40% higher than the U.S. rate.[17] Alarmingly frequent is one horrific result of tight family structures: "family suicides" in which a parent kills the children and then commits suicide. The Japanese authorities count these family deaths all as suicides, not homicides.[18]

6. According to some Japanese researchers, Japanese individuals feel perennially insecure, and feel a "dread of power." People feel that dread, at least in part, because individuals cannot count on others in Japanese society to help them against violence or against authority -- and because individuals themselves are forbidden to possess weapons for self-defense.[19]

Is The Ruler's Conscience Enough?

Using language ordinarily applied to tyrannical and totalitarian governments, Kopel wrote about Japan in 1992: "There is hardly any check on the power of the state, save its own conscience."[20]

What about the conscience of the Japanese government? Is *conscience* enough to prevent genocide? Consider the historical record of Japan in the 20th Century.

In the early 1900's, the Emperor and the civilian government installed Shinto as a national religion and established emperor-worship (especially by members of the armed forces). Shinto was formulated into "an endorsement of a modern, totalitarian state."[21] Added in the 1920's was a warriors' code of honor known as *bushido*, which glorified extreme nationalism and militarism.[22]

In the 1920's and 1930's, the armed forces exerted increasing control over the government of the Empire of Japan, especially over foreign policy. Bribery flourished and political assassinations were common in the internal struggles for power.[23] Japan's military rulers embraced national socialism, working to exert control over the entire national economy and to direct all activities to achieve the public welfare.[24]

When the Japanese Empire went to war, the Genocide Formula came into play:

Hatred + Government + Disarmed Civilians = Genocide

Part of the Japanese culture, especially at that time, was a strong belief that the Japanese were racially superior to all other Asian peoples.[25] That view, combined with a military culture of brutality toward its own servicemen and ruthlessness toward "enemies," resulted in *Hatred* as defined in Chapter 5: the loathing and disgust for other people, the state of mind that would order, encourage or permit the intentional killing of innocent people.

As described above, the Imperial Japanese Government adopted such ideas as racial supremacy, national socialism, and the desire for national expansion and power.[26] The increasingly well-armed military largely controlled foreign affairs. Thus there existed the element of *powerful Government*.

Civilian Disarmament was a near certainty in Japan at that time. Nearly five centuries ago, Hideyoshi conquered and unified Japan, and in 1588 he announced "the Sword Hunt" — the ban on possession of swords and firearms by anyone other than noblemen. All other privately-held weapons were confiscated.[27] The *Samurai*, warriors of the noble class, retained a right to carry swords ...and held a privilege to kill without consequences members of the lower class who might show disrespect.[28]

For centuries in Japan, weapons were reserved for the ruling

256

class, not for the subjects. At the same time, the concept of individual freedom was non-existent; the concept of opportunity, such as to travel or better oneself, was extinguished.[29] There has been in Japan no culture of individual rights or healthy distrust of government.[30] As the militarist rulers acquired greater control in the 1920's and 1930's, the "army and the navy were vast organizations with a monopoly on physical violence. There was no force in Japan that could offer any resistance."[31]

When the elements of the Genocide Formula came together, it resulted in the astonishingly savage destruction of non-Japanese between 1937 and 1945. In China alone, the Japanese Empire's military killed 400,000 prisoners of war and others in custody, 142,000 forced laborers, and 2,850,000 others by massacres and atrocities.[32] Throughout Asia and the Pacific, including the Philippines, French Indochina, Malaysia, Indonesia, Singapore, Burma, and other islands, the Japanese military butchered another estimated 1.7 million civilians.[33] Apparently no element of conscience slowed the murderous frenzies of victorious Imperial Japanese troops.

So, what about the conscience of the Japanese government? Iris Chang, author of *The Rape of Nanking,* documented how for decades after World War II the Japanese government and academic institutions have continued steadfastly to deny the aggression, barbarism and atrocities committed by the Imperial Japanese military in 1937 to 1945.[34] For example, Ms. Chang quoted the leading member of Japan's Liberal Democratic Party, Ishihara Shintaro, who said: "People say that the Japanese made a holocaust there [in Nanking], but that is not true. It is a story made up by the Chinese. It has tarnished the image of Japan, but it is a lie."[35]

According to Ms. Chang, textbooks used in Japan must be approved by the Japanese Ministry of Education, and the history texts have typically white-washed or ignored the wartime aggression and atrocities committed by the Imperial government. Many Japanese academics have avoided even discussing the Rape of Nanking, for example, and others have tried to minimize or excuse the massacre of civilians there.[36]

Unlike the government of Germany, which has admitted the Nazi experience and vowed to prevent it from recurring, the government of Japan has not fully admitted and explored the Imperial government's heinous past crimes against humanity.[37] *The present government of Japan seems to lack a conscience on matters of genocide.*

Is the Future Secure?

Japan:

* A nation of unarmed citizens trained to obey authority
* A society that embraces police state policies
* A government that fails to admit the historical fact of genocide

Will the people of Japan be able to detect a looming genocide? Will the unarmed citizens have any means to resist a future tyranny in their own land ...or to stop a future military regime from launching a murderous rampage again?

The example of Japanese "gun control" does not disprove the Genocide Formula. If anything, the history of the Empire of Japan in the 20th Century tragically proves the formula true.

Defenseless in a Sacred Zone

Bursting into a second-grade music class, a man began stabbing children randomly at the elementary school using a six-inch kitchen knife. In just 10 minutes on June 8, 2001, the man had killed eight children and injured 15 other pupils and two teachers.[38] Mass murder – by knife – in Japan, where, as one Japanese teacher put it, "schools were always regarded as sacred zones."

Intense social pressures upon Japanese individuals to conform to group norms, coupled with close police monitoring of private lives, have created a nation that can boast a very low murder rate. Trusting the social system to deter crime, the Japanese schools have left their pupils and teachers undefended against violent attackers.

In this case, the school attacker, a 37 year old man, confessed to police and told them: "I want to die ... If I killed children, I knew I would get the death penalty." His attack was an attempted suicide. His victims were defenseless children. He knew they were undefended by law and custom.

A knife-wielding Japanese woman invaded a kindergarten classroom just two weeks later, stabbed a teacher and fled.[39] This woman, too, knew her victim(s) would be unarmed and unprotected against violence.

Japanese officials worry that the system of social restraints is falling apart. In the previous year, a 17-year-old boy attacked and bludgeoned people with a baseball bat. Another teenager, also 17, beat his mother to death with a metal bat. Yet another teenager murdered an elderly neighbor with a knife just for the experience of killing someone. In 1999, a man attacked and stabbed a 7-year-old boy in a schoolyard with a kitchen knife. A 14-year-old murdered and beheaded a younger boy in 1997.[40]

Japan, the nation that almost totally prohibits its citizens from possessing firearms, leaves its people defenseless to vicious or suicidal murderers. As increasing numbers of dangerous individuals ignore the laws and customs in Japan, so also will increase the numbers of innocent and defenseless victims hurt and killed. Tragically, people who most trust the "gun control" idea will suffer and die by its effects.

End Notes

[1]Kopel, David B. 1992. *The Samurai, The Mountie, and The Cowboy.* Buffalo, NY: Prometheus Books.

[2]Ibid., p. 23.

[3]Ibid., p. 41.

[4]Ibid., pp. 42-43.

[5]Ibid., pp. 39-40.

[6]Ibid., pp. 26, 37, 44-45.

[7]Ibid., p. 26.

[8]Ibid, p. 45.

[9]Ibid., p. 24.

[10]Landers, Peter. 2000. Second Thoughts: A False Confession Jailed Mr. Yakushiji; Then Fate Intervened. *The Wall Street Journal.* October 6, p. A1.

[11]Kopel 1992, p. 25.

[12]Landers 2000, p. A1.

[13]Kopel 1992, p. 25.

[14]Ibid.

15Ibid., pp. 23, 26.

16Ibid., p. 43.

17United Nations. 1998. 1996 Demographic Yearbook.

18Kopel 1992, pp. 43-44.

19Ibid., p. 44 (citing Iga, Mamoru and Kichinosuke Totai, "Characteristics of Suicide and Attitudes toward Suicides in Japan," in Farberow, Norman L. (ed). 1975. *Suicide in Different Cultures.* Baltimore: University Park Press.)

20Ibid., p. 26.

21Johnson, Paul. 1991. *Modern Times.* Revised edition. New York: Harper Collins, pp. 180-181.

22Ibid., p. 181.

23Ibid., pp. 183-186.

24Rummel, R.J. 1994. *Death by Government.* New Brunswick, NJ: Transaction Publishers, p. 144.

25Ibid.

26Johnson 1991, 189-190.

27Kopel 1992, pp. 29-30.

28Ibid., p. 30.

29Ibid., pp. 31-33.

30Ibid, pp. 38-39, 46.

31Ibid., pp. 34-35 (quoting a Japanese scholar).

32Rummel 1994, p. 148 (table).

33Ibid., 148-149.

34Chang, Iris. 1997. *The Rape of Nanking.* New York: Basic Books, pp. 199-214.

35Ibid., p. 201 (quoting interview in *Playboy* magazine, October, 1990).

36Ibid., pp. 205-210.

37Ibid., pp. 200-201, 222-224.

38Kanai, Keiko. 2001. Seven Children Dead in Japan School Stabbing. *Reuters.* June 8.

39Ueno, Teruaki. 2001. New Attack in Japan Raises Alarm on Violent Crime. *Reuters.* June 19.

40Ibid.

Visualize World Bondage

Chapter Twenty-two:
The United Nations: Governments Helping Governments Disarm Citizens

A key element in the Genocide Formula is *powerful government*. So what happens when there is *world government?* The United Nations, founded in 1945, has been advertised as a union of nations designed to prevent war and facilitate world peace. As popularly understood, the UN was "an attempt to stabilize world politics ... by bringing the nations of the planet into a single, cooperative, deliberative forum with sufficient authority to resolve international disputes peacefully."[1]

In reality, the United Nations more accurately should be dubbed the United Governments. There has never been a worldwide vote of the people to ratify the UN Charter. There has never been a world election to select representatives from each nation to the UN. Rather, the delegates to the UN are appointed by their respective governments.

And who are these governments? Surveys of civil and political rights by Freedom House show that 55% of the world's nations are not "free" countries.[2] Most of the "free" nations themselves labor under varying forms of "democratic" socialism (welfare statism). Perhaps a better name for the UN is the Union of Socialist and Military Regimes: a collection of entities, in Tom Paine's terms, ranging in degrees of evil from "necessary" to "intolerable."

Not surprisingly, the UN member governments seek to preserve and enlarge their powers. To concentrate political power into the hands of national and then world governments, UN policy has lately shifted toward "microdisarmament" — which means disarming individual citizens within its member states.

Two Faces of Microdisarmament

There are two types of microdisarmament: *post-conflict disarmament* and *population disarmament*. In recent years, post-conflict disarmament comes into play when the United Nations has intervened to stop internal or civil wars.

At its inception in 1945, the UN worried about preventing international or global wars (e.g., World War III). The United Nations Institute for Disarmament Research (UNIDR) has stated that after the end of the Cold War, however, "the main objective of global action" has become "to stabilize domestic situations."[3]

"Global action" here refers to situations where the UN has sent military forces into a nation to quell an insurrection or civil war, or to enforce a truce or a cease-fire. As soon as the UN has established some kind of peace in the nation (termination of armed conflict), the UNIDR suggests that UN forces create a "situation of stability."[4] "Such stability can be facilitated by troop withdrawals, the demilitarization of border zones, and effective disarmament, demobilization and demining."[5] The plan makes some sense: if you want to prevent a flare up of conflict between armed factions, then you move the armies away from each other, and then disband them and remove their weapons.

The UNIDR states that "the way to implement peace, defined in terms of long-term stability, is to focus not just on the sources of violence (e.g. social and political development issues) but also on the material vehicles for violence (weapons and munitions)."[6] Moreover, "weapons that are not managed and controlled in the field will invariably flow over into neighboring countries, becoming a problem in themselves."[7] Here the UNIDR embraces the idea that weapons by themselves cause problems — the same idea that underlies the "public health" arguments for "gun control" in America.[8]

Fatal Flaws In Disarmament Agenda

Post-conflict disarmament seems to be a reasonable way for a neutral party (UN) to quiet a civil war between armed factions. Two fatal flaws make such disarmament dangerous.

First, the UNIDR assumes that firearms (weapons) cause violence. This assumption appears often in UN discussion of microdisarmament. *The Report of the Panel of Government Experts on Small Arms* presented to the United Nations in 1997, refers to "the excessive and destabilizing accumulation of small arms and light weapons."[9] Perhaps to defuse criticism, the *Report* remarks that the "accumulation of small arms and light weapons by themselves do not cause the conflicts in which they are used."[10] The rest of the Report deals almost entirely with the problems of the existence or "accumulation" of weapons, as though the weapons themselves do actually cause the problems.

Starting by assuming that the presence of weapons does cause violence, the *Report* quietly expands that premise from civil wars to also include ordinary criminal violence. "The excessive and destabilizing accumulation and transfer of small arms and light weapons is closely related to the increased incidence of internal conflicts and *high levels of crime* and violence."[11] "Small arms" refers to ordinary firearms: revolvers, semi-automatic pistols, rifles of all types, and machine guns.[12] Once "small arms" can be linked with "high levels of crime and violence," the door opens to global "gun control."

The second fatal flaw in the UN post-conflict disarmament agenda is its moral emptiness. UN disarmament agencies cannot tell the difference between aggressor and victim; between government oppression and popular resistance; between government genocide and victim defense. The proof of the UN's moral blindness shows in its careful choice of morally neutral words — words that erase the distinction between evil aggression and righteous defense, and between beneficial government and evil government. Consider these examples:

- "Since weak states are susceptible to ethnic tensions, secession, and outright criminality, many regions are now afflicted by situations of violent intrastate conflicts. Intrastate conflict occurs at immense humanitarian cost."[13]

  NOTE: This language does not distinguish between aggressive versus defensive use of force. A rebellion against a tyrant is an "intrastate conflict." The American Revolutionary War was an "intrastate conflict" involving a desire for "secession."

- "The UN has necessarily shifted its focus from a supporting role, in which it could ensure long-term national and international stability, to a role which involves obtaining a quick peace and easing humanitarian pressures immediately."[14]

NOTE: A "quick peace" does not indicate, let alone guarantee, a morally right result. Communist Chinese military forces obtained a "quick peace" after killing over 3,000 mostly unarmed demonstrators at Tiananmen Square, Beijing, on June 3-4, 1989. Shooting escaping slaves obtains a "quick peace."

- "Small arms and light weapons" play prominent roles in "several of the armed conflicts dealt with by the United Nations, particularly where fighting involves irregular troops among the conflicting parties. Many of these conflicts have inflicted heavy casualties on the people involved. The vast majority of these casualties have been civilians, mostly women and children."[15]

NOTE: Seemingly neutral language referring to "armed conflicts" involving "irregular troops among the conflicting parties" makes no distinction between marauding government death squads and parties of resistance fighters trying to stop the squads and protect towns.

- "The availability of [small arms and light weapons], however, contributes towards exacerbating conflicts by increasing the lethality and duration of violence, by encouraging a violent rather than a peaceful resolution of differences, and by generating a vicious circle of a greater sense of insecurity, which in turn leads to a greater demand for, and use of, such weapons."[16]

NOTE: This logic of a "vicious circle" of using weapons does not distinguish between aggression and self-defense. It does not allow the possibility that the "greater demand" for weapons to defend a persecuted minority might be entirely justified on moral grounds.

- "In many instances, weapons procured at an earlier stage for purposes of national liberation have become available for the violent overthrow of new Governments by insurgent forces or terrorists, or for acts of criminality for personal gain."[17]

NOTE: This language assumes that "new Governments" are the product of "national liberation," and that these governments are legitimate, non-aggressive and beneficial.

The "insurgents" must be disarmed because they oppose the government — yet there is no consideration for the possibility that the government is oppressive and ought to be stopped by the armed citizenry.

- "[W]here [non-military and home-made] weapons are used and accumulated in numbers that endanger the security and political stability of a state, the [UN] Panel considered them relevant" to the microdisarmament agenda.[18]

NOTE: Weapons that "endanger the security and political stability of a state" are those that must be taken away, according to the UN. The "states" must be protected from accumulations of non-military and home-made weapons — that are held by non-government parties. What about the accumulation of weapons in the hands of governments and their agencies that endanger the people? Hardly a word.

Protecting Governments First

The above examples show how the UN views post-conflict disarmament as a means to protect governments first. Protecting people's lives, liberty and property rights falls in at lower priority. Consider also that several of the "governmental experts" consulted for the UN's 1997 *Report* represented countries that Freedom House does not consider "free": Egypt, Russian Federation, Iran, Belarus, and Colombia.[19]

"Guidelines for international arms transfers" were published with the 1996 *Report of the Disarmament Commission*.[20] Among the statement of "Principles" was the following:

[Paragraph 14:] States should respect the principles and purposes of the Charter of the United Nations, including the right to self-defense; the sovereign equality of all its members; non-interference in the internal affairs of States; ...and continue to reaffirm the right of self-determination of all peoples, taking into account the particular situation of peoples under colonial or other forms of alien domination or foreign occupation, and recognize the right of peoples to take legitimate action in accordance with the Charter of the United Nations to realize their inalienable right to self-determination.

By this wording, the Disarmament Commission has affirmed

the sanctity of governments and the right of "self-determination" of peoples (not individuals), especially if they are under colonial or foreign domination.

The "right to self-defense" refers to defense of nations, not of individuals. The 1996 *Report of the Disarmament Commission* stated: "All States have the inherent right to self-defense, as enshrined in the Charter of the United Nations, and consequently the right to acquire arms for their security."[21] The same paragraph slams the brakes on popular resistance to established governments:

> This shall not be construed as authorizing or encouraging any action that would dismember or impair, totally or in part, the territorial integrity or political unity of sovereign and independent States conducting themselves in compliance with the principle of equal rights and self-determination of peoples and thus possessed of a Government representing the whole people belonging to the territory without distinction of any kind.

The principle of "equal rights" preserves no rights in particular. All citizens can be equally unfree and have "equal rights." The idea of "self-determination" has no real substance, especially considering how the large majority of the world's nations are not "free." Having a "Government representing the whole people" also has little meaning when the government is a military junta, central communist party or other domestic dictator.

As a matter of historical fact, the United Nations Security Council (the select body where each permanent member has veto power) long included Communist Russia and still includes Communist China. Neither country has been known for human rights, liberty, or a free society, and post-Cold War Russia is still not classified as a "free" country. There can be little doubt that the UN microdisarmament concept works largely to protect governments in unfree countries from uprisings of their own people.

World "Gun Control" Propaganda Technique

UN strategists for microdisarmament cleverly weaved a world government mandate for "gun control" by small shifts in language. At first the UN targeted weapons of international war, then weapons of civil war, then weapons of "intrastate conflict," then weapons of crime. Watch how the UN expanded its mission by gradual steps:

1. The UN tries to prevent war between nations by discussion

and negotiation.

2. The UN works to prevent war between nations by cutting back the stockpiles of weapons of war that each nation has.

3. When wars between nations are fairly rare, the UN turns its attention to "intrastate conflicts" or "civil wars." The UN tries to stop such violence by brokering peace talks and agreements.

4. The UN forcibly intervenes in "intrastate conflicts" to stop violence. To make sure that peace (cessation of violence) is maintained, the UN tries to reduce or eliminate the stockpiles of weapons of war possessed by the various factions.

5. To protect "stability" of governments after "intrastate conflicts," the UN disarms those parties that oppose the governments.

6. Parties that oppose governments frequently are equipped with small arms and light weapons. Therefore, the UN must confiscate as many such weapons as possible in regions of former "intrastate conflict."

7. Small arms play a major role in "intrastate conflicts" and rebellions against governments, as well as criminal violence and crime, so the UN must confiscate small arms where such conflicts and rebellions have recently taken place.

8. To prevent future "intrastate conflicts" in countries where no such conflict has occurred recently, to prevent shipments of weapons from nations at peace to factions in civil wars, as well as to prevent criminal violence and crime, the UN must confiscate small arms from citizens of countries at peace.

Using these eight steps over a period of years, the UN has moved from a world body seeking to prevent huge wars, to an interventionist world power that works to disarm nonviolent citizens in nations at peace. Consider next the UN world population disarmament proposal.

Disarming Populations

UN-sponsored microdisarmament's second face is *population disarmament*. Post-conflict disarmament aims at ending civil wars and keeping peace (cessation of violence), but population disarmament more clearly aims to keep governments in power and their peoples in submission.

The reasons for population disarmament start with the idea that the mere physical presence of weapons causes or stimulates violence in everything from international war to street crime. To make firearms ownership an international issue, the UN and other microdisarmament advocates frame the problem as "illicit traffic in arms."

Read how the 1996 *Report of the Disarmament Commission* treats war and street crime as the same, and blames "illicit traffic in arms" for making them happen:

> The problem of the illicit traffic in arms has a social and humanitarian component in addition to its technical, economic and political dimensions. The human suffering that is caused, inter alia, by the devastating consequences of war, destabilizing violence and conflicts, terrorism, mercenary activities, subversion, drug trafficking, common and organized crime and other criminal actions cannot be ignored.[22]

The solution to "illicit arms trafficking"? All governments must enact "gun control":

- by restricting import and export of weapons:

   > States should ensure that they have an adequate system of national laws and/or regulations and administrative procedures to exercise effective control over armaments and the export and import of arms in order, among other goals, to prevent illicit arms trafficking.[23]

- by restricting the manufacture, sales and possession of weapons:

   > States should scrutinize their national arms-control legislation and procedures, and, where necessary, strengthen them in order to increase their effectiveness in preventing the illegal production, trade in and possession of arms in their territory that can lead to illicit arms trafficking.[24]

- by authorizing government agent access to firearms while restricting civilian ownership and possession of firearms:

   > States should define... which arms are permitted for civilian use and which may be used or possessed by the military and police forces.[25]

World Gun Control Lobby: BASIC

The British American Security Information Council (BASIC) lobbies the UN for global disarmament, which includes population disarmament.[26] Using the "illicit arms traffic" as its starting point, BASIC takes the "guns cause violence" line: "The internationalization of the gun trade enables gun control measures in one country to affect the levels of gun-related crime and violence in other countries."[27] To implement world "gun control" there must everywhere be national "gun control." BASIC urges, "It will be difficult, if not impossible, to control the illicit international market in light weapons without also monitoring and controlling domestic access to weapons."[28]

In parallel with its efforts to end the threat of nuclear war, BASIC targets "light weapons" which include pistols, revolvers, rifles, machine guns and other portable weapons systems.[29] BASIC wants international laws to ban the manufacture, sale and possession of "junk guns" (handguns lacking "essential safety features)" and "other dangerous weapons such as Saturday Night Specials (non-sporting, low quality handguns)."[30]

BASIC's position teaches a key lesson. The goal of population disarmament is to make it extremely difficult for average citizens and poor people to obtain the weapons necessary to stop a Rape of Nanking or to overthrow a Hitler, Stalin, or Pol Pot. When an international disarmament lobby busies itself trying to get the United Nations to ban "junk" and inexpensive handguns, then you know that **governments fear a citizenry armed with anything.**

The BASIC Strategy: Global Norms, Local Outcry

BASIC not only recommends "gun control" proposals, it also has published a strategy to push worldwide population disarmament.[31] The BASIC Plan suggests:

1. "Improving domestic gun control," and employing "gun guy-back programs." The buy-back programs are "not at all assured" of success; they serve instead a propaganda goal because "they tie control of weapons transfers to an issue that is much more readily understood — violence in the streets."

2. "Eliminating or restricting certain types of weapons. The

prospects for success of these measures are greatest when global norms against particular weapons and their effects have been established. ... This approach can also be undertaken in the domestic sphere, as with assault weapons and the 'Saturday night special' pistol in the United States."

3. "When such control measures are well-defined and linked directly to specific problems, they tend to generate more support than more sweeping measures. Later on, **when the principle of controlling particular weapons or ammunition has been accepted, broader measures may be more easily implemented.**"[32]

4. Banning specific weapons has tactical advantages: "There are several advantages to outright bans on certain types of weapons. Perhaps most prominent is that such bans are much easier to monitor and enforce than are qualitative or quantitative limits. ... Focusing on particularly harmful or indiscriminate weapons can also mobilize public outcry."

Under the category of "making the argument," BASIC teaches how to sell population disarmament: "the issue ...is frighteningly obvious: light weapons kill, maim and destroy; they cause instability and prolong wars; they promote a culture of violence ...and they divert much-needed resources away from social and economic development."[33]

As described above for post-conflict disarmament, BASIC's arguments focus on firearms as the cause of violence and war. BASIC scarcely recognizes the possibility that individuals must use force righteously to repel invaders or to stop tyranny. Yes, "light weapons kill" — but they kill attackers and murderers and death squads, too. By failing to account for the morality of individual self-defense, BASIC itself advocates immorality.

The United Nations "Gun Control" Plans

The United Nations is expanding its mission from international peacekeeper to the arbiter of family disputes. In its April 1998 session, the UN Commission on Crime Prevention and Criminal Justice ("Crime Commission") issued its report entitled *Criminal Justice Reform and Strengthening of Legal Institutions: Measures to Regulate Firearms ("Firearms Regulation Report")*.

That report responded to the Economic and Social Council's request to develop "a programme of continuing education for criminal justice administrators and of public education and awareness-building in relation to the links between firearms in civilian use and the unacceptable levels of violence in cities, communities *and families.*"³⁴ Evidently, the UN now considers "violence in families" to be within its scope of concern.

To develop suggestions for world "gun control," the UN Crime Commission conducted several multi-national "regional workshops on firearm regulation." Participants in these workshops included representatives from such decidedly non-free and totalitarian countries as Communist China, Gambia, Guinea, Iran, Kenya, Qatar, Saudi Arabia, Sudan, Swaziland, Viet Nam.³⁵ *The Firearms Regulation Report* collected and summarized the results of the workshops. Here are some of the key points and suggestions from the participants as published in that report:³⁶

- "Participants recommended that ownership of firearms should be authorized for specific purposes only" and "that firearms should be used strictly for the purpose for which they were authorized."

- Purposes of firearms that might be authorized included: "sports," "hunting," "protection of life and property," "collections," and corporate private security services.

- "Persons applying for authorization to use firearms for personal protection should be obliged to establish real and serious reasons for their use."

- "Only when a State could not protect its citizens adequately" would the citizens have a right to possess firearms.

- When considering applicants for possession or ownership of firearms, the governments might decide the question based on considerations of the applicants'
  - age
  - proof of need for firearms
  - knowledge of firearms use
  - prior criminal record
  - prior record of drug or alcohol abuse
  - prior record of domestic violence
  - "mental fitness"

- ○ "physical fitness"
- ○ "payment of all taxes"
- ○ "community approval through letters of reference"
- ○ spouse's approval
- ○ proficiency in firearms use
- ○ ability to store firearms in a "safe place"
- "Authorization for firearm ownership or possession should be renewed every year or two."
- "Intensive media campaign to urge residents to register their firearms."
- Require registered firearms owners to verify residence, prove their knowledge of firearms laws and restrictions via written tests, and submit to periodic inspection.
- Require firearms owners over age 60 to undergo annual physical exams as a condition of keeping their license.
- "Strong emphasis on firearms training."
- "Intensive background checks."
- Limits on the number of firearms one person could buy.
- Applicants for firearm license must provide picture identification, birth certificate, firearm training certificate, proof of payment of license fee, fingerprinting record, and results of intensive background check.
- As a condition of keeping the firearm license, the gun owner must comply with restrictions on lending firearms, strictly obey limits on carrying, renew the license periodically, register all firearms, obtain a liability insurance policy for firearms use, and establish "real and serious reasons for requesting authorization to use firearms for personal protection."
- Necessary elements of any "firearm control" program would have to include "regular inspection, proper supervision, periodic audits and prosecution for negligence."
- To recover and remove "illegal firearms" from the population, governments could offer amnesty surrender and "buy-back" programs, destroy all surrendered and confiscated firearms, and outlaw all private firearm collections.

Visualize World Police

Who would enforce all of this world "gun control?" *The Firearms Regulation Report* answers that question: "global law enforcement cooperation and assistance." Government law enforcement agencies helping one another, exchanging intelligence and technical data on firearms tracking, and using Interpol to share information.[37]

Imagine: your local police chief and your FBI will be helping the Minister of Death Squads in a killer State to track down "illegal gun traffickers" and unlicensed gun owners. Your tax money at work.

End Notes

[1]Axelrod, Alan and Charles Phillips. 1998. *What Everyone Should Know about the 20th Century.* Holbrook, MA: Adams Media Corp., p. 158.

[2]Freedom House. 2000. *Table of Countries - Comparative Measures of Freedom.* www.freedomhouse.org.

[3]UNIDR, Disarmament and Conflict Resolution Project, *Microdisarmament: A New Agenda for Disarmament and Arms Control.* Extracted from the 1995 Progress Report. (www.bicc.de) ("Microdisarmament Agenda") Sec. I, (italics in original.)

[4]Ibid., Sec. II.

[5]Ibid.

[6]Ibid.

[7]Ibid.

[8]Kates, Don B. et al., 1995. Guns and Public Health: Epidemic of Violence or Pandemic of Propaganda? *Tennessee Law Review* 62, pp. 513-596. (www.2ndlawlib.org);Suter, Edgar A. 1994. Guns in the Medical Literature — A Failure of Peer Review. *Journal of the Medical Association of Georgia* 83 (March), pp. 133-146. (http://www.dipr.org) ; Stevens, Richard W. 1997. Disarming the Data Doctors: How to Debunk the "Public Health" Argument for "Gun Control." *The Firearms Sentinel,* (Winter), pp. 2-6. (www.jpfo.org)

[9]General and Complete Disarmament: Small Arms, *Report of the Panel of Governmental Experts on Small Arms,* Doc. No. A/52/298, August 27, 1997, ("*Report*"), ¶ 13.

[10]Ibid., ¶ 17.

[11]Ibid., ¶ 14 (italics added).

[12]Ibid., ¶ 26.

[13]UNIDR, *Microdisarmament Agenda,* Sec. I.

[14]UNIDR, *Microdisarmament Agenda,* Sec. I.

[15]*Report,* ¶ 15.

[16]*Report,* ¶ 17.

[17]*Report,* ¶ 19.

[18]*Report,* ¶ 28.

[19]Freedom House at www.freedomhouse.org.

[20]UN Disarmament Commission, General Assembly Official Records, Fifty-first Session, Supplement No. 42, Doc. No. A/51/42, 1996, Annex I.

[21]Ibid., Annex I, ¶ 1.

[22]Ibid., Annex I, ¶ 3.

[23]Ibid., ¶ 23.

[24]Ibid., ¶ 24.

[25]Ibid., ¶ 30.

[26]www.basicint.org. A coalition of governments, including those of Brazil, Mali, the Netherlands and the United Kingdom, has created the International Action Network on Small Arms (IANSA) to agitate for worldwide civilian disarmament. IANSA explains its agenda on its Internet website at www.iansa.org.

[27]Geraldine O'Callaghan, Statement of BASIC to the European Regional Workshop on Firearm Regulation for the Purposes of Crime Prevention and Public Safety, Sept. 22, 1997. *("Firearm Regulation Report")*

[28]Ibid.

[29]Ibid., n. 1.

[30]Ibid.

[31]British American Security Information Council, Project on Light Weapons. *Controlling Global Light Weapons Transfers: Working Toward Policy Options,* prepared for the International Studies Association annual meeting, April 16, 1996. The Ford Foundation provided "generous support" for the Project.

[32]Emphasis added.

[33]Ibid.

[34]*Firearm Regulation Report,* ¶ 1 (emphasis added).

[35]*Firearm Regulation Report,* ¶¶ 6-9.

[36]Ibid, ¶¶ 11-25.

[37]Ibid, ¶¶ 39.

The Issue Is Self-Defense

Chapter Twenty-three:
Is Self-Defense Rocket Science?

Human experience, Judeo-Christian tenets of belief, and simple reasoning together show Seven Basic Truths:

1. There is a difference between good and evil, and evil exists among mankind.[1]
2. Aggression means initiating force against people to deprive them of life, liberty or property without just cause.
3. Aggression by one person or group against another is evil.
4. All things being equal, an aggressor with superior force will defeat a victim who employs less force in defense.
5. Evil people who aggress will generally prevail over good people who cannot defeat the aggression.
6. For good people to protect their lives, liberty and property, they must be able use superior force to defeat aggression.
7. Ideas that inhibit good people from being able to defeat aggression are ideas that confer an advantage to aggressors, and thereby reduce good people's ability to protect their lives, liberty and property.

Are these Seven Basic Truths difficult to understand?

The Genocide Formula described in this book does no more than illustrate these seven truths in the context of government megamurder. "Gun control" schemes are simply laws that give authority to governments to enforce the idea of disarming citizens. Cesare Beccaria, one of the founders of modern criminology, pointed out the perverse silliness of "weapons control" about 350 years ago, when he wrote:

> The laws that forbid the carrying of arms ... [act to] dis-
> arm those only who are neither inclined nor determined
> to commit crimes. . . . Such laws make things worse for
> the assaulted and better for the assailants; they serve
> rather to encourage than to prevent homicides, for *an
> unarmed man may be attacked with greater confi-
> dence than an armed man.*[2]

The danger of civilian disarmament ("gun control") seems to
have been obvious for centuries. Yet some people in the modern
era cannot grasp the simple fact.[3]

Let's bring the problem close to home. In recent years there
have been several publicized cases where civilian disarmament
laws and anti-firearms ideas made it not only possible, but actually easier, for a violent person to kill innocent people.

Unarmed Victims Murdered at Yosemite

Three women visiting Yosemite National Park were abducted
and killed in February 1999 by a lodge employee. A few months
later the same employee also brutally killed and decapitated
another woman who worked at Yosemite.[4] Did these women have
the means to defend themselves against this killer? No — for at
least one reason: possession of firearms in Yosemite is prohibited
(except for authorized government employees).[5]

If the women had been carrying a firearm, would their lives
have been saved? There is no certain answer, but statistics show
that women who do not resist an attack face a 250% higher risk
of injury than women who resist using a firearm.[6] When people do
use firearms for self-defense, studies show that 19 out of 20
defenders escape injury.[7]

Statistics are not the only proof. When aggressors suspect
their victims are armed, the aggressors shy away from attacking.
During the Los Angeles riot in spring of 1992, attackers used crow-
bars and sledgehammers to smash into a shuttered but otherwise
undefended store owned by Korean-Americans in Hollywood, and
looted and burned it. Rioters avoided businesses that were defended by armed merchants — even, as in one case, where the merchants were dressed up as "commandos" and their "Uzi" machine
guns were toy guns.[8] One teenager explained why houses and

apartment buildings near the riot area were mostly left alone: "They (the residents) got guns and everybody knows that. Nobody's going to want to mess with folks in houses."[9]

Suppose the women at Yosemite had been each carrying a sidearm in a holster. Would the evil man have even approached them? Human experience says he likely would have looked for other, less well-defended, prey.

Suppose the evil man had reason to worry that the women might be carrying *concealed* sidearms? Professor John Lott investigated that very question by examining the effect of changes in laws to make it easier for decent citizens to carry concealed weapons for defense. His exhaustive study of nationwide data, published in his book, *More Guns, Less Crime,* strongly suggested that liberalizing the concealed-carry permit laws on average resulted in:[10]

- an 8% decrease in murders
- a 5% decrease in rapes
- a 7 % decrease in aggravated assaults.

Statistics don't predict an individual's behavior. Still, the evil man might have thought twice about approaching the women at Yosemite if he had thought there was a chance they were "packing heat." As it was, the women were forbidden to possess firearms at all at Yosemite.

Schools As Defense-Free Zones

If an aggressor has a choice between a group of defenseless victims and a group of possibly armed victims, which group is he likely to attack? Unless the aggressor is suicidal, the answer is obvious: attack the defenseless people.

Where in America can an aggressor be nearly certain to find large numbers of potential victims cornered, unarmed and undefended? The answer: elementary and secondary schools.

What practically guarantees that people in schools are unarmed and undefended? The federal Gun Free School Zones Act that forbids possession of a firearm in "a school zone."[11] Making sure the civilians were disarmed in schools allowed tragedies such as:[12]

- Moses Lake, Washington, February 2, 1996: Teenager walks into a junior high classroom and with a rifle kills the unarmed and defenseless teacher and two students.

- West Paducah, Kentucky, December 1, 1997: Teenager enters school, shoots and kills three and wounds five defenseless students praying in a school hallway.
- Jonesboro, Arkansas, March 24, 1998: Two boys, aged 11 and 13, set off a false fire alarm and from hidden positions snipe at unarmed teachers and students filing out into the yard; four students and one teacher killed, 10 others wounded. The boys faced no return fire.
- Springfield, Oregon, May 21, 1998: In a possible copycat incident, a 15-year old first murders his parents and then opened fire in a high school cafeteria, killing two unde-fended students and wounding 19 others.
- Littleton, Colorado, April 20, 1999: Two young men plant bombs and then, heavily armed, invade a high school and methodically shoot and kill 13 people and wound 28 others. The single armed guard only briefly fired at the killers but did delay them until he had to seek cover from homemade grenades.[13] A teacher who heroically tried to rescue and save students from the attackers was unarmed and thus unable to prevent his own murder.[14]

Reacting to calls for even more "gun control" laws after the April 20, 1999 mass murder at Columbine High School in Littleton, one student's father wrote:

> I wonder: If two crazy hoodlums can walk into a "gun free" zone full of our kids, and police are totally inca-pable of defending the children, why would anyone want to make it harder for law-abiding adults to defend themselves and others? ...Of course, nobody on TV men-tions that perhaps gun-free zones are potential magnets for crazed killers.15

Now consider the *saving effects* when responsible adults use firearms to stop killers in the schoolyard:

- Pearl, Mississippi, October 1, 1997: A 16-year old boy stabs his mother, then attacks his high school where he kills two undefended students and injures seven others. In this case, however, the assistant principal, Joel Myrick, runs to get his Colt .45 pistol gun from his car after he hears the first shots. As the killer is driving away from the high school, Myrick catches up with him and points the gun at him.

Seeing the gun through his windshield, the killer crashes the car. Myrick gets close and holds a gun to the killer's head until police arrive over four minutes later. Lives are saved because the killer's plan was to invade the nearby junior high school next.[16]

- Edinboro, Pennsylvania, April 24, 1998: A 14-year old boy shoots a teacher at a middle-school graduation dance. While the killer is reloading, a nearby restaurant owner, James Strand, points a shotgun at the boy and prevents further violence. Police arrive 11 minutes later.[17]

In these two high-profile cases, **anti-firearms laws did not and could not save anyone.** What stopped the killing and protected other possible victims? Citizens with firearms. Ironically, Mr. Myrick, who heroically intervened to capture the killer, was forced to violate the federal "Gun-Free School Zone Act" and risk a federal felony prosecution.

Dr. Thomas Sowell, fellow at the Hoover Institution, observed that all of the highly-publicized school shootings occurred at "affluent, predominantly white schools." Why had the multiple murder sprees not occurred at otherwise more violent low-income or "ghetto schools"?

Dr. Sowell suggested the answer: "there are likely to be more armed people in or near [such] schools ... some have armed guards ...some have armed gangs." A criminal who opens fire in a school in a high crime neighborhood is "likely to face more bullets coming back." Only in "nice, wholly disarmed, affluent white schools" does having a gun on campus make you "instant king of the hill." Dr. Sowell counts the school shooting deaths and injuries as part of the "high cost already being paid for the fetish of disarming law-abiding people."[18]

"Safe Storage" Law Helps Murderer Kill Children

Touted as eminently "sensible," so-called safe storage laws require firearms owners to secure their guns at home so that juveniles and others cannot get them. Such laws exist in 17 states. But, like many "gun control" laws, these storage requirements impair a person's ability to speedily obtain a firearm for defense.

Safe storage laws helped kill two young children in Merced, California. Wednesday morning, August 23, 2000, a 27-year-old man came to the Carpenter family home carrying a pitchfork.[19] The man, reportedly naked, cut the phone lines and then invaded the house. Jessica Carpenter, 14, tried to dial 911, but that was no use.

Jessica ran to where the family guns were stored. She knew how to shoot because her father had taught her. But the guns were locked up.

The attacker stabbed and killed John, 7, in his bed. As the killer turned to attack again, Ashley, 9, grabbed his leg and begged him to stop. He stabbed her against a wall, and Ashley died. Two older daughters were stabbed but escaped from the house.

Jessica ran to a neighbor's house and pleaded with him to use his rifle to "take care" of the attacker. The neighbor refused; Jessica then called 911 from there. Police deputies eventually arrived and shot the attacker as he charged them with his bloody pitchfork.

Reverend John Hilton, the children's great-uncle, later told reporters: "If only [Jessica] had a gun available to her, she could have stopped the whole thing. If she had been properly armed, she could have stopped him in his tracks."

Does Self-Defense Work for Children?

At one o'clock in the morning on March 11, 2001, a man awakened the Starling family by beating on the patio door and shouting. The man got into the family truck, beat on the dashboard, then went back to the house, tearing open the patio door and beating on the glass. Seth Starling, 16, fetched a hunting rifle from the closet. From the inside of the glass doors, Seth and his parents shouted at the man to leave. Seth pointed the rifle at the man who then flew into a rage, now even more violently punching and kicking the glass doors. Fearing the man would smash through and attack the family, Seth fired a single shot through the glass and stopped the attack cold. The family called 911, and the injured attacker was airlifted shortly to a hospital.[20]

Just as Seth Starling did, Jessica Carpenter could possibly have saved her young siblings had she been able to readily reach for a loaded firearm. Only because her parents obeyed the "gun control" law was she stopped from using adequate force in self-defense.

Tale of Two San Diego Area Schools

March 5, 2001: Santana High School, Santee, California. High school freshman, 15, entered the school where there were 1,900 students. Using a .22 caliber revolver, he killed two students and injured 13 other people, including an on-campus officer who was unarmed. The killer had time to step into the bathroom and reload at least once. He surrendered when surrounded by police responding to calls.[21]

March 22, 2001: Granite Hills High School, El Cajon, California. High school senior, 18, took up a position in front of the school where 2,900 students attend. Using a shotgun, the attacker injured four people. Others were injured in the process of fleeing. An armed officer assigned to the campus responded almost immediately, engaged in a gun battle, shot the attacker, and terminated the attack.[22] Calling the officer her "personal hero," the school's principal said she was "glad he was in the office, because if he wasn't there, a lot of people would have died."[23]

The difference: A responsible armed person can stop a school attacker. Unarmed people are just victims.

What's the Answer?

We must understand one thing very clearly: ***people are always at risk of violent crime.*** Some people face a high risk, others a much lower one, depending upon circumstances. For example, statistics show that 1,634,773 serious violent crimes were committed in America in 1997, including:[24]

- 1,022,492 assaults (63%).
- 497,950 robberies (30%)
- 96,122 rapes (6%)
- 18,209 murders (1%)

Thus, in 1997, every 31 seconds an American was assaulted, every minute an American was robbed, every five minutes an American (typically, a woman) was raped, and every 29 minutes an American was killed.[25] These figures are based on crimes *reported* to police. The U.S. Department of Justice has estimated that victims overall report crimes only 38% of the time, and about half of all rape, robbery and burglary victims report those crimes.[26]

The risk of violent crime exists. Knowing that the risk exists, what should citizens do? That's a personal question, and the answer depends upon many factors. Some people will choose not to prepare for the possibility of violent crime, believing or hoping it won't happen to them. Others will consider their risks and will lock windows and doors, avoid risky situations, install intruder detection and alarm systems, obtain defensive firearms, hire bodyguards, or do whatever they believe to be enough.

Will the defense strategies always work? No; there is no perfection on this Earth. Will accidents happen? Yes; and most people will work to minimize them.

But the Seven Basic Truths always apply. Evil people exist and some will aggress on others. Forceful defense is necessary to stop aggressors. Whether the evil person is swinging a pitchfork at children, charging with a lynch mob, killing classmates, assaulting a woman, smashing into a home, beating a spouse, torturing prisoners, captaining a death squad or ordering genocide — nothing has ever changed those truths.

To the person who does not value self-defense, or who wants to ban firearms or to enact "gun control" laws that make it harder for people to defend themselves, we ask this question:

What moral authority do you have to tell others not to defend against aggression?

"But We're Talking About Safety"

Saying that a particular "gun control" law aims to increase safety does not answer the question. If obeying the law increases the risk that the citizen cannot effectively use his defense system when the need arises, then the law endangers people. People cannot depend solely on the government or "911" emergency response. The government has no legal duty to protect individual citizens against violent crime.[27] The government typically does not pay compensation to crime victims whom the government has endangered by its laws.

So increasing "gun safety" for some citizens imposes costs and danger on others. That result is bad enough, but the moral results are worse. Aggressors profit; defenders lose.

The "gun safety" laws unquestionably only affect people who are willing to abide by them. Non-violent, peace-loving, decent people tend to obey safety laws. Criminals by definition have already chosen not to obey laws. There is no special place for "gun safety" laws in the criminal heart.

Thus, decent people bear the costs and face the dangers of "gun safety" laws. The aggressors benefit directly from "gun safety" laws that make their targets easier to attack. To the anti-self-defense person, we must then ask:

What moral authority do you have to make aggression easier and righteous defense harder?

End Notes

[1]For a psychological analysis of evil, see Peck, M. Scott. 1983. *People of the Lie: The Hope for Healing Human Evil.* New York: Simon & Schuster. Dr. Peck there defined "evil" as "that force, residing either inside or outside of human beings, that seeks to kill life or liveliness." Ibid., p. 43.

[2]Beccaria, Cesare. 1963 [1764]. *On Crimes and Punishments.* Indianapolis: Bobbs-Merrill, pp. 87-88 (emphasis added).

[3]See Dowlut, Robert. 1997. The Right to Keep and Bear Arms: A Right to Self-Defense Against Criminals and Despots. *Stanford Law and Policy Review.* Vol. 8, pp. 25-40 (examining American and world history, concludes that the personal right to arms is fundamental and necessary to deter aggression from any source).

[4]Drawn from information at http://historychannel.com.

[5]Drawn from information at www.jrabold.net/yosemite.

[6]Lott, John R., Jr. 2000. *More Guns, Less Crime: Understanding Crime and Gun Control Laws.* Second edition. Chicago: University of Chicago Press, p.4 (discussion with sources); Lott, John R. 1998. Myths Destroyed. Chicago Tribune. May 8.

[7]Stolinsky, David C. and Timothy W. Wheeler. 1999. *Firearms: A Handbook for Health Professionals.* Claremont, Calif: The Claremont Institute, p. 5 (citing Kleck, G. *Point Blank: Guns and Violence in America.* 1991. New York. Aldine de Gruyter. P. 124-26, 149; and Kleck G. and M. Gertz. 1995. "Armed Resistance to Crime: The Nature and Prevalence of Self-Defense with a Gun." *Journal of Criminal Law and Criminology.* Vol. 86, p.185). Both authors are physicians.)

[8]Reynolds, Morgan O. and W. W. Caruth, III. 1992. *Myths About Gun Control.* National Center for Policy Analysis (NCPA). (www.ncpa.org) Citing *New American,* June 15, 1992, pp. 14-15; *Wall Street Journal,* June 16, 1992, p. A5.).

[9]Ibid., citing *New American,* June 15, 1992, p. 15.

[10]Lott 2000, p. 51.

[11]18 U.S.C. § 922(q)(2)(a).

[12]Stories listed with links at www.washingtonpost.com.

[13]Lott 2000, p 195.

[14]Lott 2000, p. 236.

[15]Lott 2000, p. 243, quoting Anema, Dale. 1999. A Father at Columbine High. *American Enterprise*. Sept./Oct., pp. 48-50.

[16]Laugesen, Wayne. "A principal and his gun." Reprinted at www.keepandbeararms.com.

[17]Lott 2000, pp. 236-37.

[18]Sowell, Thomas. 2001. School Disasters. Syndicated column, March 12. (www.jewishworldreview.com)

[19]Story and quotes taken from Suprynowicz, Vin. 2000. If it'll save a single child ... repeal the gun laws. *Las Vegas Review-Journal*. Sept. 24. (www.lvrj.com); and Maxwell, Lesli A. 2000. Terminal Madness - Man Kills Children with Pitchfork. *The Fresno Bee*. Aug. 25. (www.fresnobee.com)

[20]Alleged intruder shot, in critical condition. *The Gainesville Sun*. March 11, 2001. (www.keepandbeararms.com)

[21]Adler, Jeff and William Booth. 2001. Two Students Die in Calif. Shootings. *The Washington Post*. March 6, p. A-1.

[22]Adler, Jeff and William Booth. 2001. Five Wounded in Month's Second Calif. School Shooting. *The Washington Post*. March 23, p. A-3.

[23]Preventing School Violence. *The Washington Post*. March 25, p. A-4. (Associated Press story.)

[24]United States Dep't of Justice, Federal Bureau of Investigation. 1998. *Uniform Crime Reports for the United States 1997*. Pp. 9, 12, 19, 22.

[25]Ibid., p 6.

[26]United States Department of Justice, Bureau of Justice Statistics. 1993. *Criminal Victimization in the United States - 1991*. P. 102.

[27]Stevens, Richard W. 1999. *Dial 911 and Die*. Hartford, WI: Mazel Freedom Press. (Collecting cases and laws, e.g. *Warren v. District of Columbia,* 444 A.2d 1 (D.C. 1981) (en banc), *Ford v. Town of Grafton,* 693 N.E.2d 1047 (Mass. App. 1998), *Barillari v. City of Milwaukee,* 533 N.W.2d 759 (Wis. 1995), *DeShaney v. Winnebago County Dep't. of Soc. Servs.,* 489 U.S. 189 (1989).

Appendices

Appendix One:

Nazi Justiz teaches how to detect and prevent genocide – Is America listening?

By Richard W. Stevens*

(Originally published in The Firearms Sentinel, *Fall 1997. End Notes are in the style of the original article.)*

Of the Nazi Holocaust we say: *Never again!* But what if the machinery for genocide were being installed right now in America? How would we detect the signs of the deadly tornado before it strikes?

Richard Lawrence Miller's 1995 book, *Nazi Justiz: Law of the Holocaust*[1] explains the five major steps leading from the 1933 election of Adolf Hitler to the calculated mass murder of Jews (and others) that started in 1941. *Nazi Justiz* shows how the Nazi laws and legal philosophy converted, in five steps, Hitler's anti-Jewish hatred into genocide.

Public Health, Nazi Style

Regardless of whatever underlying reasons might have existed, Hitler outwardly believed and convinced others that Jews endangered public health. Hitler wrote in *Mein Kampf*, for example, that Jews were menaces to society, they were "dirty," great masters of the lie, sneaking parasites on all of humanity, filthy, unwashed, "maggots in a rotting body." Jews were the lowest form of life, would corrode German culture, and could infect Aryans. Jews could cause "blood poisoning" to Aryans by their proximity, their ideas and their spoken words.[2] Racially-correct science developed theories and scholars published papers proving these accusations. Generous government funding flowed to

291

build think tanks and huge libraries to focus on race issues. German academic staffs gained prestige and comfortable careers working to protect the public health from Jews.[3]

For Nazis, to hate Jews was as natural as fearing an epidemic or avoiding an open cesspool. Who can argue against public health? Aryan actions to eliminate the Jews were sensible — the Nazis were just doing it to protect themselves and their children.

Five Steps to Genocide

The Nazis used the German legal system to implement their plans to rid Germany of the public health menace (Jews). Accordingly, the Nazi government enacted statutes, generated regulations, and enforced them all through the police and courts. *Nazi Justiz* describes how the lawful persecution moved Germany through the five steps that led to the genocide.

STEP ONE: IDENTIFICATION[5]	
Elements	**Implementation / Effect**
Legally defining the "menace"	Define "Aryan," "Non-Aryan," "Jew"
Classifying persons as "menace" or "non-menace" to society	Everyone is either Jew or Aryan
Physically locating, marking and tracking the movements of the "menace"	Race identity papers, special passports, requiring Jews to wear a yellow star

STEP TWO: OSTRACISM[6]	
Elements	**Implementation / Effect**
Coordinating government efforts to generate public awareness of the "menace"	Media campaigns against the Jews. School lessons about Jews
Stimulating private citizens to avoid the "menace" and to purge the economy of its influences	Boycott anyone and anything connected with Jews

Elements	Implementation / Effect
Enacting laws and regulations to prevent the "menace" from existing in society	Deny Jews the right to practice professions, hold government jobs, live in certain neighborhoods, use public facilities, obtain public education, receive charity.
	Industrial codes that prohibit whole industries from employing Jews Revocation of all drivers' licenses
Stripping the "menace" of any legal protection	Impose curfews and restrictions on travel
	Exclusion from military forces
	Loss of citizenship and voting rights
	Judicial presumption that Jews' testimony was untrustworthy

STEP THREE: CONFISCATION[7]	
Elements	**Implementation / Effect**
Emigration tax broadened to tax the "menace" as they leave	Impoverish Jews Enrich the state
Death penalty for smuggling property out	Cause Jews to leave property behind
Registering all personal property imported into Germany	Jews file and update exhaustive inventory for government agency
Registering all personal property of the "menace"	Trace assets for later forfeiture or confiscation

Elements	Implementation / Effect
Reporting all banking transactions above a certain limit	"Jew-tainted" property was subject to forfeiture because of assumed connection with Communism or anti-Naziism
Civil forfeiture laws to confiscate property used in a way that "threatened" society	Jews' cars were confiscated for minor traffic violations Whole business and factories were forfeited because one Jew was employee Jews forced to sell personal and real property at huge discounts to Aryans[8] Placing all property into Aryan hands so that rioters and storm troopers would not destroy it during attacks on Jews

STEP FOUR: CONCENTRATION[9]	
Elements	**Implementation / Effect**
Excluding the "menace" from some areas	Expulsion of Jews from rural areas Eviction of Jews from government-funded housing Confiscation of Jewish-owned orphanages and homes for elderly and infirm Refusals by Aryan individuals and businesses to rent to Jews Laws denying legal rights to Aryans who rent to Jews
Gathering the "menace" into segregated housing	Jews de-facto forced to live only with other Jews Jews rendered homeless had to share with other Jews in common housing

Elements	Implementation / Effect
Creating concentration camps to solve the housing shortage and to collect the "menace" away from society	Mass roundup of easily identified and located Jews for deportation to camps

STEP FIVE ANNIHILATION[10]	
Elements	**Implementation / Effect**
Preventing the birth of the "menace"	Prohibit marriage between Jews and Aryans
	Forced divorces of married Jews and Aryans
	Removal of children from families of "mixed race"
	Denial of tax benefits and subsidies for Jewish families with children
	Sterilization of medically-certified "genetically inferior" Jews
Inflicting death on the "menace"	Abortion of Jewish (or mixed race) babies was allowed and promoted
	Euthanasia for institutionalized Jews
	Mobile killing units
	Central killing stations

Lethal Lawgivers

Bizarre as it may seem to Americans, the five steps to Nazi genocide were *entirely legal* under German law. The German judicial system was not merely a weak protector of Jews' rights — it actively supported the Nazi persecutors.[11] Many pre-Nazi and post-Nazi factors combined to make this so:

• Germany's legal profession dated only from 1870, and a large proportion of lawyers were already affiliated with the government.[12]

- Germany lacked any tradition of lawyers opposing government power. Judges and prosecutors were practically united against the defendant.[13]

- Judges were civil service bureaucrats on a career track, not necessarily accomplished lawyers or scholars.[14]

- Germany's written constitution (like the U.S. counterpart) protected personal liberties, but any law passed by a two-thirds vote of the legislature (*Reichstag*) would supersede any constitutional provision that conflicted with the law.[15]

- The German President, in an emergency, was authorized to suspend parts of the constitution. Before Hitler's election as Chancellor, the President had suspended the constitution more than once without causing public alarm.[16]

- Citing a national emergency, Chancellor Hitler caused the German President in 1933 to issue an emergency decree which suspended "until further notice" several sections of the constitution. The decree declared it a criminal act to "provoke or incite an act contrary to public welfare," and eliminated "freedom of the person," the freedoms of speech, press, assembly, association, the right to privacy in mail and telephones, and the warrant and due process requirements for searches and seizures of private property.[17]

- The *Reichstag* passed an "enabling act" to empower Hitler's cabinet ministers to make laws with the same validity as those passed by the Reichstag, and those laws could disregard the constitution.[18]

- The Nazi Party, by decree, became the source of law. Party statements and Hitler's speeches attained the force of law that guided judge's decisions.[19]

- The first principle of Nazi legal authority was "civic duty." The courts "had a civic duty to uphold the law, and the law's purpose was to protect the state."[20]

- The second principle of Nazi legal authority was the "educational nature of law." Under this principle, the courts were expected to use the law to teach the people a lesson. One Nazi theorist announced the rule: "No crime without punishment."[21]

- Combining the first and second principles, Nazi judges and bureaucrats were expected to read Nazi decrees as guides and minimums. These Nazi officials received the authority to fashion the law to "promote the public good" as defined by the Nazis. Punishments were supposed to exceed the stated minimums to prove the judge's commitment to his civic duty. One Nazi thus declared: "He who sticks to the letter of the law or refuses to go beyond it, because the orders are not given to do so, confirms the fact that he is willing to do only the minimum of what the community asks of him."[22]

This framework of laws and traditions encouraged Nazi officials to zealously carry out the Nazi plans. When the law was aimed at the Jews (and other non-Aryans and "defectives"), the officials had every reason to read all laws liberally and creatively, and to impose all penalties excessively and punitively.

Parallels in America?

America is not yet overtly following the Nazi path to genocide. But the key question is: "Is the social and governmental machinery in place to make genocide possible?" Using the elements set forth in *Nazi Justiz,* the following chart shows how some of the machinery might be in place right now.

Element Supporting Holocaust Process (from *Nazi Justiz*)	Feature of American Society/Government
Identification	
Defining persons or groups as a menace to public health (and convincing the populace of the rightness of the definition)	*Tobacco smokers:* policies and laws aimed at imposing stigma and penalties on persons engaging in otherwise legal behavior.[23]
	Firearms owners: federally funded activities to establish "ownership" of firearms as "public health" issue; marking firearms owners as belonging to particular social classes; "guns turn people into criminals;" associating guns with "extremist patriots" and "enemies of the people."[24]

	Politically-incorrect persons: state and private university policies and speech codes prohibiting "offensive" or "insensitive" speech, are selectively enforced against speakers who hold certain views.[25]
Physically locating, marking and tracking persons	*Social security numbers:* required from birth; track through income tax records throughout life; track real property location by county records; used on motor vehicle licenses and registrations, gun registrations, and records for household utilities, telephone, financial accounts and credit history. All of these aid in locating individuals. *Passports:* track movement in and out of the country; also used to prove citizenship on employment applications. *National Identity Cards:* proposed to "simplify" medical record keeping, to aid national law enforcement, and to deter immigration.[26] *Private databases:* contain identity and location data, plus financial information and consumer preferences.[27]
Ostracism Stimulating public outcry, private shunning and discrimination against the menace	*Tobacco smokers:* currently endure public humiliation and scorn.[28]

	Firearms owners: painted by media as abnormal, criminal, extreme, or on the fringe of society.[29]
	Politically incorrect persons: face ridicule, sanctions, and expulsion.[30]
Enacting laws to exclude the menace from society	Laws to prevent smoking on public and private property, in workplaces, even if no one is affected by the smoking.[31]
Confiscation	
Registration of personal property	*Firearms owners:* Many state laws require registration of firearms owners. President agrees with proposed federal registration of firearms owners. New York City first registered many rifles, then confiscated them using the records.[32]
	Federal Bureau of Alcohol, Tobacco & Firearms has built a national database of firearms owners, using gun dealer records.[33]
Reporting citizens' banking transactions to government	Federal regulations require financial institutions to report transactions of $10,000 (domestic or international); same rule applies to **Postal money orders.** Banks must also report transactions of $5,000 or more which appear "suspicious." Proposed new rules will require money

	transfer services (other than banks) to report international wire transfers of just \$750 or more.[34]
Civil forfeiture laws to confiscate property implicated in anti-social or anti-government activities	Federal civil forfeiture laws allow government to take property without charging a crime. Police can seize property if they believe it was bought with money from illegal activity or used to "facilitate" a crime. Amount of property forfeited does not depend on size of crime. Seizure is allowed based on "probable cause," which may be based on hearsay evidence. To get property back, the owner usually must file suit and then *prove* the "innocence" of the property.[35]
Concentration Capability of relocating and interning large segments of "menace" population	Presidential executive order (not Congress) imposed curfew, relocation, and detention of Americans of Japanese descent living on the West Coast during World War II.[36]
Annihilation Preventing the birth of children to persons considered part of a menace.	Some prominent Americans have favored birth control, sterilization, and abortion to "purify the race" or decrease poverty.[37]

Legal / Judicial Support for Concentrating Power in Central Government	
Power of Government to centralize power on declaration of emergency	Presidents can issue executive orders without Congress' express approval. [38] Upon a presidential declaration of emergency, existing executive orders would grant broad powers to 28 federal cabinet and other agencies *to directly control all industries and resources, and to control all electronic media.*[39]
Constitutional limits on federal power relaxed by judicial interpretation and custom	Supreme Court decisions have vastly broadened federal government power to regulate individual conduct under "commerce clause" of Constitution.[40]
Direct discretionary power to carry out government aims is delegated to agency bureaucrats.	Tremendous growth in federal agencies and their power. Judicial presumption that agency actions are legal.[41]
Power of judges to create or interpret law to enact social/political agendas	Modern "instrumentalist" legal theory allows judges to decide cases by "giving expression to community mores or ideals," or "when the political process is not working properly."[42]

Eternal Vigilance is Key

Richard Miller, author of *Nazi Justiz*, sums up the lessons from his study of the Nazi institutions with these messages:[43]

* "Disregard identifying labels on victims; remember them as ordinary persons. ...Holocaust victims differed in no way from you and me."

* "The outcome of the destruction process is lethal.

Annihilation of victims can be avoided only by abandoning the destruction process. In the beginning it looks so limited, every new increment so reasonable."

* "To prevent another Holocaust our task must be to recognize any destruction process that is underway and to stop it, perhaps before its perpetrators even realize what they are doing. ...As soon as we see our productive, ordinary next-door neighbors somehow being identified as deviant by our government, we now know enough to leap to their defense before they are ostracized, before their property is seized, before they are concentrated in certain areas, before they are annihilated."

Author's note: The process of ostracizing people because of their thoughts about firearms, or because of even the most remote connection to firearms, is accelerating. See the discussion of "zero tolerance" policies in Chapter Four.

End Notes

[1]Richard Lawrence Miller, *Nazi Justiz: Law of the Holocaust* (Praeger Publishers: 1995) (referred to here as *"NJ"*).

[2]Adolf Hitler, *Mein Kampf* (Boston: Houghton Miflin Co., 1971), pp. 57, 59, 91, 123, 150, 232, 289. See also *NJ*, pp. 31-35, 70.

[3]*NJ*, pp. 14, 36-40

[4]*NJ*, p.3; drawing from Raul Hilberg, The Destruction of the European Jews (1967), p. 1189.

[5]*NJ*, pp. 9-18, 24, 36-40, 73-75.

[6]*NJ*, pp. 43, 54-95.

[7]*NJ*, pp. 97-129.

[8]An estimated $8 billion worth of property was confiscated by Nazis from Jews. *NJ*, p. 131. Proceeding for a least 10 years, huge amounts of property (everything from business interests to personal belongings) were transferred, by "Aryanization," forfeiture and auction, or outright confiscation, to ordinary German citizens. *Ibid*, pp. 113-129. There is no way many Germans could have honestly claimed later that "we didn't know" what was happening to the Jews.

[9]*NJ*, pp. 133-141.

[10]*NJ*, pp. 143-170.

[11]*NJ*, pp. 43.

[12]*NJ,* p. 44.

[13]*NJ,* p. 44 & n.4.

[14]Ibid.

[15]Ibid.

[16]*NJ,* pp. 44-45.

[17]*NJ,* pp. 44-45.

[18]*NJ,* p. 45.

[19]*NJ,* p. 46.

[20]*NJ,* p. 47.

[21]*NJ,* p. 48.

[22]*NJ,* pp. 48, 50. This expectation of harshness itself became law in 1935.*NJ,* p. 49.

[23]Liz Spayd, Puffing and Persecution; New Laws, Warnings Make Smokers Feel Under Siege, *Washington Post,* March 15, 1994, p. B-1 (laws, stigma, and exclusion); Jessica Lee & Richard Benedetto, $34M to fight teen smoking OK'd. But congressional leaders take little action on settlement deal, *USA Today,* Sept. 4, 1997, p. 8A (laws targeting smokers).

[24]Richard W. Stevens, Disarming the Data Doctors: How to Debunk the "Public Health" Argument for "Gun Control," *Firearms Sentinel* (JPFO, Inc: Winter 1997), p.2 (citing sources);

David B. Kopel, *The Ideology of Gun Ownership and Gun Control in the United States,* 18 Qtly. J. of Ideology 3, 14 (1995), *citing* Barry Bruce-Biggs, *The Great American Gun War,* 45 The Pub. Interest 37, 61 (1976) (stereotypes about firearms owners); Arthur L. Kellermann, et al., *Gun Ownership as a Risk Factor for Homicide in the Home,* 329 New Engl. J. Med. 1084 (Oct. 7, 1993) (example of "public health" research and conclusions); Eunice Moscoso, "Popular gun shows attracting criminals, extremists, study says," *Atlanta Journal & Constitution* (July 18, 1996), p. A8 ("gun control" advocates' study); William Norman Grigg, "Crackdown on Extremism," *The New American* (July 7, 1997) pp. 15-17 (describing movement, in parallel with Soviet KGB program, to identify all militias as "extremist patriots" who are "enemies of the people").

[25]John W. Whitehead, *Politically Correct: Censorship in American Culture* (Chicago: Moody Press, 1995), p. 12-16, 18, 21 (citing original sources).

[26]Peter Cassidy, "We have your number: the push for a national ID card," *The Progressive* (Dec. 1994), p. 28-30. See Jay Simkin, et al., *Lethal Laws: "Gun Control" is the Key to Genocide* (JPFO: 1994) pp. 28-29 (describing government databases).

[27]Rajiv Cahandrasekaran, "Database firms set privacy plan; Personal information curbs intended to preempt regulation," *Washington Post* (June 10, 1997), p. A1.

[28]Liz Spayd, *Puffing and Persecution, supra* note 23.

[29]David B. Kopel, *The Ideology of Gun Ownership, supra* note 24; W. N. Grigg,

Crackdown on Extremism, supra note 24, p. 17 (plans to emphasize "extremism"). For examples of media stereotyping with government help, *see* Eunice Moscoso, "Popular gun shows attracting criminals, extremists, study says," *Atlanta Journal & Constitution* (July 18, 1996), p. A8 (Rep. Charles Schumer (D-N.Y.) touting "gun control" advocates' study); *but see,* Jack Levin, "Militias reflect public's mistrust," *USA Today* (March 31, 1997), p. 15A (discusses how stereotypes unfairly portray some militia groups). See documentation of media bias and hostile portrayal of firearms owners in Jay Simkin, et al., *Lethal Laws, supra* note 26, pp. 34-37.

[30]John W. Whitehead, *Politically Correct, supra* note 25; "Professor attacked for racist comment," *Washington Times,* Sept. 16, 1997, p. A6; Mary Ann Roser, "Texas professor's remarks on minorities irk Jackson," *Washington Times,* Sept. 17, 1997, p.A6 (describing protests and denunciations of college professor for stating his views).

[31]Liz Spayd, *Puffing and Persecution, supra* note 23; Jessica Lee & Richard Benedetto, *$34M to fight teen smoking OK'd, supra* note 23.

[32]James Bovard, *Lost Rights: The Destruction of American Liberty* (St. Martin's Press, 1994), pp. 216-224 (state registration laws and New York City confiscation); Jay Simkin, et al., *Lethal Laws, supra* note 26, p. 37, 70 (President Clinton's position; New York City's program). In the 20th Century, the first seven major genocides in the 20th Century were preceded by gun registration or "gun control" laws. *Lethal Laws, supra* note 26, pp. 14, 87, 91, 98-99, 150-52, 188-89, 230-33, 283-99, 305-06,

[33]Neal Knox, "BATF Again Registering Guns," *American Rifleman,* (April 1995), p.14 (BATF agent admits computer database contains 60 million records); James L. Pate, "Gun Gestapo Gang-Bangers," *Soldier of Fortune* (July 1995), p. 59 (ex-BATF agent describes BATF "Firearms Tracing Center" in West Virginia).

[34]See 31 C.F.R. § 103.21 ("suspicious" transactions); 31 C.F.R. § 103.22 ($10,000 transactions); 31 C.F.R. § ($10,000 international transactions); 31 C.F.R. § 103.26 (power to enforce stricter requirements where "necessary"); 31 C.F.R. § 103.29 (records of cash or draft transactions of $3,000 or more); *see also,* "Clinton to hit drug dealers with new money-transferring rules, report says," *Atlanta Constitution,* May 9, 1997, p. A1 ($750 transactions).

[35]See, *United States v. Parcel of Real Property at 6109 Grubb Road,* 886 F.2d 618, 110 A.L.R. Fed. 553 (3d Cir. 1989) (overview of the law); Daniel A. Klein, *Supreme Court's views as to due process requirements, under Federal Constitution's Fifth and Fourteenth Amendments, concerning forfeitures of property to government as a result of unlawful conduct,* 126 L.Ed. 2d 799 (1996) (detailed legal article with comprehensive list of cross-references); James R. Healy, "Facts on forfeiture," *USA Today,* March 5, 1996, p. 10A (forfeiture in a nutshell). See also, Leonard W. Levy, *A License to Steal: The Forfeiture of Property* (University of North Carolina Press, 1995); Steven B. Duke, Albert C. Gross, "Casualties of war:

Drug prohibition has shot gaping holes in the Bill of Rights," *Reason* (February 1994), p. 20 et seq. The U.S. Attorney General has directed all federal prosecutors and FBI agents to "reinvigorate their efforts in using asset forfeiture as a law enforcement tool." William R. Schroeder, "Civil forfeiture: recent Supreme Court cases," *65 FBI Law Enforcement Bulletin* (October 1996), p. 28 (encouraging use of civil forfeiture).

36Two Supreme Court cases explain the legal and practical rationales given to justify this program: *Hirabayashi v. United States,* 320 U.S. 81 (1943), and *Korematsu v. United States,* 323 U.S. 214 (1944). A thorough study is found in: Peter Irons, *Justice at War* (Oxford Univ. Press, 1983).

37For examples of eugenics rhetoric in the 20th century (from the founder of Planned Parenthood), see Margaret Sanger, *Woman, Morality, and Birth Control* (New York: New York Publishing Company, 1922), p. 12; Margaret Sanger, *The Pivot of Civilization* (Swarthmore College Library ed. 1922), pp. 116, 122, 189 (cruelty of charity); and see Margaret Sanger's statements in the periodical *Birth Control Review,* October 1921 (eugenics and birth control), April 1932 (segregation or sterilization of inferiors), and April 1933 (eugenics to eliminate "bad stock" of Latins, Slavs, Blacks, "Hebrews"); *see also* the speech of Margaret Sanger quoted in "Birth Control: What It Is, How It Works, What It Will Do", The Proceedings of the First American Birth Control Conference (*Birth Control Review,* Gothic Press, 1921) (eugenic purpose of birth control). A bold statement of eugenic ideals is found in F. Kennedy, *The problem of social control of the congenital defective Education, sterilization, euthanasia,* 99 Am. J. Psychiatry 1316 (1942) (advocates killing of "defective" children at age 5; view endorsed by unsigned editorial of same publication). A long list of names of directors and members of American Eugenics Society (now the Society for the Study of Social Biology) is available at www.africa2000.com/ENDX/aedata.htm. Other Internet sources for eugenics information and Margaret Sanger's books are available at www.all.org/eugenics.htm.

38*See,* 77 Am. Jur. 2d *United States* § 24 (1997) (discussion with citations).

39Executive Order 11490, "Assigning Emergency Preparedness Functions to Federal Departments and Agencies," 34 Fed. Reg. 17567-17599 (October 30, 1969) [reprinted in full at 41 Fed. Reg. 24301 (June 15, 1976)] (assigns all planning and control duties to 28 executive agencies). Section 102(b) states that the Order is designed to assure the continuity of the federal government "in any national emergency type situation that might confront the nation." Section 105 of this Order implies the unilateral power of the President to invoke the plans: "[These plans] may be effectuated only [when] authority...is provided by a law enacted by the Congress or by an order or directive issued by the President pursuant to statutes or the Constitution of the United States."

40The Commerce Clause is found in the U.S. Constitution, Art. I, § 8, cl. 3. Key cases broadening federal power under this clause were *United States v. Darby,* 312 U.S. 100, 61 S.Ct. 451 (1941) and *Wickard v. Filburn,* 317

U.S. 111, 63 S.Ct. 82 (1942). See also Robert H. Bork, *The Tempting of America* (Free Press: 1990), pp. 51-58 (brief but clear explanation of this point).

[41]James Bovard, *Lost Rights, supra* note 32, pp. 49-52.

[42]Randall Kelso & Charles D. Kelso, *Studying Law: An Introduction* (St. Paul, Minn: West Publishing, 1984), pp. 274, 286-87, 395.

[43]*NJ,* pp. 172-73 (author's italics omitted here).

Appendix Two

The Psychology of "Gun Control" Believers

As discussed earlier in this book, the term "gun control" is a slogan that collects together the ideas and policies that work against widespread private ownership and possession of firearms. What kind of mind favors "gun control"?

Dr. Sarah Thompson examined this question in her path-breaking article, "Raging Against Self-Defense — A Psychiatrist Examines the Anti-Gun Mentality."[1] She identified four mental processes that lead an otherwise normal person to oppose so emotionally the private right to firearms ownership.

Projection

The first of the four mental processes that leads to strong "anti-gun" feelings is *projection*. Dr. Thompson defined it:

> Projection is a *defense mechanism*. Defense mechanisms are unconscious psychological mechanisms that protect us from feelings that we cannot consciously accept. They operate without our awareness, so that we don't have to deal consciously with "forbidden" feelings and impulses.[2]

An anti-gun person might say, for example, "people shouldn't be allowed to carry guns because I don't want to be murdered by my neighbor who is having a bad day." The statistics show that the average person is not at all likely to be killed by an otherwise law-abiding neighbor.[3] That fact won't matter to the anti-gun person, because the real risk of harm is not what worries him.

In the projection case, the anti-gun person is actually saying he fears "that if *he* had a gun, *he* might murder his neighbors if he had a bad day, or if they took his parking space, or played their stereos too loud."[4] He fears that he might misuse a gun in a moment of frustration or rage, so everyone else is likely to do the same.

Everyone has violent, sometimes homicidal, impulses at one time or another, but some people "are unable consciously to admit that they have such 'unacceptable' emotions."[5] Rather than admit and deal with strong feelings of rage, frustration or fear, the person *projects* those kinds of feelings — and violent impulses — on everyone around him. The defense mechanism of projection "not only prevents a person from dealing with his own feelings, it also creates a world where he perceives everyone else as directing his own hostile feelings back at him."[6]

So, the person sees the neighbor who owns a gun for hunting, target shooting, or home defense, as a hostile enemy liable at any moment to shoot him down. If guns are eliminated, that hostile enemy cannot hurt anyone.

Denial

Supporters of "gun control" might also use the defense mechanism of *denial*. Dr. Thompson explained: "Denial is simply refusing to accept the reality of a given situation."[7] This defense mechanism works psychologically to protect the person from feeling anxious, helpless or vulnerable.

The facts are that we live in a world where criminals attack and hurt people, burgle homes and cars, and steal property. The police cannot protect everyone, and as a legal matter, they don't owe a duty to protect any particular individual from crime.[8] Research shows that personal firearms are effective tools for personal and family defense.[9] The anti-gun person who uses *denial* will banish all such information from his mind, preferring to believe that "this is a safe neighborhood," or "the police will protect you," or the idea that crime "can't (or won't) happen here."[10]

A person who denies the risks must also deny the need for the defense tools. That leads such a person to say (and seem to believe) things like "nobody needs a gun in America" — a textbook case of denial.

When ordinary non-violent Americans have and use guns, seeing that can upset the person who has denied any need for guns.

The illusion of safety, created by the denial of reality, is threatened — so the person in denial reacts strongly. Guns must be eliminated so that the illusion can survive unchallenged.

Reaction Formation

A third psychological factor within the mind of the anti-gun person can be *reaction formation*. This defense mechanism is complex and difficult to explain and spot. Dr. Thompson indicated that "Reaction formation occurs when a person's mind turns an unacceptable feeling or desire into its complete opposite. For example, a child who is jealous of a sibling may exhibit excessive love and devotion for the hated brother or sister."[11]

A person who feels rage toward other people may claim to be a devoted pacifist, even refusing to eat meat or kill cockroaches. That person might get involved in spiritual or activist groups that disdain violence of any kind. "In the case of anti-gun people," Dr. Thompson observed, "reaction formation keeps any knowledge of their hatred for their fellow humans out of consciousness, while allowing them to feel superior to 'violent gun owners.'" In working to deny people the right to have and use tools for self-defense, the anti-gun person can actually harm those people while at the same time feeling morally superior.[12]

Victim Identity Cycle

The fourth psychological factor is *identity as a victim*. Dr. Thompson summarized this factor in three sentences as it applies to the anti-gun person:

(1) People who identify themselves as "victims" harbor excessive amounts of rage at other people whom they perceive as "not victims."

(2) In order psychologically to deal with this rage, these "victims" utilize defense mechanisms that enable them to harm others in socially acceptable ways, without accepting responsibility or suffering guilt, and without having to give up their status as "victims."

(3) Gun owners are frequently the targets of professional victims because *gun owners are willing and able to prevent their own victimization.*[13]

A person who views himself as a victim, especially within a

group of victims, can demand special treatment and consideration. Organizations that cater to victims will prosper if they can expand the number of victims, so these organizations have every incentive to keep the victims feeling insecure, fearful or oppressed. Victims and their organizations must oppose firearms ownership, because having the tools and ability to protect yourself is the quality of a *non-victim*.

Non-victims prove by their existence that victimhood is not necessary. That fact unsettles the professional victim and endangers the victim organization.[14] It is no surprise that "gun control" organizations and victim organizations both oppose firearms ownership, and seek to demonize and destroy gun owners.

The facts offered in this book show that civilian disarmament creates real victims: dead bodies, shattered lives. Millions of them. The "gun control" mentality must be defeated or changed, but it cannot be ignored.[15] The human cost of "gun control" is far too high.

End Notes

[1]Thompson, Sarah. 2000. "Raging Against Self-Defense — A Psychiatrist Examines the Anti-Gun Mentality." *The Bill of Rights Sentinel*. (Fall), pp. 7-12. Copies available from Jews for the Preservation of Firearms Ownership, P.O. Box 270143, Hartford, WI 53072. (www.jpfo.org)

[2]Ibid., p. 7 (footnote omitted).

[3]Kates, Don B. And Daniel D. Polsby. 2000. "The Myth of the 'Virgin Killer': Law-abiding Persons Who Kill In a Fit of Rage." Paper to be delivered at the American Society of Criminology Annual Meeting, San Francisco, November 2000. (Copy on file with authors.) "Forty years of further homicide studies document that murderers are almost never the 'ordinary, law-abiding' citizens ...the great majority are extreme aberrants whose life histories are full of crime, pscyhopathology, substance abuse, and other hazardous behavior and dangerous accidents. The whole corpus of research shows murderers 'almost always have a long history of involvement in criminal behavior.'" Ibid, p. 11, citing Elliott, Delbert S. 1998. Life Threatening Violence is Primarily a Crime Problem: A Focus on Prevention. *Colorado Law Review*. Vol. 69, pp. 1081, 1089.

[4]Ibid.

[5]Ibid.

[6]Ibid. (footnote omitted).

[7]Ibid.

8Stevens, Richard W. 1999. *Dial 911 and Die.* Hartford, WI: Mazel Freedom Press. (Analyzes the law in 54 U.S. jurisdictions).

9Kleck, Gary and Marc Gertz. 1995. Armed Resistance to Crime: The Prevalence and Nature of Self-Defense with a Gun. *Journal of Criminal Law & Criminology.* Vol. 86 (Fall), pp. 150-187.

10Thompson 2000, p. 8.

11Ibid.

12Ibid.

13Ibid, p. 9 (italics added).

14Ibid.

15Dr. Thompson has developed a one-on-one program for communicating with anti-gun people that can help change hearts and minds by addressing psychological needs and relaxing defenses. Ibid., pp. 10-12.

About the Authors −

Aaron Zelman learned about freedom and self-reliance growing up in the Arizona desert. A Vietnam veteran (he was a Navy Corpsman assigned to Fleet Marine Force, Third Marine Airwing) he's also the co-author of *The Life Insurance Conspiracy, The Consumer's Guide to Handguns, "Gun Control," Gateway to Tyranny, Hope, The State vs. The People* and *The Mitzvah,* now being made into a motion picture. Aaron is the creator of the educational series of "Gran'pa Jack" freedom booklets, and publisher of the *Bill of Rights Sentinel.* He's perhaps best known as the founder and Executive Director of Jews for the Preservation of Firearms Ownership, regarded by many as America's most aggressive civil rights organization, and director of its sister organization, Concerned Citizens Opposed to Police States (CCOPS). He lives with his wife and children in the Kettle Moraine region of Wisconsin, to which he says they've successfully escaped from "Naziwaukee."

Richard W. Stevens graduated with high honors from the University of San Diego School of Law in 1988, practiced civil litigation in California, then for several years taught legal research and writing at George Washington University Law School and George Mason University School of Law. He comprehensively revised and annotated the *Standardized Civil Jury Instructions* for the District of Columbia, the standard reference for D.C. courts. In 1999, he wrote *Dial 911 and Die,* a book that assembles the laws and actual cases from 53 U.S. jurisdictions to show that government owes no legal duty to protect individual citizens from crime. Richard is editor of the *Bill of Rights Sentinel,* and has authored numerous articles on a variety of subjects in legal and other publications. One booklet he wrote, entitled "It's Common Sense To Use Your Bill of Rights," has well over 100,000 copies in print. He has been a frequent guest on local and national radio and television talk shows to discuss his writings, the Bill of Rights and the freedom philosophy. He now lives in Phoenix, Arizona.

Index

Index (continued)

Index (continued)

Index (continued)

Index (continued)

Index (continued)

"One of the best books ever written about the right to keep and bear arms."

David Kopel
*Research Director,
Independence Institute*

"Although the stories of governmental persecution are heart-breaking, this book is a pleasure to read because of its clear-sighted and humanitarian concern for the victims who were stripped of self-defense."

Wendy McElroy
*Author and regular columnist for
FOXNews.com*

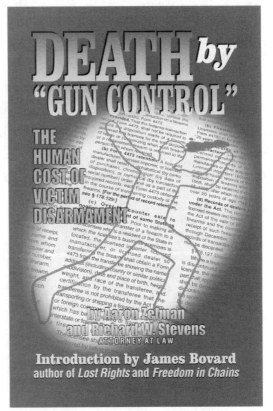

"How I wish that the information in this book were not true. Nevertheless, this book speaks to the irrefutable truth: *police do very little to prevent violent crime.* We investigate crime after the fact. I applaud Richard Stevens for his tremendous research and his courage to tell this truth."

Richard Mack, former Sheriff, Graham County, Arizona

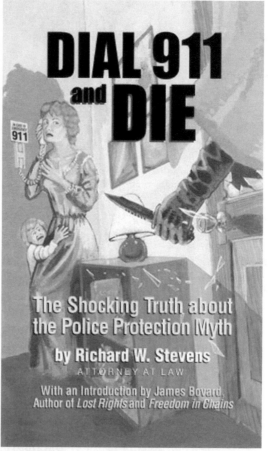

DIAL 911 and DIE

The Shocking Truth about the Police Protection Myth

by Richard W. Stevens
ATTORNEY AT LAW

With an Introduction by James Bovard, Author of *Lost Rights* and *Freedom in Chains*

$11.95 each • 6 copies **$44.95** • 12 copies **$79.95** • 58 copies **$349.95**
One copy FREE with your order of 125 or more Gran'pa Jack booklets
(No other discounts or free books with this offer. Price includes shipping.)
For delivery to Canadian addresses, please add 10% to cover additional postage cost.

ORDER FORM
JPFO • P.O. Box 270143 • Hartford, WI 53027 • 262-673-9745 • fax 262-673-9746
www.jpfo.org
Total enclosed $ _____
Wisconsin residents add 5.6% sales tax

AMEX / VISA / MC #_____ Exp. Date _____

- -

SHIPPING LABEL – PLEASE PRINT CLEAR BLOCK CAPITAL LETTERS

Name _____ Phone _____

Address _____

City _____ State / Province _____

Postal / Zip Code _____

320

THE STATE vs. THE PEOPLE

THE RISE OF THE AMERICAN POLICE STATE

by Claire Wolfe and Aaron Zelman

Introduction by James Bovard

MAZEL FREEDOM PRESS, INC.

Coming soon –

The State vs. The People;
The Rise of the American Police State,

by Claire Wolfe and Aaron Zelman

Reserve your copy today! Send the information below to:
JPFO • P.O. Box 270143 • Hartford, WI 53027

- -

PLEASE TELL ME WHEN THIS BOOK IS PUBLISHED

Name _____ Phone _____

Address _____

City _____ State / Province _____

Postal / Zip Code _____

CCOPS

CONCERNED CITIZENS OPPOSED TO POLICE STATES

Concerned Citizens Opposed to Police States, Inc. (CCOPS)

Why is CCOPS needed? Why should you support CCOPS?

Most Americans don't understand their Constitution and Bill of Rights. Many don't even know what the Bill of Rights contains. Ignorance of fundamental rights will lead to loss of those rights. When America ceases to beam the light of liberty, the rest of the world will have little hope of preserving it.

On the other hand, many Americans instinctively fear a police state. *CCOPS will help Americans to understand how the Bill of Rights is the barrier to a police state in America.* CCOPS will help Americans learn to spot, and then effectively oppose those trends, policies and laws that destroy our rights and establish a police state.

Preserving fundamental rights and opposing a police state. Can you think of any more important effort to safeguard the American way of life?

CCOPS aggressively works to influence politicians and public opinion. For that reason, dues and contributions to CCOPS are not tax-deductible. A subscription to the CCOPS newsletter, the *Police State Policies Alert,* is included with your membership. Annual Dues: $25.00.

Sign up to support CCOPS today because your life and liberties are being threatened. CCOPS will show you what can be done to save them.

- -

Name _____

Address _____

City _____ State _____ Zip _____

E-mail: _____ Phone: _____

Circle one: **VISA**   MasterCard   AMERICAN EXPRESS

Name on Card: _____

Card No. _____

Expiration Date: _____

CCOPS

CCOPS, Inc.
P.O. Box 270205
Hartford, WI 53027
(262) 670-9920 (voice)
(262) 670-9921 (fax
www.ccops.org

CONCERNED CITIZENS OPPOSED TO POLICE STATES

Get one copy of #2 and #6 FREE
when you order Death by "Gun Control"

PRICE CODE "A"
Gran'pa Jack #1, 2, 4, 5, 6 & 7

(24 pages)	Booklets					
	#1	#2	#4	#5	#6	#7
1 Copy US $3.00 ppd.						
25 Copies US $15.00 ppd.						
50 Copies US $20.00 ppd.						
100 Copies US $38.00 ppd.						
250 Copies US $93.00 ppd.						
500 Copies US $180.00 ppd.						
1000 Copies US $350.00 ppd.						

PRICE CODE "B"
Gran'pa Jack #3
(48 pages)

1 Copy US $4.00 ppd.	_____
25 Copies US $20.00 ppd.	_____
50 Copies US $30.00 ppd.	_____
100 Copies US $49.00 ppd.	_____
250 Copies US $120.00 ppd.	_____
500 Copies US $210.00 ppd.	_____
1000 Copies US $390.00 ppd.	_____

All seven booklets FREE
when you order three or more books of your choice.

JOIN JPFO TODAY! *Only $20.00 – Tax deductible!*
(Jews for the Preservation of Firearms Ownership, Inc.)
For delivery to Canadian addresses, please add 10% to cover additional postage cost.

ORDER FORM
JPFO • P.O. Box 270143 • Hartford, WI 53027 • 262-673-9745 • fax 262-673-9746
www.jpfo.org

Total enclosed $ _____   ❏ Membership
Wisconsin residents add 5.6% sales tax

AMEX / VISA / MC #_____ Exp. Date _____

- -

SHIPPING LABEL – PLEASE PRINT CLEAR BLOCK CAPITAL LETTERS

Name _____   Phone _____

Address _____

City _____   State / Province _____

Postal / Zip Code _____

JPFO:
Fierce Defender of American Liberty

To destroy "gun control" and to encourage Americans to understand and defend all of the Bill of Rights for everyone. Those are the twin goals of Wisconsin-based Jews for the Preservation of Firearms Ownership (JPFO). Founded by Jews and initially aimed at educating the Jewish community about the historical evils that Jews have suffered when they have been disarmed, JPFO has always welcomed persons of all religious beliefs who share a common goal of opposing and reversing victim disarmament policies while advancing liberty for all.

JPFO is a non-profit tax-exempt educational civil rights organization, not a lobby. JPFO's products and programs reach out to as many segments of the American people as possible, using bold tactics without compromise on fundamental principles.

To help protect the Bill of Rights now and for future generations, JPFO offers a complete action kit for citizens to celebrate December 15 as Bill of Rights Day annually in their home, city or state. The kit includes a video, promotional materials and a sample Bill of Rights Day resolution passed in other localities. A copy of the Bill of Rights in English, French, German or Spanish is also available free for community and international outreach efforts.

To contact JPFO for more information, call the national headquarters at **(800) 869-1884** or **(262) 673-9745,** fax to **(262) 673-9746,** or click on **www.jpfo.org.** Dues are only $20 year year and are tax-deductible.

- -

Name _____

Address _____

City _____ State _____ Zip _____

E-mail: _____ Phone: _____

Circle one: VISA   MasterCard   AMERICAN EXPRESS   **JPFO, INC.**

Name on Card: _____   P.O. Box 270143
Hartford, WI 53027
Card No. _____   (262) 673-9745 (voice)
(262) 673-9746 (fax)
Expiration Date: _____   www.jpfo.org

326

The following is a special excerpt from the forthcoming blockbuster from Mazel Freedom Press, Inc.—

The State vs. The People

The Rise of the American Police State

By Claire Wolfe and Aaron Zelman

Chapter One
What is a police state?

[C]itizens were deprived of all rights and privileges. Every existence was comprehensively subordinated to the purposes of the State, and in exchange the State agreed to act as a good father, giving food, work, and wages suited to the people's capacity, welfare for the poor and elderly, and universal schooling for children.

– John Taylor Gatto[1]

Goose-stepping jackboots in an old documentary. Enforcers hiding behind faceless masks. Demonstrators clubbed to their knees. Dissidents "detained" without charges. These are the images of a police state.

Secret dossiers kept on enemies of powerful men. Sophisticated electronic tracking devices. Ever-more-present surveillance. These, too, signal a police state.

A professor loses a job for vague, political reasons. A scientist is defunded after publishing unpopular findings. People fear to reveal opinions in front of their own children, who may be spies for some hazy, but terrifying, government apparatus. Neighbors are dragged from their homes in midnight raids, charged with vaguely defined crimes. Their property is seized; their reputations trampled, their finances ruined.

We worry that these point toward a police state. We suspect that a government whose friendly face we see on television is, in some dark reality, far different than we're told – a government of secrets, disinformation, black budgets and lethal "wet work."

---

[1]Gatto, John Taylor. *The Underground History of American Education: A Schoolteacher's Intimate Investigation into the Problem of Modern Schooling.* The Oxford Village Press, pre-publication edition, 2000. Gatto is writing about the Prussian police state under Frederick William II, nephew and successor of Frederick the Great.

What is a police state? Like pornography or "good art," everybody knows a police state when they see one. Pundits right and left accuse opponents of "police-state" tactics. The media designates one foreign government as a police state while extolling another, equally brutal, regime as a democracy. We often use the term "police state" as a synonym for tyranny, forgetting that a police state is actually a complex system and philosophy of government (which can indeed be tyrannical).

Precise definitions are hard to come by. In the 1970s, Praeger Publishers issued a series of textbooks that analyzed commonly used political terms. Its book *Police State*[2] showed in detail the origins and nature of such governments. But nowhere did the book's author, Brian Chapman, even hint at a concise definition of the term.

Similarly, David Wise, writing his book *The American Police State* in the wake of Watergate, described "…wiretapping, bugging, break-ins, burglaries, opening of mail, cable interception, physical surveillance, clandestine harassment, widespread use of informants, detention lists, and political tax audits"[3] as characteristics of a police state. But what made them characteristics of a police state? Wise didn't say.

In *Police State: Could It Happen Here?* Jules Archer used this definition:

> A police state … is a state in which a dictatorship imposed by a single ruler, party or group exercises total, rigid and repressive controls over the social, economic and political life of its citizens, usually by means of terror through a secret police force.[4]

Attorney Richard W. Stevens, who has written extensively on tyranny and justice, offers this:

> A police state exists where (1) the state imposes its comprehensive vision of economic welfare and correct behavior upon the citizens, (2) the police apparatus serves the state (instead of serving the citizens), (3) the police apparatus takes upon itself to actively enforce the will of the state [rather than respond to criminal misdeeds], and (4) the citizens serve the state and the police apparatus because of pervasive fear of punishment.[5]

All these definitions are useful. There are excellent reasons why it

[2]Chapman, Brian. *Police State.* Praeger Publishers, 1970.

[3]Wise, David. *The American Police State: The Government Against the People.* Vintage Books, 1978.

[4]Archer, Jules. *Police State: Could It Happen Here?* Harper & Row, 1977.

[5]Stevens, Richard W. "What Is a Police State?" *Police State Policies Alert,* Winter 2000.

is difficult to arrive at a single comprehensive definition for a police state. One reason: The nature of police states has changed as societies, technologies, and the temper of the times have altered. Just as the police state of Robespierre's France was different from the one in Hitler's Germany, so the nature of a police state is altered in any new country or new era. Within this book, we will need to add to existing definitions to reflect some twenty-first century realities – such as burgeoning electronic surveillance systems no Hitler, Machiavelli, or Stalin could have imagined.

Modern police statists are learning some subtleties their jackbooted predecessors never knew. Yet the electronic Big Brother states of the future will still be police states, as long as they rigorously oversee the everyday activities of citizens, mold individuals to the state's purposes, and suppress political dissent, independent thought, or independent non-violent action through tactics of fear.

To truly understand police states – and to learn whether we are in the midst of one or in danger of ending up in one – we first need to come to terms with what police states *have been* in philosophy and history. Then we need to examine what one might look like if it rises up in our path to the future. This first chapter will examine the past. The rest of the book will look at today and see what it portends for tomorrow.

Polizeistaat: Original meaning of police state

Our phrase "police state" is a literal translation from the German *Polizeistaat*. The term was used in Prussia as far back as the seventeenth century, when Frederick William, Elector of Brandenberg (1620-88) and his successors crafted the first modern police state. The term wasn't commonly used in English until the rise of Hitler, when it entered our language with connotations of evil and insane brutality it didn't originally have.

It's easy for English speakers to misinterpret the term, because, to us, "police" generally signifies "the cop on the beat." Historically, police in American and British commonwealth countries have been uniformed officers who investigate (and ideally aim to prevent) crimes such as murder, rape, and burglary.

In parts of Europe the term "police" has different and broader

---

(Newsletter of Concerned Citizens Opposed to Police States, P.O. Box 270205, Hartford, Wisconsin 53027, http://www.ccops.org.) Stevens adds that "police apparatus" doesn't necessarily mean traditional peace officers, but a special class of functionaries with extensive power and the will to actively pursue the government's goals — not merely to respond when an act of theft or violence has been committed.

significance, deriving from ancient Greek roots – the same roots that gave us the English terms "policy" and "politics." As Brian Chapman explains:

> The [Greek] term *politeia* was a comprehensive one, touching on all matters affecting the survival and welfare of the inhabitants of the city [polis]. It comprised within itself the whole notion of "the art of governing the city." ... Plato and Aristotle regarded the officials responsible for "the police" as being involved with the ultimate responsibility for ensuring the safety of the republic. This involved the power to regulate the affairs of the city in the general interest of public order, security, morality, food supplies and welfare.[6]

Therefore the term "police state" relates directly to our verb "to police" (to surveil or oversee). That same connotation is found in our legal term "police power."[7] This meaning of "police" is much different from, and related only peripherally to, the concept of a police force of uniformed officers.

While tyranny is an ancient curse of humanity, the police state is a relatively modern phenomenon and – surprising though it seems – grew out of Enlightenment efforts to reform and improve political systems.

Just as we better understand the definition of "police state" if we go back to the Greeks, we must also return to the Greeks – Plato, specifically – for an early insight into why police states develop. Two millennia before the Prussians constructed the first police state on earth, Plato had created a proto-police state in words.

The police state of Plato

In his dialog *The Republic*,[8] Plato envisioned what he called the "Just City."[9] It was the highest form of government and the highest form of human society he could conceive.

Plato's ideal society would be run by a class of guardians, chosen in

---

[6]Chapman, op. cit.

[7]*Black's Law Dictionary* defines police power as (in part): "The power of the State to place restraints on the personal freedom and property rights of persons for the protection of the public safety, health, and morals or the promotion of the public convenience and general prosperity." In *Black's*, this definition is part of a larger one that deals with the U.S. Constitution and the scope of federal and state powers.

[8]Plato's *Republic* is available in a variety of print editions from Amazon.com or local bookstores. It may also be dowloaded free in text form from Project Gutenberg, http://promo.net/pg/.

[9]To the Greeks, the city was the fundamental independent political entity, just as the nation is to the modern world.

childhood and raised to their task. Directly beneath them would be a class of brave warriors. All property would be communal and all wives and children shared.[10] The people would support the guardians and warriors, and in return these superior classes would guide and protect the state.

The first concern of this society would be education, especially music and art. By law, however, artists would be forbidden to depict any but "virtuous things." No portrayals of evil or discord, or of anything disruptive to public order, would be tolerated.

Plato's next concern was physical training, and after that the character of doctors and judges. In Plato's world, however, doctors would deal only with the temporary ills of healthy people. Chronically ill people would be left to die. The insane would be put to death.

Plato called for strict regulation of sex so that the Just City could achieve the finest genetic stock. Citizens could have sexual intercourse only within their own group and only after a relationship received the sanction of the rulers. All babies would be taken by the rulers. Children of "inferior people" would be left to die, while those judged to have superior eugenic qualities would be taken care of by nurses. In reality, people would never choose their own sex partners because the guardians would run a rigged lottery to make sure the "best" men bred with the "best" women. Plato believed it would be moral for the guardians to deceive the common people because of their greater wisdom and understanding.

All citizens would refer to each other as "son," "daughter," "brother," "sister," "father," or "mother." Plato asserted that this system would bring rulers and common people together as one cohesive family, free of any "us" vs "them" rivalries. In this vision of a "perfect" republic, the bounds of the nuclear family would be broken, as would ties to dynasties or classes. They would be replaced by utter devotion to society where "…the desires of the inferior many are controlled by the wisdom and desires of the superior few."

How would all this be enforced? Although modern readers will

---

[10]Plato sometimes writes as though communal marriages and shared children apply only to the top two classes; but elswhere he writes as though they apply to all of society; it's impossible to tell what he actually intends. But he does say "no man would call anything his own," and has a discussion about why it would be moral for leaders to lie to the common people to get them to agree to his ideal breeding scheme. So it appears likely he wished to extend these relationships to all. Plato also stated in *The Republic* that man-boy relationships were the highest form of love; but he opposed man-boy sexual relations on the grounds that they compromised educational benefits such relationships might otherwise offer.

recognize that nearly everything Plato envisioned has been tried, in one variation or another, in modern police states like Nazi Germany or the Soviet Union, there are no police in *The Republic*. (The warriors apparently only protect against external enemies.) As Plato (via the character of Socrates) blandly asserts, the Just City would function harmoniously because the guardians would all be philosophers – the famous philosopher kings.

At this point in the dialog, one of the participants astutely objects that the public will "never accept a philosopher as king, because all philosophers are either vicious or useless." Socrates explains that philosophers in his state would be so wise and well-qualified that no one would question their will. End of argument. "Until philosophers bear rule," he asserts, "States and individuals will have no rest from evil."[11]

More's vision of Utopia

Eighteen hundred years after Plato, in 1516, another philosopher envisioned an ideal society. Sir Thomas More, now St. Thomas More, patron of statesmen and politicians, composed *Utopia*.[12] *Utopia* is also a dialog, with a nod to Plato. In it, a traveler named Raphael Hythloday describes the marvelous island of Utopia.

More – a man of contrasts – makes it clear he's not quite as serious about Utopia as Plato was about the Just City. The name "Hythloday" is Greek for "talker of nonsense," and in some parts of the book the reader can't be sure whether More agrees with the fictional Hythloday or is merely speculating on various means of improving European culture.

Nevertheless, *Utopia*, like *The Republic,* describes one man's ideal society and government. Once again it's an ideal that leaves a state-weary twenty-first century reader asking, "How many enforcers would it take to make everybody so 'happy'?"

As with the Just City, Utopia is a homogeneous society, based on

---

[11]To his credit, Plato noted that this ideal city – which he identifies as a kingship or an aristocracy – is doomed. As it decays, it will fall through four lesser stages: timocracy (rule by brave and noble warriors); oligarchy (rule by the rich); democracy (mob rule); and tyranny (dictatorship). Ironic as it seems – looking back on the catastrophic twentieth century in which most of Plato's ideas were tried by Hitler, Pol Pot, Stalin, and others – Plato had no clue that tyranny would be necessary to *implement* the rigid society he considered the height of perfection. Plato's blindness to this fact is evidence that governing should definitely *not* be left to philosophers. Interestingly, although he lists tyranny as the lowest form of degenerate government, Plato saves his most biting contempt for democracy – the type of government under which he himself lived.

[12]More's *Utopia* is available in a variety of print editions from Amazon.com or local bookstores. It may also be downloaded free in text form from Project Gutenberg, http://promo.net/pg/.

More's idea of rational thought. It features communal property, no greed, no serious class distinctions, no poverty, and little crime or immoral behavior (all immoral behavior is, in fact, outlawed). It imposes a strict and utter uniformity upon its citizens.

Utopia is an island of 54 cities, so much alike as to be virtually indistinguishable – same size, same architecture, same customs, same ideas, same behavior on the part of all citizens. Each house is identical. No locks and keys are allowed. No private spaces exist. Hythloday, More's spokesman, considers elimination of privacy a fine way to promote friendship and reduce harmful gossip.

More envisioned homogeneity as the key to justice.[13] He believed that rational thought would lead all rational people toward the same values.

Each household in Utopia consists of a group of thirty people – once again, no nuclear families – who choose their own administrators. These managers operate within a detailed administrative hierarchy (a prototype of our modern bureaucracy which, as we shall see, was a key component of the first and all subsequent police states).

Anyone caught discussing issues of state outside of the ruling committees is put to death. (More, soon to become Henry VIII's chancellor of England in a turbulent era, believed this would eliminate plots and conspiracies.) No officials can be bribed because there is no money.

City-dweller More spells out an agricultural labor plan that would make any full-time farmer laugh or cry. City residents perform two-year stints "on the land." Harvests take about a day. All surplus is shared at no charge. Utopians spend their plentiful free time on intellectual pursuits, music, gardening, and physical exercise. As Plato did, More also exempts intellectuals from the need for physical labor.

Sick Utopians receive excellent care, but those too ill to perform their duties are gently urged to let themselves be killed in their sleep rather than be a burden to society. As in Plato's Just City, sex is rigidly controlled by the state, as are marriage and religion – with harsh penalties, including death or slavery, for violators.

Of course, everyone is happy and lives in harmony under a just government that operates more on "reason" than on specific laws. More,

---

[13]It is notable that many writers since – Orwell, Huxley and Ayn Rand among them – have seen such uniformity as a key component of the most oppressive forms of injustice. Ironically, followers of the Rand mythos also know that Rand famously attempted to impose exactly that type of uniformity on her circle of friends, and for precisely the same reasons More advocated it – because she believed that all rational people, by definition, would share her beliefs and preferences.

like Plato, expends almost no ink explaining *how* such uniformity and perfection would be enforced. We can excuse More. Unlike Plato, he may have been "just kicking around ideas" rather than describing his desired real-world system. But philosophers' ideas tend to end up in the hands of politically powerful people.

Eventually, through the winding channels of history, More's conceptions flowed through the minds of French revolutionary thinkers and to Karl Marx, where they sprang to life in the doctrines of communism. It seems odd but appropriate that More eventually became the only Christian saint honored with a statue at the Kremlin.

Common elements

More and Plato have a great deal in common – with each other, and with modern police states:

- They begin with a philosophical ideal imposed by an elite.
- They presume that there is one "right way" to live and think, and that all reasonable people will agree. Individuality is devalued and may be severely punished. (As horror writer Dean Koontz quipped about this mentality, "Apparently, utopia requires the absolute uniformity of thought and purpose exhibited by bees in a hive."[14])
- The "ideal" government reaches into every aspect of human life from sex to education to commerce to religion – to the very design of houses.
- People are focused on "betterment," and betterment of the self is secondary to betterment of the whole.
- People unable to meet the rulers' standards for quality are judged disposable.
- Privacy is non-existent.
- Though brotherhood is presumed to reign, in fact there are distinctly privileged classes (philosophers, warriors, intellectuals).
- These ideals require a complete makeover of society and assume extraordinarily high expectations for individual behavior; yet both authors avoid discussing the measures that would be necessary to bring about such change.

Many other philosophers contributed to the development or eventual refinement of police states. Two of the foremost were Jean-Jacques Rousseau (1712-1778) and Jeremy Bentham (1748-1832).

Rousseau taught that man was noble, free and happy in a "state of nature," and that only society brought about vice, corruption and misery. He believed that the "general will" of a new type of society was capable of

---

[14]Koontz, Dean. *Seize the Night*. Bantam, 1999.

"forcing a man to be free" again.[15] Thus Rousseau laid the groundwork for the Marxist contention, two centuries later, that a government can customize human mentality and behavior to its specifications, simply by changing a person's circumstances. In decrying property as the chief corrupting influence, Rousseau also helped give the Communists their justification for abolition of private property. Finally, Rousseau's ideas are the origin of the widely held contemporary belief that society, not the individual, is responsible for crime, poverty, and evil.[16]

Bentham, an Englishman of the Enlightenment, was more pragmatic, less theoretical. He was among the first to promote the use of law to engineer a desired form of society. Bentham reduced human motivation to two factors: pain and pleasure. He considered the desire to avoid pain the stronger motivator of the two, and therefore viewed threats of punishment as an effective prod toward "good" behavior. In the name of producing "the greatest good of the greatest number"[17] (the only standard by which right and wrong were to be judged, in Bentham's view), government could legitimately practice any method – from extreme regulation of daily life to torture. Not surprisingly, this philosophy – Utilitarianism – was promoted in a time and place where government was generally benevolent (at least to members of Bentham's race, sex, and class). Bentham had no working concept of what government could do given the unlimited power he advocated to inflict pain or deliver pleasurable rewards.[18]

As we shall see, the ideals of Plato, More, and Rousseau, combined with the legal theories and enforcement methods advocated by

---

[15]Rousseau's two major works on these topics, *Discourse on the Origin of Inequality* (1755) and *The Social Contract* (1762) are available in a variety of editions from Amazon.com or major book stores. Both works can also be found in compilations of his major writings. In his diary of life in Nazi Germany, *I Will Bear Witness* (Random House, 1998) Victor Klemperer wrote on July 19, 1937: "Rousseau has never triumphed to such a degree nor been taken ad absurdum to such a degree as today. The posthumous unmasking of Rousseau is called Hitler."

[16]Ironically, another philosopher with a starting point the opposite of Rousseau's also influenced police-state development. Thomas Hobbes wrote (in Leviathan, 1651) that life in a state of nature was "poor, nasty, brutish, and short." His solution? Like Rousseau's – government. Hobbes advocated a state so all-powerful it could control even a person's inner mental and emotional life.

[17]Sometimes written as "the greatest happiness for the greatest number."

[18]An essay, "Bentham's Utilitarianism in Victorian England," by Paul Roach, gives a pocket glimpse of Bentham's work and influence. It can be found at http://www.gober.net/victorian/reports/utilitar.html. Paul Craig Roberts and Lawrence M. Stratton give a long explication of Bentham's influence in their book *The Tyranny of Good Intentions: How Prosecutors and Bureaucrats are Trampling the Constitution in the Name of Justice.* Forum, 2000.

Bentham, became the inspiration – even the script – for some of the world's most tyrannical police states. But the first real-world police states didn't set out to be that barbarous.

Prussia: The first police state

There have been brutal, rapacious regimes throughout human history. But the first government to bear the designation police state – *Polizeistaat* – appeared three and a half centuries ago in Prussia.[19] It was certainly repressive by American and English standards, but it wasn't characterized by brutality or terror, nor was it the kind of greed-driven marauder state that thinkers from Aristotle onward had considered synonymous with tyranny. On the contrary, it was an effort at modern social and organizational management. To a Europe weary of squabbling princes and unstable principalities, the first police state must have seemed a relief.

As Brian Chapman explains:

> The *Polizeistaat* as it was developed in Prussia ... was the product of economic, social, and military policies. ... The municipal economies of medieval times came to be replaced by territorial economies, and mercantilism involved the creation of a balanced national economy, a favorable balance of trade, a buoyant national revenue and the means of war under state control.

> This economic doctrine was reinforced by social and dynastic considerations. The devastation of the Thirty Years War in Europe predisposed large sections of the population of central Europe to prefer order to liberty, and protection to freedom. The dynastic interests of rulers favored the creation of strong, internally stable and strictly disciplined states. In a Hobbesian world political survival seemed to be dependent on military strength placed at the service of the state.[20]

The Prussian state was so highly militarized that Mirabeau, the French Revolutionary-era orator, called war "the national industry of Prussia." Nearly a century later a French military attaché wrote that "other countries possessed an army, but in Prussia the army possessed the country."[21]

---

[19]Descriptions of the early Prussian and French police states are adapted largely from Chapman, op. cit. Interpretation and interpolation are our own.

[20]Chapman, op. cit.

[21]Quoted in Gerard, James W. (U.S. ambassador to Germany). *My Four Years in Germany.* George H. Duran Company. 1917. Found at http://www.ukans.edu/~libsite/wwi-www/Gerard/4yrs1.htm.